L.S.E. Essays on Cost

The Institute for Humane Studies Series
in Economic Theory

Distributed by New York University Press

Published by New York University Press

L.S.E. Essays on Cost

Edited by J.M. Buchanan and G.F. Thirlby

New York University Press • New York and London
1981

©1973 by London School of Economics and Political Science

First published 1973 for the London School
of Economics and Political Science by
Weidenfeld and Nicolson, U.K.

Library of Congress Cataloging in Publication Data

Buchanan, James M   comp.
   L.S.E. essays on cost.

   "The Institute for Humane Studies Series in Economic Theory."
   Includes bibliographical references and index.
   1. Cost—Addresses, essays, lectures. 2. Cost accounting—Addresses, essays, lectures. I. Thirlby,
G. F. II. London School of Economics and Political Science. III. Title.
HB199.B824   1980   338.5'1'01   80-24921
ISBN 0-8147-1034-4
ISBN 0-8147-1035-2 (pbk.)

MANUFACTURED IN THE UNITED STATES OF AMERICA

Contents

Acknowledgements

Beyond making the typography and general lay-out of each more or less uniform, these papers are reprinted as they first appeared in their respective books and journals.

The London School of Economics gratefully acknowledges permission to reprint copyright material from the following:

From Lord Robbins and from the Royal Economic Society for 'Remarks upon Certain Aspects of the Theory of Cost', published in the *Economic Journal*, March 1934.

From Professor F. A. Hayek and from the Editorial Board of *Economica* for 'Economics and Knowledge', published in *Economica*, February 1937.

From Professor Sir Ronald Edwards and from Sir Arnold Plant for 'The Rationale of Cost Accounting', published in A. Plant (ed.), *Some Modern Business Problems*, Longman, 1937.

From Mr G. F. Thirlby and the Editorial Board of *Economica* for 'The Subjective Theory of Value and Accounting "Cost" ' (*Economica*, February 1946), for 'The Economist's Description of Business Behaviour' (*Economica*, May 1952), and for 'Economists' Cost Rules and Equilibrium Theory' (*Economica*, May 1960).

From Mr G. F. Thirlby and the Editorial Board of the *South African Journal of Economics* for 'The Ruler', published in that journal, Vol. 14, No 4, December 1946.

From Professor J. Wiseman and the Editorial Board of *Economica* for 'Uncertainty, Costs and Collective Economic Planning', published in *Economica* May 1953.

From Professor J. Wiseman and the Clarendon Press for 'The Theory of Public Utility Price – an Empty Box', published in *Oxford Economic Papers*, Vol. 9. Oxford University Press, Oxford, 1957.

Preface

When I originally suggested the idea for this book, I had hoped to be able to include a considerably wider range of papers with which to underline James M. Buchanan's challenge on p. 35 of his *Cost and Choice,* where he regrets the demise, and calls for a resurrection, of the L.S.E. opportunity-cost tradition (see p. 6 of this book). However the limitations of finance compelled a stricter selection, and, even so, the emergence of the book would not have been possible without institutional as well as personal support and encouragement. The Center for Study of Public Choice, Virginia Polytechnic Institute, has cooperated fully with the L.S.E. Publications Committee throughout the planning and production of the book, which is institutionally a joint product. For this purpose the Center itself was supported by the Earhart Foundation, whose assistance is gratefully acknowledged.

I do not adhere entirely to Buchanan's Introduction: I am not a grand designer! My own pedestrian idea of the next goal towards which economic theorists should direct their own steps is indicated in an unpublished paper called 'After Cost and Choice', namely towards the construction of a multi-entrepreneur firm together with a theory of the account.

G. F. Thirlby

I

Introduction: L.S.E. cost theory in retrospect

JAMES M. BUCHANAN

In his paper, 'Economics and Knowledge', included in this volume, Hayek scarcely mentioned 'cost'. Nonetheless he provides indirectly the strongest argument for attempting, through the publication of this collection of essays, to focus the attention of modern economists on the elementary meaning of cost. Hayek emphasized the differences, in principle, between the equilibrium position attained by a single rational decision-maker in his own behavioural adjustments, given his preference function and the constraints that he confronts, and the equilibrium potentially attainable through the interaction of many persons. To Hayek the latter 'is not an equilibrium in the special sense in which equilibrium is regarded as a sort of optimum position'.

Despite Hayek's warning, since the 1930s, when his essay along with some of the others in this collection was written and when the l.s.e. tradition in cost theory was developed, economists have increasingly analysed equilibrium states in terms of their optimality or non-optimality properties, defined by criteria for maximizing some objective function. It is somewhat paradoxical that Robbins, whose contributions to London cost theory cannot be questioned, should also have been at least partially responsible for the drift of modern economic theory towards the mathematics of applied maximization, variously elaborated, and away from the analysis of exchange processes. In *The Nature and Significance of Economic Science*,[1] Robbins supplied the methodological paradigm within which modern micro-economics has been developed. Elementary textbooks throughout the world soon came to define 'economics' in terms of 'the economic problem',

[1] London 1932.

the allocation of scarce resources among alternative ends. So defined, the 'problem' faced by the individual on the desert island, the Crusoe so familiar to us all, is, at base, quite similar to that faced by the society or the community of persons. The paradigm was somewhat differently put, but with the same effect, by Paul A. Samuelson in his influential *Foundations of Economic Analysis,* when he stated :

> They [meaningful theorems in diverse fields of economic affairs] proceed almost wholly from two types of very general hypotheses. The first is that *conditions of equilibrium are equivalent to the maximization (minimization) of some magnitude.*[2] [Italics supplied.]

The increasing conceptual quantification in economic theory was almost necessarily accompanied by increasing conceptual 'objectification'. Once the magnitude to be maximized is symbolically defined, attention is quite naturally diverted to the manipulation of the symbols and away from the initial leap into presumed objectivity itself. The increasing conceptual quantification need not have introduced confusion save for the simultaneous developments in theoretical welfare economics. Within what Hayek called the 'Pure Logic of Choice', the formal theory of utility maximization, mathematical rigour has offered aesthetic satisfaction to the sophisticated without loss of explanatory potential. More importantly, the increasingly elegant and formalistic content of general-equilibrium theory, and notably its emphasis on existence proofs and stability conditions, yields pleasure to the talented, criteria to the critical, and convictions to some who have remained unconvinced about the overall efficacy of market order.

So long as the object for discussion, and for theorizing, is either the individual decision-maker or the interactions of separate decision-makers *in markets,* no harm is done and perhaps some good is added by conceptual objectification. Confusion arises only when the properties of equilibrium, as defined for markets, are

[2] Paul A. Samuelson, *Foundations of Economic Analysis* (Cambridge, Mass. 1947), p. 5. Samuelson's Nobel lecture provides evidence that his own position has not substantially changed. See 'Maximum Principles in Analytical Economics', *American Economic Review,* 62 (June 1972), pp. 249-62.

transferred as criteria of optimization in *non-market* or political settings. It is here that the critical distinction between the equilibrium of the single decision-maker and that attained through market interaction, the distinction stressed by Hayek, is absolutely essential to forestall ambiguity and analytical error. The theory of social interaction, of the mutual adjustment among the plans of separate human beings, is different in kind from the theory of planning, the maximization of some objective function by a conceptualized omniscient being. The latter is equivalent, in all respects, to the problems faced by Crusoe or by any individual decision-taker. But this is not the theory of markets, and it is artificial and basically false thinking that makes it out to be. There are properties or characteristics of equilibria in markets that seem superficially to be equivalent to those attainable by the idealized optimization carried out by the planner. But shadow prices are not market prices, and the opportunity costs that inform market decisions are not those that inform the choices of even the omniscient planner. These appear to be identical only because of the false objectification of the magnitudes in question.

This is what the great debate on socialist planning in the 1930s was all about, comment to the contrary notwithstanding. And modern economic theorists measure their own confusion by the degree to which they accept the alleged Lange victory over Mises, quite apart from the empirical record since established. The central issue in this debate should not have been the possibility or impossibility of socialist calculation. All the participants were wrong in concentrating on this. The difference in data confronted by decision-makers in different institutional settings is quite sufficient to prove that the properties of market equilibrium cannot in the nature of things be duplicated under non-market institutional structures. This is not of course to say that 'efficiency', defined in a different but legitimate planning sense, cannot be defined in an ideal-type socialist model. Of course it can. But it is a wholly different 'efficiency' framework that is involved here, informed by the marginal-value estimates of the planner and not by the participants in markets.

I think that it is legitimate to trace the sources of error to fundamental misconceptions in the theory of opportunity cost, misconceptions that the London (and Austrian) scholars were attempting to clarify, and which later I tried similarly to rectify with my little book, *Cost and Choice*, in 1969.[3] Unfortunately neither the London contribution nor my book seems to have exerted much effect on mainstream thinking in economic theory.

But I am getting ahead of my story. As I noted above, the increasing conceptual quantification, and objectification, of economic theory need not have sown confusion without the accompaniment of developments in theoretical welfare economics. Precisely at the time that methodologists were effective in formalizing economic theory within a more rigorous maximization framework, interest in 'market failure' rather than 'market success' was at its peak, and, with this, interest in the extension of economic theory to socialist organization became widespread. The Robbins definition of the allocation problem, with its implied emphasis on the universality of scarcity, supported such an extension. It was predictable that economists, trained professionally to analyse market equilibria, and increasingly adept at formalizing the maximization paradigm, should begin to discuss planning problems and solutions as if these required the same set of tools as those applicable to market phenomena. In retrospect it seems singularly unfortunate that the institutionalists should have lost favour precisely when their emphasis on and expertise in the functioning of organizational-institutional structures, and the impact of differing structures on behaviour of decision-makers, might have, with some intrusion of analysis, yielded their highest marginal product in effective critical scholarship. Instead the mathematically sophisticated analytics of such scholars as Hotelling were allowed to go unchallenged despite their vulnerability in this most fundamental sense. And young economists everywhere learnt to appreciate the beauty of the mathematical models of what they called 'an economy'. Theirs was not the role of sceptic, and to question quantification and objectification itself quickly came to be the mark of eccentricity rather than excellence.

[3] Chicago 1969.

6

Is it any wonder that, in the idealized fully quantifiable and fully objectifiable 'economy' that commanded all attention, the market itself should come to be regarded as a 'mechanism', as an 'analogue computing device', to be legitimately treated as one among several alternative means of allocating resources, to be evaluated comparatively in terms of some criteria of accomplishment? And so it should be in such a world.

The quest for objectivity is eternal and perhaps praiseworthy, but what has modern scholarship to offer where the classical economists tried and failed? There seems little harm in speculating about the properties of an economy whose only scarce resource is a homogeneous glob of something (putty clay or little Abner's schmoos) that may be instantly convertible into any one of a large number of final goods upon which consumers place value. In this setting the cost of any one good becomes the displaced physical alternative, measurable separately in any one of the other n goods potentially available from the single homogeneous source. If a unit of good X uses up twice as much of the scarce resource as a unit of good Y, the cost of X is properly defined as $2Y$, and the cost of Y as one-half X. In such a model it is meaningful to consider the planner's problem of maximizing output, defined in values or prices of goods, from the single scarce input. The norms of theoretical welfare economics can be applied directly to this purpose. The omniscient planner can solve his maximization problem quite simply by setting the prices of goods at their relative marginal costs, arbitrarily choosing one good as numeraire. As the final consumers adjust quantities demanded to the announced set of prices, the value of total output, denominated in the numeraire, will be maximized.

Nor need we limit analysis of such a conjectural economy to the planner's problems. As an alternative speculative exercise we may suppose that our homogeneous glob of scarce resource (putty clay or schmoos) is initially and arbitrarily parcelled out among persons under a private-property-rights arrangement. By assumption, the individual owners are completely indifferent as to just what set of final goods their own assigned input becomes in the transformation. These owners are motivated solely by their own desire for final goods, command over which is measured by income, denominated in some commonly agreed numeraire good. The only difference between this model and the one described earlier is that this one 'works on its own', once private-property-rights are defined and protected. The scarce resource will be allocated among uses; final goods will be 'produced'; prices will be set. The 'market' equilibrium that emerges will in this case be equivalent in all respects to the solution of the maximization problem posed for the planner in the earlier model. Prices will equal marginal costs, not because some hidden planner has now drawn on the norms of welfare economics, but because this equality is descriptive of the end of the trading process. If this equality is not satisfied, further gains from trade would be possible; potentially realizable surplus would remain unexploited. Not only can we deduce the equivalence in results between these two models on some *a priori* basis. We could also *observe* such equivalence in an objectively verifiable sense.

I do not think it a caricature to describe modern economic theory as being grounded on the two conjectural models that I have briefly sketched, and on the equivalence between their 'equilibrium-optimality' properties. Viewed in this simplistic perspective, however, the models paradoxically suggest that economic theory has advanced little, if at all, over that advanced almost two centuries earlier by the classical economists. In one respect at least, the classical writers were more honest in their efforts. They sought to explain relative prices by relative-input ratios of homogeneous labour. They fell short precisely because the deficiency in their common objective standard for measurement was revealed for all to see. This prompts the question as to why modern theorists have been so much more successful in concealing the fundamental flaw in their structure 'Camouflage by complexity' provides only a part of the answer here. The classical economists failed because their standard for measurement was demonstrably deficient, but also because their logical structure was not complete. One must read much into classical structure if any general-equilibrium theory of markets is to be discerned. They did not close the circle, and the lacunae in their essentially one-sided explanatory model provided the source for the familiar normative critique associated with Marx. The circle was completed by the subjective-value theorists, by the Marshallian synthesis, and, more explicitly, by the Walrasian theory of general equilibrium. These several contributions represent a major conceptual advance over classical economic analysis by criteria of logic and coherence. But the logical symmetry achieved in explaining the workings of the economic process was secured at a cost which is reflected by drainage of empirical, objective content. The classical economists offered us a positive-predictive theory of relative prices; this theory was falsified. But the neo-classical model contained no comparable predictive hypotheses; there was no externally measurable standard which allowed the scientist to make predictions from observable data. This post-classical theory described an interaction process and allowed the identification of certain properties of equilibrium positions. But there was nothing upon which the economist could have based objective predictions about relative-price formation.

This was surely sensed by Alfred Marshall as witnessed by his lingering adherence to classical models, and the desire for some restoration of predictive content offers a motivation for his time-period analysis. Frank Knight was also unwilling to disregard fully the classical precepts, and, despite his affinity with some of the Austrians, students of students of students of Knight continue to learn, and to learn well, the lessons of the deer and beaver. The reaction of the Austrians was quite different. They seemed quite willing to jettison the putative objective content of the classical hypotheses. The full implications of this may not have been recognized by the early Austrians, but in Mises and his followers economic theory is explicitly acknowledged to be wholly non-objective. Intellectual tidiness rather than empirical or explanatory content seemed to be the purpose of both earlier and latter-day Walrasians.

As I have suggested above, confusion emerged only when 1) theorists overlooked the absence of objective content in neo-classical and general-equilibrium analysis, *and* 2) when they attempted to utilize the properties of market equilibrium as

norms for the optimizing solutions of problems posed in non-
market institutional settings. The presence or absence of objective
content assumed instrumental significance only when the planner
was introduced, whether in the administration of state or public
enterprises (piecemeal or *in toto*) or in levy of corrective taxes
and/or subsidies on production in markets. The control or correction of allocation requires that norms be invoked, and these
norms must come from somewhere. The presumption of modern
economic theory that such norms are readily identifiable must be
attributed to the acceptance of the paradigm one-resource model
sketched above.

In any plausibly realistic market process, however, only prices
have objective content. This being so, how can prices be settled by
reference to 'costs' or to anything else? It will be useful to discuss
briefly the precise relationships between prices and 'costs' in full
market equilibrium. (In this treatment I shall follow closely the
discussion in *Cost and Choice*, page 85.)

In full market equilibrium expected marginal benefit for each
participant will be equal to marginal opportunity cost, both
measured in terms of the person's subjective valuation. All persons
confront uniform relative prices for goods; this is a necessary
condition for the absence of further gains-from-trade. Since each
participant is in full behavioural equilibrium, it follows that each
person must also confront the same marginal cost. As a demander
the individual adjusts his purchases to insure that marginal benefit
equals price. Hence the anticipated marginal benefits of a good,
again measured in the numeraire, are equal for all demanders.
As a supplier the individual adjusts his sales to insure that anticipated opportunities forgone, marginal opportunity cost, equals
price. Hence marginal opportunity cost in the numeraire is equal
for all suppliers.

Prices tend to equal marginal opportunity costs in market
equilibrium. But costs here are fully analogous to marginal
benefits. Only prices have objective, empirical content. Neither
the marginal valuations of demanders nor the marginal costs of
suppliers can be employed as a basis for determining or setting
prices. The reason is that both are brought into equality with

prices by behavioural adjustments on both sides of the market. Prices are not brought into equality with some objectively measurable phenomena on either the demand or supply side.

The implications of this basic, and in one sense, elementary fact for applying economic theory's tools to the making of control decisions for a wholly or partially socialized institutional structure have not been fully recognized, even by those who have partially escaped the dominance of the single-resource model. To an extent the blame for this lies in the failure of the London economists, and of the latter-day Austrians, to develop a full-blown 'subjectivist economics' that commands intellectual respect while seeming to retain explanatory relevance. Mises and his followers have been too prone to accept the splendid isolation of arrogant eccentrics to divorce their teaching too sharply from mainstream interests, and too eager to launch into polemic: epistemological, methodological, ideological. Certain members of the London group, although profoundly influenced by the Austrians via both Hayek and Robbins, had the merit of maintaining more practical interest in business decision problems. But unfortunately their interest was too pedestrian to allow them to attempt the 'grand design' that might have been produced from the cost-theory foundations which they developed.

As a result, we find Hayek (and Mises even more emphatically) talking largely to the disciples of the Austrian faith, and alongside we find Coase, Edwards, Thirlby and Wiseman taking up the cudgels against orthodoxy in detailed and particularistic applications. In their later papers both Thirlby and Wiseman seemed to recognize the grander implications but both men were perhaps discouraged by their failure to secure acceptance of their particularistic arguments, discouraged to the extent that neither made the attempt to draft the 'treatise' that seemed to be required, and which still seems to offer challenge.

Perhaps the most significant L.S.E. impact on modern economics has come through an indirect application of opportunity-cost theory rather than through an undermining of basic cost conceptions. 'Marginal social cost', enthroned by Pigou as a cornerstone of applied welfare economics, was successfully challenged by

R. H. Coase a quarter-century after his initial work on cost. His now-classic paper on social cost,[4] which reflects essentially the same cost theory held earlier, succeeded where the more straight-forward earlier attacks on the marginal-cost pricing norm – attacks by Coase himself, by Thirlby and by Wiseman – apparently failed. Nonetheless the still-provisional success of Coase's modern challenge should be noted. As this is written, in mid-1972, the implications of Coase's attack on the Pigovian concept of social cost for the elementary textbook discussions of opportunity cost have not yet been realized. Advanced textbooks, and notably those written in what may loosely be called the 'Chicago–Virginia' tradition, devote some space to the 'Coase theorem', but the standard chapters on cost in these same textbooks remain as if the more fundamental critique in the Coase paper had never been published.[5]

A primary purpose of this summary of doctrinal developments has been to emphasize the general importance of the theory of opportunity cost, and the London contributions to the development of a fundamentally correct theory which has not yet come to inform mainstream thinking in economics. The significance may, I fear, be hidden from those who glance only at the volume's title, *L.S.E. Essays on Cost*, and whose subjective image of 'cost' calls up carefully specified algebraic functions, sharply etched geometrical figures, or actual numbers carried to at least two decimal points in accountants' worksheets. Such an image may unfortunately be reinforced by a superficial survey of titles of some of the independent essays included here. Coase, Edwards and Thirlby, in some of the papers reprinted here, were interested in practical problems faced by business decision-makers in business administration as such. They were attempting to use economic

---

[4] R. H. Coase, 'The Problem of Social Cost', *Journal of Law and Economics*, 3 (October 1960), pp. 1-44.

[5] This summary of the impact of the London cost theory should include mention of G. L. S. Shackle. Although Shackle does not specifically present his ideas in opportunity-cost terms, his whole approach to decision is fully consistent with that developed by the London theorists. Shackle was both directly and indirectly associated closely with the London group. For Shackle's most appropriate treatment of decision, see his *Decision, Order, and Time in Human Affairs*, Cambridge 1961.

theory in this severely practical setting, to apply opportunity-cost notions to the problems faced in everyday economic choices. In this effort the London economists did not themselves fully appreciate the uniqueness and originality of their approach. To an extent they looked on themselves as writing down, in the context of practical-problem situations, what 'everyone knew' about cost, at least everyone around L.S.E. during the period in question.

As the norms drawn from the description of competitive equilibrium came to be presented more and more as 'rules' for socialist planners, and 'marginal-cost pricing' was elevated into a paradigm for the management of public enterprise, the significance of getting the elementary confusions identified, and with this the relative importance and uniqueness of the London approach, came to be recognized. Both Thirlby and Wiseman, in the most recently published papers in this volume, recognized the depth of mainstream intellectual error, but their plaints were largely ignored. One reason perhaps lies in the fact that the critique of orthodoxy is too fundamental; to accept fully the implications of the theory of opportunity cost that is implicit in these essays requires the modern economist to throw overboard too much of his invested intellectual capital. How can we write the elementary textbooks and teach the elementary course if we cannot draw the standard cost curves? How can we carry out benefit-cost analysis and pretend that we are assisting in social decision-making? How can we say anything at all about managing nationalized public enterprises?

What is so 'revolutionary' in the theory of opportunity cost that threatens the very foundations of modern applied economics? This introductory essay is not designed to summarize the papers reprinted in the volume, and I do not propose to develop my own interpretation and application of the theory. I have done the latter in *Cost and Choice*. But brief elaboration of the central argument may offer some support to my assertions about significance. The basic idea is at once extremely simple and profound. *Cost* is inherently linked to *choice*. This notion did not of course originate with the economists associated with the L.S.E. in the 1930s or before or since. As students of Frank Knight learnt, elements of the correct theory of opportunity cost are found in Adam Smith's deer-and-beaver model. Even before the subjective-value revolution, Francesco Ferrara in Italy was sharply critical of classical theory on opportunity-cost grounds.[6] The opportunity-cost conception was explicitly developed by the Austrians, by the American, H. J. Davenport, and the principle could scarcely have occupied a more central place than it assumed in P. H. Wicksteed's *Common Sense of Political Economy*.[7] This book was independently influential at L.S.E., and it properly deserves mention here.

At the L.S.E. there was the beginning and the widening recognition of the implications of elementary opportunity-cost theory for applications of economics. Herein lies the contribution of the economists who are represented in this volume. Almost all professional economists, old and new, can provide a rough working definition of opportunity cost that is tolerably acceptable for pedagogic purposes. But very few economists, new or old, have been consistent. Almost none of them beyond the London–Austrian axis has recognized just what his own definition suggests for the application of his discipline.

Simply considered, cost is the obstacle or barrier to choice, that which must be got over before choice is made. Cost is the under-side of the coin, so to speak, cost is the displaced alternative, the rejected opportunity. Cost is that which the decision-maker sacrifices or gives up when he selects one alternative rather than another. Cost consists therefore in his own evaluation of the enjoyment or utility that he anticipates having to forgo as a result of choice itself. There are specific implications to be drawn from this choice-bound definition of opportunity cost :

1 Cost must be borne exclusively by the person who makes decisions; it is not possible for this cost to be shifted to or imposed on others.

---

[6] See my *Fiscal Theory and Political Economy* (Chapel Hill, North Carolina 1960), pp. 27-30 for a summary treatment. One of my own unfinished projects is a critical analysis of Ferrara's work, with a view towards making his contribution more widely known to English-language readers.

[7] London 1910.

2 Cost is subjective; it exists only in the mind of the decision-maker or chooser.

3 Cost is based on anticipations; it is necessarily a forward-looking or *ex ante* concept.

4 Cost can never be realized because of the fact that choice is made; the alternative which is rejected can never itself be enjoyed.

5 Cost cannot be measured by someone other than the chooser since there is no way that subjective mental experience can be directly observed.

6 Cost can be dated at the moment of final decision or choice.[8]

In any general theory of choice cost must be reckoned in a *utility* rather than in a *commodity* dimension. From this it follows that the opportunity cost involved in choice cannot be observed and objectified and, more importantly, it cannot be measured in such a way as to allow comparisons over wholly different choice settings. The cost faced by the utility-maximizing owner of a firm, the value that he anticipates having to forgo in choosing to produce an increment to current output, is not the cost faced by the utility-maximizing bureaucrat who manages a publicly owned firm, even if the physical aspects of the two firms are in all respects identical. As the London economists stressed, cost is that which might be avoided by not making choice. In our example the private owner could avoid the explicit incremental outlay *and* the incremental profit opportunity should he fail to produce the output increment. The socialist manager, by our assumptions, could avoid the same objective consequences by taking the same course of action. These consequences could be measured in monetary terms. But the opportunity cost relevant to choice-making must be translated into a utility dimension through a subjective and personal evaluation. The private owner may evaluate the objectively measurable consequences of choice quite differently from the bureaucrat, although both are utility-maximizers.

I am not suggesting that the contributors to the London tradition in cost theory fully appreciated and understood all the implications of their own conception, nor that even now they

---

[8] For a detailed discussion of each of these attributes of opportunity cost see my *Cost and Choice*, chapter 3.

would endorse my interpretation of this conception. I suggest only that their several papers mark a beginning of such appreciation, that they reflect an early critical questioning of aspects of modern economic theory, a questioning that is more urgently needed in the 1970s than it was when they wrote.

While the contribution of the L.S.E. group of economists should be emphasized, the constructive content of their work should not be exaggerated. Taken as a whole, the London effort is largely negative in its impact. Properly interpreted, it demonstrates major flaws in the applications and extensions of economic theory. But there is little in this work which assists us in marrying 'subjectivist' and 'objectivist' economic theory. Few modern economists would be willing to go all the way with the latter-day Austrians and convert economics into a purely logical exercise. Most of us want to retain, and rightly so, positive and predictive content in the discipline, to hold fast to the genuine 'science' that seems possible. To accomplish this, however, *homo economicus* must be returned to scientific respectability, and economists must learn to accept that hypotheses may be falsified. Finally, and more importantly, we must try to construct meaningful, if limited, norms for decision-making in non-market institutional structures. In competitive markets prices tend to equal marginal costs, but do we want to *make* prices equal 'marginal costs' in non-market settings, when we fully realize that marginal costs can only be objectified by the arbitrary selection of some artificially homogenized measure? Do we really want to make one beaver exchange for only two deer when poisonous snakes abound near the beaver dams? Of course not! But how do we know that the snakes are there? Because the beaver hunters think they are?[9]

[9] I am indebted to my colleagues, Thomas Borcherding and Gordon Tullock for helpful comments.

2

Remarks upon certain aspects of the theory of costs

LIONEL ROBBINS

A lecture delivered before the Nationalökonomischen Gesellschaft, Vienna, 7 April 1933. First published in the *Economic Journal* (March 1934).

The theory of costs is not one of those parts of economic analysis which can properly be said to have been unduly neglected. It has always occupied a more or less central position, and in recent years it has been the subject of a quite formidable body of new work. There is, indeed, no part of his subject about which the contemporary economist may legitimately feel more gratified, either as regards the quality of the work which has been done or as regards the temper in which it has been undertaken. Yet, in spite of this, the present state of affairs in this field is not altogether satisfactory. The various problems involved have been tackled by different sets of people; and the conclusions which have been reached in one part of the field have sometimes a rather disquieting appearance of incompatibility with conclusions which have been reached elsewhere. No doubt some of this apparent incompatibility is real. It is not to be expected that here – any more than elsewhere – economists should have reached finality. But some of it is probably illusory; and if in discussing these matters we were to state more decisively the problems which we are attempting to solve, and the assumptions on which we proceed, it seems likely that not only should we be able to clear up our outstanding real points of difference more quickly, but that, in the course of doing so, we should also discover that many of them depended essentially upon subtle differences of object and assumption, hitherto insufficiently stated. At any rate, it is in the belief that this would be so that these very tentative remarks are put forward.

The paper falls into four parts. In the first I discuss the fundamental nature of costs; in the second the relation between this conception and the Marshallian supply curve; in the third the relation between costs and technical productivity. I conclude with some notes on cost variation through time.

I

I start, then, with fundamentals. The conception of costs in modern economic theory is a conception of displaced alternatives: the cost of obtaining anything is what must be surrendered in order to get it. The process of valuation is essentially a process of choice, and costs are the negative aspect of this process. In the theory of exchange, therefore, costs reflect the value of the things surrendered. In the theory of production they reflect also the value of alternative uses of productive factors – that is, of products which do not come into existence because existing products are preferred.[1] Such is the conception of costs first systematically developed by Wieser[2] and made familiar in English-speaking areas by Green, Wicksteed, Davenport, Knight and Henderson.[3] Following the usage of Pantaleoni[4] and many others, we may refer to it for short as Wieser's Law.

It is probably true to say that at the present day the broad outlines of this conception are generally acceptable.[5] The work of

[1] This somewhat roundabout way of putting matters is deliberate. The money costs of production in any line of industry are a reflection of 1) the value of factors of production wholly specialized to that line of production (Wieser's 'specific' factors) and 2) the value of transferable ('non-specific') divisible factors in other uses. It is in regard to these latter ingredients that Wieser's propositions have special relevance.

[2] *Ursprung und Hauptgesetze des wirtschaftlichen Werthers*, pp. 146-70; *Natural Value*, pp. 171-214; *Theorie der gesellschaftlichen Wirtschaft*, pp. 61-4, 73-81, 142-6; also the juvenile work *Über das Verhältnis der Kosten zum Wert* ('Gesammelte Abhandlungen', pp. 377-404).

[3] See D. L. Green, 'Opportunity Cost and Pain Cost', *Quarterly Journal of Economics* (1894), pp. 218-29; P. H. Wicksteed, *The Common-sense of Political Economy*, p. 373; Davenport, *Value and Distribution*, pp. 551-2; *The Economics of Enterprise*, pp. 106-49; Knight, *Risk, Uncertainty and Profit*, p. 92; 'Fallacies in the Interpretation of Social Cost', *Quarterly Journal of Economics* (1924), p. 582; Henderson, *Supply and Demand*, p. 162.

[4] *Pure Economics*, p. 184.

[5] It is sometimes held that Wieser's Law is only true of a state of affairs in which the supplies of the factors of production are fixed. If these supplies are flexible, it is urged, then the disutility principle – the concept of real cost as real pains

22

Wieser's successors in this field – in particular the various writings of Professor Mayer – have brought home to us all its central importance as a unifying principle in the structure of modern analysis. And, in the sphere of applied economics, it becomes more and more clear that many of the most urgent problems of the day can be understood only in the light of the knowledge that it furnishes.[6]

and sacrifices – comes into its own as an independent principle of explanation. (See Edgeworth, *Papers Relating to Political Economy*, 3, pp. 56-64; Robertson, *Economic Fragments*, p. 21; Viner, 'The Theory of Comparative Costs' in *Weltwirtschaftliches Archiv*, 36, pp. 411 ff.). The objection is plausible but it is not ultimately valid. Even when we are contemplating a situation in which the total supplies of the factors actually used in production are flexible, it is quite easy to show that Wieser's Law is still applicable. Variations in the total supply of labour in productive industry are accompanied by variations in the amount of time and energy which is available for other uses. Variations in the supply of land in production are accompanied by changes in the supply of land put to consumptive uses. Variations in the supply of capital are accompanied by variations in present consumption. All economic changes are capable of being exhibited as forms of exchange. And hence, as Wicksteed has shown, they can be exhibited further as the resultant of demand operating within a given technical environment. (See Wicksteed, *Common-sense of Political Economy*, especially I, chapter ix; also F. X. Weiss, 'Die moderne Tendenz in der Lehre vom Geldwert', *Zeitschrift für Volkswirtschaft, Socialpolitik, und Verwaltung*, 19, p. 518; and Wicksell, *Vorlesungen*, 1, p. 159). It has been said that this becomes impossible if account be taken of the so-called other advantages and disadvantages of different occupations. Professor Viner in the article cited above has urged this particular objection. The difficulty however seems to be capable of a simple solution. If the other advantages and disadvantages are treated as joint products, the Wicksteed constructions can still be maintained.

[6] An example should make this quite plain. The introduction of improved methods of production sometimes has the effect of causing the price of the particular line of product concerned to fall below costs of production, and observation of this fact has often led to the belief that therefore the mechanism of free markets is incapable of dealing with the effects of scientific invention. But what does such a situation imply? Prices are below costs; the products fetch less than the amounts which have to be paid for the factors which produce them. But why is this? If the factors were completely specialized to the line of production in question – i.e. if they had no mobility – then in a free system their prices would fall automatically with the fall in the prices of their products. There could be no lasting disparity between prices and money costs. But the costs of transferable factors, according to Wieser's Law, are a reflection of their value in other possible uses. If therefore in one line of production costs of production are higher than prices, this means under our assumptions that there are factors of production in that line which are more urgently demanded elsewhere – that the change in technique creates a new equilibrium of factors. As the transfer takes place under the pressure of the costs disparities, there will be movements of prices and costs tending to a restoration of profitability. It follows therefore that, if technical progress is accompanied by more extensive disequilibrium, the causes must be sought outside the area covered by our assumptions; the market is not free, the monetary mechanism is not functioning properly.

But there is one matter on which there is not yet full agreement. It relates to the precise *mode* in which the displaced alternatives are to be conceived. Wieser's usage is clear. They are to be conceived in terms of *values* – in terms of the values of the goods of the first order displaced. 'The cost of production of one thing', said Wicksteed, 'is the marginal value of another thing.'[7] This is the sense in which it has usually been understood. In recent years, however, it has been suggested in some quarters that they should be conceived in terms of technical *quantities* – in terms of the quantities (as distinct from the values) of the goods of the first order which might have been produced. This is the procedure suggested by Professor Knight in his 'Suggestion for Simplifying the Statement of the General Theory of Price'.[8] He invokes Adam Smith's parable of the beaver and the deer and concludes: 'In sum, the cost of beaver is deer and the cost of deer is beaver, and that is the only objective and scientific content of the cost notion.' The same procedure is adopted by Dr Haberler in his recent article on the theory of comparative cost.[9]

Now there can be no doubt that there is much that can be said for this suggestion. The conception of costs as technical displacement has an objectivity and precision which is in itself an advantage. It has none of that elusiveness which seems to inhere in concepts involving subjective valuation. Moreover it is true that in equilibrium the values of goods produced with common factors of production and variability of technical coefficients are necessarily in harmony with their displacement-cost ratios. It has been well known since the time of the classical economists that this was the case with the products of simple unskilled labour. This is, of course, the moral of the parable of the beaver and the deer. It is the achievement of Professor Knight and Dr Haberler to have shown that the same generalization can be extended to cover the

---

There is nothing in the institutions of exchange as such which makes technical progress necessarily self-frustrating. This conclusion, which follows directly from Wieser's Law, is surely a conclusion of considerable practical importance.

[7] *Common-sense of Political Economy*, p. 382; cf. also, Rosenstein-Rodan, 'Grenznutzen' in *Handworterbuch der Staatswissenschaften*, 4, pp. 1198 ff.

[8] *Journal of Political Economy*, 36 (1928), pp. 353-70.

[9] *Weltwirtschaftliches Archiv*, 32, pp. 353-70, especially the note on p. 358.

case of production with more than one factor of production. If the amount of a commodity produced by a combination of factors of production is not the same as can be procured by devoting the same combination to the production of something else and procuring the first commodity by way of exchange, then clearly, if the conditions of production are technically variable, there will be evoked movements which tend to bring about this harmony.

So far so good. The argument seems overwhelmingly convincing. But on closer inspection certain difficulties present themselves. In the first place it is important to recognize that there are wide areas where the conception of costs as technical displacements clearly has no application. This is the case if the productive process involves fixed technical coefficients. The imputation problem (and hence the cost problem) here can only be solved in value terms. Costs of production in value terms can and will change with changes in demand.[10] But the idea of changes in technical displacements in this instance has no meaning. The same is true where we are considering commodities produced with different factors of production. If A and B are produced with n and m and C and D with p and q, there will exist exchange ratios *between* members of the first group and members of the second, but it is impossible to conceive of technical displacement cost ratios save *within* them. There may be an exchange ratio between A and D, but when A is produced there is no technical quantity of D sacrificed. Yet there will certainly exist costs of production in the value sense.

Moreover – and this is even more important – it is the central requirement of any theory of cost that it shall explain the *actual* resistances which production in any line of industry encounters;

[10] We can see this most clearly if we contemplate an extreme case. Suppose a state of affairs in which two commodities are produced by the aid of two classes of factors of production – the factors entering into the manufacture of the two commodities in proportions which are different for each commodity. (For example, PA involves $2x$ and $1y$ and PB $1x$ and $2y$.) Now suppose a shift of demand. The relative scarcities of the factors and of the products will change. The cost of production (in money terms) of the commodity whose manufacture involves the higher proportion of the factor which has become relatively scarcer will rise. The cost of production of the commodity whose manufacture involves a higher proportion of the factor which has become relatively less scarce will fall. There is no movement of technical displacements which corresponds to this.

that it shall explain to us the influences determining the elements of which account is taken by those responsible for production. Now there can be no doubt that these influences are of the nature of valuations. The isolated producer thinks of the sacrifice he is making by not producing something else. The entrepreneur in the exchange economy thinks of the prices he has to pay for the factors of production. In each case, although – as with all valuations – there may be in the background a technical condition, yet the final determinant is not merely technical. The isolated producer thinks not merely of the quantity of goods he gives up, but of their place on the relative scale, compared with the place on the relative scale of the goods he acquires. The price which the entrepreneur pays for the factors of production he uses is determined not by the *number* of products which they can produce elsewhere, but by the value of such products. Indeed it is most highly improbable that he knows at all the number of products which can be produced elsewhere. All that he knows are values of the factors of production, which are, of course, reflections of the value of other products. If we reflect upon the way in which equilibrium is established, it is surely obvious that it is only through regard for cost in the value sense that any harmony between technical displacements and prices can be conceived to come about. It is only in equilibrium that such a harmony exists. In a state of disequilibrium, prices, costs and displacement ratios may all be different. If we do not keep these things conceptually discrete, we cannot understand the actual process of equilibration. This is not merely true of the Austrian approach. The condition that prices shall be equal to cost of production in the value sense is as essential a condition of equilibrium in the Walrasian system as the condition that marginal products shall be proportionate to factor prices.

For both these reasons, therefore, because there are whole areas where technical displacements are not conceivable, and because it does not focus attention on the actual process of price formation, I conclude that the conception of costs as quantities of goods forgone is not acceptable. No doubt the technical conditions of production play an important part in determining the conditions of equilibrium. But to make the cost concept purely technical is to deprive it of important analytical functions and to run the risk of misunderstanding. We shall see that a very similar procedure underlies some of the deficiencies of particular equilibrium analysis.

But this brings me to the second part of my paper: the relation between this general conception of costs and the Marshallian supply curve.

II

According to Wieser's Law, costs of production under competitive conditions are a reflection of the value of the alternatives which are displaced in order that the goods in that line of production may be produced and appropriated by the ultimate consumers. That is to say, they are essentially a reflection of the strength of excluded demands – demands both for the specific factors specialized to such lines of production and the non-specific factors capable of employment elsewhere. It seems to follow that, in the normal case, at the point of equilibrium, just as demand price will be decreasing, so will cost be increasing. This is quite obvious in the case of equilibrium of two commodities. To push production beyond that point would involve a product of diminishing relative utility – that is, a sacrifice of increased relative utility. I do not think that the situation is fundamentally changed when we consider many commodities. Nor do I think that in this connection it is necessary to take account of the possibilities of unusual utility functions. To move in any direction from a position of equilibrium is to encounter increased resistance: this is the fundamental conception.

But if this is so, what are we to say of the constructions, so familiar in the Marshallian system of what is sometimes called – in my opinion not very helpfully – 'partial equilibrium analysis' : the supply curve parallel to the x axis, and the supply curve with a negative inclination? At first sight we seem to be faced with a complete contradiction. Here are constructions which, if *they* are valid, seem to point to a definite rejection of our fundamental conception, while if *it* is valid, seem themselves to be doomed to be rejected. Nor are we in any way reassured when, turning to post-Marshallian criticism, we find it stated on high authority that, for the analysis of competitive conditions – and of course it is competitive conditions which are in question – constant cost is to be regarded as the normal and increasing cost as the quite exceptional condition.[11] We seem to have discovered a major inconsistency in the very centre of the corpus of pure economics.

Now in circumstances of this kind, before concluding that it is necessary to make a complete break with one or other of the apparently conflicting usages, it is always advisable to inquire more closely into the implicit assumptions on which they proceed. Again and again in the history of economic thought the apparent contradiction between different usages has come to be seen to rest not upon deficiencies of logic on the one side or the other, but upon differences of assumption concerning the problem to be solved. This was notoriously so in the case of the historic disputes regarding the theory of rent.[12] A similar difference can, I think, be shown to underlie part at least of this apparent contradiction in the theory of costs.

For if we look more closely at the constructions in question, it becomes fairly clear that they are appropriate to the investigation of fundamentally separate problems. The general propositions regarding costs which spring from Wieser's Law are essentially a description of the conditions of equilibrium. They answer the question, what would happen to costs if, from a position of equilibrium – *other things remaining equal* – it were attempted to increase or diminish production in any particular line of industry. The constructions which we associate with particular equilibrium analysis, on the other hand, deal with what would happen if *other things were varied*; i.e. if production were to be increased in

---

[11] P. Straffa, 'The Laws of Costs under Competitive Conditions', *Economic Journal* (1926), pp. 535, 550.

[12] I have attempted to indicate some of the more important of such cases in an article entitled 'On a Certain Ambiguity in the Conception of Stationary Equilibrium', *Economic Journal* (1930), pp. 194-214. The present paper is to be regarded as essentially a continuation of the same train of thought – but applied to a wider area than the simple analysis of final equilibrium.

response to an increase in demand. That is to say, that they are essentially germane to a theory of variations. They relate not to forces which maintain equilibrium once it is established, but rather to the differences between one equilibrium position and another.

Once this is realized the apparent contradiction which we have been considering vanishes. If other things do not change and it is attempted to increase the supply of a certain product, from the point of equilibrium, then it is natural that costs should rise, for the increase must be brought about by the use of factors which are more urgently demanded elsewhere. But if other things change – if, for instance, there is an increase in the demand for this line of product – then an increase of production to meet it need not encounter such an increased resistance. The change in the data which is characterized by the increase in demand here must be accompanied by a diminution of demand elsewhere, and this may be such as to release factors of production in such measure as to permit the necessary extension at constant, or even at diminishing cost. Once the data change, there is no presumption that an increase in output of a particular kind must be accompanied by more than proportionately increased outlay.

There is therefore no fundamental incompatibility between the implications of Wieser's Law and the constructions of 'particular equilibrium' cost analysis. But it still remains to decide what degree of validity is to be attributed to these constructions in the actual connections in which they are most frequently employed.

If what I have been urging is correct, it seems clear that we cannot regard the Marshallian supply curves as serving the exact purposes of any causal explanation. They are rather to be regarded as providing schemata of certain possibilities of price variation. *If* the demand varies in this way and *if* the cost varies in this way, then it is implicit in these assumptions that the price will change in this way. They provide, as it were, a convenient shorthand note of different ways in which particular changes may be regarded. According to Edgeworth, 'movement along a supply and demand curve of international trade should be regarded as attended with rearrangements of internal trade: as the movements of the hand of a clock corresponds to considerable unseen movements of the machinery'.[13] It is the implication of what I have already said, that this too must be the way in which we should view the supply curves of the theory of domestic values, if our usage is not to be out of harmony with the more precise implications of general-equilibrium analysis. They are notes of the implications of given changes of the general conditions of demand *and* supply, even though one curve is not shifted.

If this is true, it follows that the construction in question must have a very limited validity for the analysis of the ultimate conditions of equilibrium. Its essential function is to facilitate the examination of what happens when certain conditions are varied. The assumption which underlies its use in descriptions of final equilibrium, that all possible variations outside the particular industry or market under consideration may be neglected, is essentially incompatible with the assumptions upon which any exhaustive description of such conditions must necessarily be based. This, indeed, is only another way of putting the point which has already been made. The assumption that the factors of production have an infinitely elastic supply leads to a concentration on the purely technical features of the situation which *necessarily* misleads when the conditions of final equilibrium have to be determined. The objection made earlier to the Knight–Haberler method of treating technical displacements as equivalent to value costs applies much more strongly to a treatment of value costs which proceeds as if only technical determinants were relevant. It is quite true that, in a condition of competitive equilibrium, the prices of factors common to different industries are the same for the different industries concerned. But this is one of the *results* of the equilibrating process. It cannot be assumed to be a *condition* which would necessarily persist, were the other

---

[13] *Papers Relating to Political Economy*, 2, p. 32. Of course this usage of the integral curves, which assumes other commodities besides those registered on the co-ordinates to be produced in the economy under consideration, must be distinguished from the use of similar curves under the assumption that only two commodities are capable of coming into existence. There are objections to the use of such an apparatus, well known to all readers of Pareto, but it is arguable that if Marshall had proceeded on these lines he would have been much more reluctant to adopt his compromise constructions than in fact he was.

relations in the equilibrium disturbed. Yet this, of course, is the implication of a 'constant cost' supply curve which is prolonged on either side of the point of equilibrium intersection.

Now, no doubt, once we get away from the hypothesis of pure competition, there are many problems in which the technical element is so predominant that for certain purposes constructions which focus attention upon such elements are permissible and helpful. It is well known that this is so in the case of the theory of monopoly. Recent work suggests that it is so in the case of the analysis of imperfect competition.

But such uses have their limitations. It is clear that they may be very definitely misleading when it is a question of deciding the significance for the economic system as a whole of one equilibrium position as compared with another. As I have argued elsewhere,[14] I am of the view that most investigations of this sort beg other, more fundamental, methodological questions. But, putting this on one side, it is surely clear that constructions which depend on the assumption that other things elsewhere remain unchanged, must necessarily lead to false conclusions when it is a question of estimating the total significance of changes which, by definition, *cannot* be unaccompanied by changes elsewhere.

A simple example will make this clear. In the analysis of monopoly, for certain purposes the apparatus of intersecting demand-and-supply curves provides first approximations which are acceptable. But in any attempt to discover the significance for the economic system as a whole of monopoly in any line of industry it is open to very grave objections. For the assumption on which it proceeds – the assumption that other things remain equal – is incompatible with the most obvious implication of monopolistic restrictions; namely, the assumption that, since the number of factors employed in the monopolized industry is different from what would otherwise have been the case, their productivity in price terms *must necessarily be different*. It is illegitimate to argue that this change is of the second order of smalls. It may be of the second order of smalls for the monopolist's price policy. It may be

---

[14] See my *Essay on the Nature and Significance of Economic Science*, chapter vi, para. 2.

of the second order of smalls in each of the other branches of industry affected; but for all the other branches of industry taken collectively it must be of a magnitude comparable in the universe of discourse – the 'social' effect of the policy – with the magnitude of the primary variation. The objection, it will be noted, is almost exactly symmetrical with the fundamental objection to the use of the concept of consumers' surplus.

The case I have chosen is, of course, a very simple one. I should be very sorry to be understood as suggesting that those who use the apparatus I am discussing more frequently than I would care to do are likely to be unaware of the proposition it exemplifies. But experience of the controversies of the last twenty years does, I think, suggest that the use of supply curves, rather than the apparatus of general-equilibrium analysis, in discussing questions of this sort, carries with it dangers which may entrap even the subtlest and acutest intellects. There is a passage in the late Professor Young's critique of Professor Pigou's former position with regard to diminishing return industries[15] which has always seemed to me to be especially significant in this respect although, curiously enough, it has not attracted as much attention as other parts of the article. 'The problem as a whole, it seems to me,' he says, 'is one to which the general theory of the diminishing productivity of individual factors is appropriate rather than the curve of marginal supply prices.'[16] A fallacy which ensnared both Edgeworth and Professor Pigou is one which must necessarily be regarded as peculiarly deceptive. But I doubt very much whether they would have been thus ensnared if, instead of approaching the problem from the point of view of the intersecting curves of particular-equilibrium analysis, they had started from the marginal-productivity theorems – the example *par excellence* of the general-equilibrium approach.

---

[15] *Wealth and Welfare*, pp. 172-9.

[16] *Quarterly Journal of Economics*, 27, pp. 676ff. See also Knight, 'Fallacies in the Interpretation of Social Cost', *Quarterly Journal of Economics*, (1924), pp. 218-29. Professor Pigou's retraction of his original proposition is to be found in the second edition of the *Economics of Welfare*, p. 194; Edgeworth's endorsement of this retraction in his review of this volume, 'The Doctrine of Social Net Product', *Economic Journal* (1925) pp. 30 ff.

I hope I have said enough to make clear my view that there are profound dangers in any approach to the cost problem which identifies cost with the merely technical or which treats costs as if only technical influences were significant. It is therefore with an easy conscience that I can advance to an examination of certain aspects of the relation between costs and productivity in the technical sense.

There is no need for me to detain the reader with an examination of those variations of technical productivity which lead to increasing supply price. This is one of those parts of economic analysis where there is little ground for disagreement on purely analytical considerations. Dr Sraffa, who is sceptical of the importance of the conception, bases his scepticism avowedly upon empirical grounds. Cases where one line of production utilizes so large a proportion of the total supply of any factor of production that changes in the demand for the product will bring about changes in its price, he thinks, are rare. This view is apparently shared by Professor Knight. Whether or not one regards this as having *prima facie* plausibility, depends in part, I think, upon one's view on the classification of the factors of production. It sounds much more plausible if one thinks of two factors of production than if one thinks of many. But, in any case, no analytical issue is at stake.

But, on the other hand, when we come to those technical conditions which lead to diminishing supply price we find a very different state of affairs. The broad considerations involved in the discussion of imperfect competition and monopoly are perhaps not open to serious question. But the problems of diminishing costs under competition are still the subject of dispute and it is interesting to linger a little in this region.

We have seen already that if demand for a particular commodity increases, it may be accompanied by changes in demand elsewhere such as to cheapen the factors of production in the line of production in question. This is a possibility which emerges from general-equilibrium theory, but it is not the possibility with which I wish to concern myself in this connection. What I want to do rather is to concentrate upon the possibility of cost reductions which are due to the operation of technical factors.

Now at the present time it is generally agreed that, under purely competitive conditions, such reductions must be the effect in the first instance of the operation of external economies. That is clear even if, with Marshall and Mr Shove, we recognize that the operation of external economies may be accompanied by changes in the optimal size of firms which themselves involve cost reduction. Unless external economies are operative, the technical influences making for diminishing costs will exhaust themselves before the first point of competitive equilibrium is reached. The influences making for cost reduction must be *outside* the firms whose costs per unit are under observation.

So far so good; but now the question arises why the external economies operate only as the scale of production increases. Clearly the answer is that it does not pay to initiate the enterprises from which they spring until the demand for the ultimate produce is of a certain size. The doctrine of external economies, as Young emphasized, is merely one way of introducing into analytical constructions the old Smithian doctrine of the advantages of division of labour. It is one of the most familiar platitudes of this doctrine that the wider the market the wider the division of labour which is made possible.

But this does not completely answer our question. For we still remain in the dark concerning the reason why the advantages of division of labour must wait upon extensions of the market. Why cannot the various cost-reducing divisions take place *ab initio*, but *each on a smaller scale*? If we put the question in this way, the answer is obvious. For technical reasons they cannot be on a smaller scale. The quantities of factors which are exploited in a progressive division of labour are *indivisible* below a certain absolute size. Division of labour, external economies, depend upon demand conditions which render indivisible potentialities of production profitable.

But to solve the question in this way is only to find ourselves confronted with another. We have explained the possibility of

34

diminishing costs in this sense by invoking the existence of indivisibility in the methods of production. But the assumption of competition seems to preclude the existence of indivisible factors; in a fully competitive situation the factors of production must be capable of infinite division – or, in practical terms, of such degree of divisibility as to preclude the existence of any increasing return combination, using the term in its technical sense. How then, as the market enlarges with a general increase of factors of production, can we assume indivisibility to be exploited?

The answer is, I think, to be found in the distinction between actual and potential uses of factors of production. It may very well be the case that, given the total conditions of production, productive factors are sufficiently divisible in all the uses to which they are put for the situation to be regarded as competitive. But it is quite possible, at the same time, that some of these factors have *potential uses of a different sort* which, because of their technical indivisibility, are not exploited until the system as a whole, or large parts of it, has expanded. This, I believe, is a proposition which throws light, not only on the questions we are discussing, but also upon wider questions of localization and general-population theory. Let me try to explain what I mean.

Let me start with the simplest possible example. Among a group of independent producers of some simple product there may be one producer who has special skill at – shall we say – marketing. As a marketer he is greatly superior to the others. As a producer of the simple product he has equal skill. But his skill as a marketer cannot be satisfactorily employed unless there is a certain minimum quantity of marketing to do. Until demand has reached that point, therefore, he appears in the system as a provider of units of simple homogeneous undifferentiated labour like the rest. The competitive situation is stable. But beyond that point he emerges in a new role. He is now another factor of production – hitherto not appearing in the equations of equilibrium. At first, of course, in this situation he may be in a monopolistic position. But until the point at which it paid to employ him in this way the situation was fully competitive.

The example I have given is one which can be supposed to

occur under conditions which, to all intents and purposes, may be regarded as *a*capitalistic – that is, a condition in which production has not yet become, in important senses, roundabout: conditions in which there is little vertical division of labour. But, of course, it is under more fully developed capitalistic conditions that the phenomena which it typifies become important. As capital accumulates, and demand increases, it pays to combine original factors of production, hitherto used in other ways, to produce technically indivisible means of production – machines, means of transport, and so on, which hitherto, because of their indivisibility, have not figured in the realized system of productive combinations at all. (If we think of the way in which capital accumulation has made possible the utilization of indivisible transport systems, we can see how important considerations of this sort must be in any theory of localization.) It is clear that the advantages of roundabout production are essentially the advantages of this vertical division of labour and that another way of describing them is to say that they consist in the progressive exploitation of potential methods of production excluded in less expanded systems by their technical indivisibility.

It is in this sense, I take it, that we are to interpret the theory of increasing returns developed by the late Professor Allyn Young in his presidential address to the British Association.[17] And it is worth noting, as he showed, how the phenomena in question escape the apparatus of particular-equilibrium analysis and, indeed, involve changes which are quite incompatible with its assumptions. Granted the assumption of the Youngian analysis, we can see how diminishing costs can be regarded as *implicit* in a situation which is actually competitive. But we see, too, that such developments are to be regarded as being much more probably the function of the development of many industries than of one of them. We see too – and this is perhaps the more important point – that the diminution of costs here contemplated is essentially the product of vertical division of labour – that is, of the dis-

[17] I ought perhaps to state explicitly that this is merely an interpretation. It is not a transmission of any esoteric oral tradition. My own views on these matters spring chiefly from reflections on the remarks on the variations of productivity in Taylor's *Principles of Economics*, pp. 141-2.

integration of industries. Neither of these things is compatible with the implications of the supply curve. This seems to constitute a presumption that the use of this instrument in the analysis of variation may well involve a concentration on the insignificant exception to the neglect of what, both from the point of view of theory and practice, must be regarded as the typical and significant cases.

IV

So far in this paper the propositions I have discussed have for the most part dealt with variations of costs in terms of what has been well called comparative statics. That is to say, they consist essentially of a comparison of two states of equilibrium, and an investigation of the causes of difference. The demand for a group of products increases so that in the new equilibrium position factor prices and costs of production are different, and so on. They do little to elucidate the actual process of change – the path followed through time between one equilibrium position and the other.[18] This is notoriously the field of theoretical economics in which least has been done and in which most remains still to do. In concluding this survey, therefore, it seems appropriate to add certain remarks on this matter.

It is not necessary in this connection to expatiate on the significance of the Austrian contribution to this theory. It is clear that, in the characteristically Austrian constructions, we have a technique which is pre-eminently suited to the explanation of the phenomena of movement. On the demand side, the conception of the dependent use (*abhängige Nutzen*); on the supply side, the conception of the displaced alternative – here we are dealing with

---

[18] The distinction between these two stages of the theory of variations is not often clearly recognized in the English and American literature. It is, however, very clearly stated by Pareto (*Manual*, p. 147), and it has recently been the subject of important studies by Mayer, Rosenstein-Rodan and Schams. See Mayer, 'Der Erkenntniswert der funktionellen Preistheorien', *Wirtschaftstheorie der Gegenwart*, 2, pp. 146-239; Rosenstein-Rodan, 'Das Zeitmoment in der mathematischen Theorie des wirtschaftlichen Gleichgewitchtes', *Zeitschrift für Nationalökonomie*, 1, pp. 129-42; Schams, 'Komparatives Statik', *Zeitschrift für Nationalökonomie*, 2, pp. 27-61. See also my article on Production in the *Encyclopedia of the Social Sciences*.

elements which are the actual focus of attention of the economic subjects through whom changes come about. No one who has followed Wicksteed's exposition of the continuous relevance of Wieser's Law to the explanation of change[19] can doubt that the main instrument of explanation in this field has already been devised.[20]

These things are well known. Rather than linger in this neighbourhood, it is more profitable to turn once more to the Marshallian system. For here we have theories in which propositions which are true and helpful are not altogether disentangled from ways of expression which sometimes give rise to misapprehension.

The Marshallian doctrine of short and long period price is essentially an attempt to provide a theory of price change in terms of the length of time which is taken to overcome various technical obstacles on the supply side. The relative specificity – to use Wieser's term – of productive factors means that the immediate response to a change in the conditions of demand or supply is not necessarily a response to an ultimate equilibrium position. To take Marshall's own example: in the short period, a change in the demand for fish will be met by an increased output from existing fishermen and a more intensive use of fishing gear already in existence. In the long period, however – I use Marshall's own words – 'the normal supply price . . . is governed by a different set of causes, and with different results'.[21] Capital and labour come into the industry or leave it; the fixed equipment involved is augmented or depleted. In the sphere of cost theory this leads to the distinction between prime and supplementary expenses; in the sphere of distribution theory, to the distinction between quasi-rents and interest.

[19] *Common-sense of Political Economy*, I, chapter ix.

[20] It is significant in this connection that historically the Austrian theories are said to have sprung from Menger's inability to explain the short-term fluctuations of produce and stock markets in terms of the classical generalizations. It is clear that for the most part the classical theories are to be regarded as theories of comparitive statics (in the sense explained above) with the differences between successive states of equilibrium explained in technical terms. The wage-fund theory in certain aspects has of course a more dynamic character.

[21] *Principles*, 8th ed., p. 370.

Now there can be no doubt that this doctrine contains much that is most valuable and important. The distinction between the immediate and more distant effects of a given change in demand, the imposition of a small tax, and so on and so forth – this is one of the most significant distinctions of the theory of variations, and it is one of Marshall's most conspicuous achievements that it has become universally recognized. None the less, as it stands, it is by no means immune from criticism. In particular two criticisms suggest themselves.

In the first place it may be suggested that it is liable to give rise to considerable misapprehension if one speaks, as Marshall does in the passage I have quoted, as if the causes operating in the long run are different from the causes operating in the short. Given a change in the data and the other fundamental conditions – including, as we shall see, what other people think about the data – the process of price change through time is determinate. The path followed by price, the rate and magnitude of the change, is determined by the total situation. Although the effects of the different conditions operative may *show themselves* at different points in the path, it is misleading to speak as if, from the moment of change onward, they were not each in operation. When the demand for fish increases, if it is supposed that the increase will be permanent, there is not an interval which elapses before the 'long period tendencies' begin to operate. They *operate* from the beginning, but, owing to their nature, their *effects* are not manifest until some time has elapsed. It is therefore arguable, I think, that to have different labels for the discussion of long- and short-period effects here is liable to veil the essentially continuous nature of the economic process. Short-period and long-period theory in this sense do not explain different processes. They explain different *sections* of the same process. It would be absurd to suggest that this was not known to Marshall. But it is none the less true that his particular mode of expressing himself has sometimes led to its being overlooked by his readers.

Secondly – and this criticism is more substantial – here too, as in other Marshallian constructions which we have examined, it may be objected that the emphasis tends to have too technical a complexion. No doubt the technical obstacles to change, the resistances through time, are fundamental. But it should be clear that, given the range of technical obstacles, the obstacles that will actually be encountered in any process of adaptation depend essentially upon *estimates* of the permanence of the change to which the adaptation is a response. The change which is expected to last for a short period invokes responses essentially different from the responses which are evoked by the change which is expected to be permanent. What are prime and what are supplementary expenses depend essentially upon the length of time over which a change of output is expected to be operative. Thus, if by long period we understand a period long enough for final equilibrium to be reached, we can say that the length of the period is not only a function of the magnitude of the technical obstacles but also of the expectations entertained by the producers. The time it takes for an industry to become adapted to a permanent shrinkage of demand depends in part upon the rate of physical depreciation. But it depends, too, upon the length of time taken by producers to become convinced that the change is permanent.

It seems therefore that in a complete theory of costs the part played by the estimates of the future of the various producers concerned will play a larger part than it plays in the original Marshallian doctrine. But, if this is so, then a further change is probable, which will necessarily bring this part of cost theory into more intimate relations with the other parts of the theory of change. There are certain cases of changes in data where different degrees of foresight on the part of producers have little effect save on the rate of adaptation. A single-line change of demand for consumer's goods in a system otherwise in even balance may be a case of this sort. Here perhaps the old single-line methods of cost analysis may be sufficient to explain the total movement. But there are other cases where the different estimates on the part of producers will themselves bring about further changes in the general situation: a simultaneous falling off of demand for the products of a large group of industries, as at the turn of a trade cycle, is an instance. Here not merely the immediate policy of the producers concerned but the future course of the general oscillation will be, in part at any rate, determined by expectations of the kind here discussed. And here single-line analysis is patently inadequate. If the cost problem here is to be handled properly, it must be dealt with in conjunction with the theory of economic fluctuations. It is probable that the extraordinary sterility of much contemporary thought on the problems of overhead costs and surplus capacity is due to the fact that this junction has not yet been satisfactorily effected.

3

Economics and knowledge

F. A. VON HAYEK

A presidential address to the London Economic Club, 10 November 1936. First published in *Economica* (February 1937).

The ambiguity of the title of this paper is not accidental. Its main subject is of course the role which assumptions and propositions about the knowledge possessed by the different members of society play in economic analysis. But this is by no means unconnected with the other question which might be discussed under the same title, the question to what extent formal economic analysis conveys any knowledge about what happens in the real world. Indeed my main contention will be that the tautologies, of which formal-equilibrium analysis in economics essentially consists, can be turned into propositions which tell us anything about causation in the real world only in so far as we are able to fill those formal propositions with definite statements about how knowledge is acquired and communicated. In short I shall contend that the empirical element in economic theory – the only part which is concerned, not merely with implications but with causes and effects, and which leads therefore to conclusions which, at any rate in principle, are capable of verification[1] – consists of propositions about the acquisition of knowledge.

Perhaps I should begin by reminding you of the interesting fact that in quite a number of the more recent attempts made in different fields to push theoretical investigation beyond the limits of traditional equilibrium analysis, the answer has soon proved to turn on one question which, if not identical with mine, is at least part of it, namely the question of foresight. I think the field where,

---

[1] Or rather falsification. Cf. K. Popper, *Logik der Forschung*, (Vienna 1935), *passim*.

as one would expect, the discussion of the assumptions concerning foresight first attracted wider attention was the theory of risk.[2] The stimulus which was exercised in this connection by the work of Professor F. H. Knight may yet prove to have a profound influence far beyond its special field. Not much later the assumptions to be made concerning foresight proved to be of fundamental importance for the solution of the puzzles of the theory of imperfect competition, the questions of duopoly and oligopoly. And since then it has become more and more obvious that in the treatment of the more 'dynamic' questions of money and industrial fluctuations the assumptions to be made about foresight and 'anticipations' play an equally central role, and that in particular the concepts which were taken over into these fields from pure-equilibrium analysis, like those of an equilibrium rate of interest, could be properly defined only in terms of assumptions concerning foresight. The situation seems here to be that before we can explain why people commit mistakes, we must first explain why they should ever be right.

In general it seems that we have come to a point where we all realize that the concept of equilibrium itself can be made definite and clear only in terms of assumptions concerning foresight, although we may not yet all agree what exactly these essential assumptions are. This question will occupy me later in this paper. At the moment I am only concerned to show that at the present juncture, whether we want to define the boundaries of economic statics or whether we want to go beyond it, we cannot escape the vexed problem of the exact position which assumptions about foresight are to have in our reasoning. Can this be merely an accident?

As I have already suggested, the reason for this seems to me to be that we have to deal here only with a special aspect of a much wider question which we ought to have faced at a much earlier point. Questions essentially similar to those mentioned arise in fact as soon as we try to apply the system of tautologies – those series of

---

[2] A more complete survey of the process by which the significance of anticipations was gradually introduced into economic analysis would probably have to begin with Professor Irving Fisher's *Appreciation and Interest* (1896).

propositions which are necessarily true because they are merely transformations of the assumptions from which we start, and which constitute the main content of equilibrium analysis[3] – to the situation of a society consisting of several independent persons. I have long felt that the concept of equilibrium itself and the methods which we employ in pure analysis, have a clear meaning only when confined to the analysis of the action of a single person, and that we are really passing into a different sphere and silently introducing a new element of altogether different character when we apply it to the explanation of the interactions of a number of different individuals.

I am certain there are many who regard with impatience and distrust the whole tendency, which is inherent in all modern equilibrium analysis, to turn economics into a branch of pure logic, a set of self-evident propositions which, like mathematics or geometry, are subject to no other test but internal consistency. But it seems that if only this process is carried far enough it carries its own remedy with it. In distilling from our reasoning about the facts of economic life those parts which are truly *a priori*, we not only isolate one element of our reasoning as a sort of pure logic of choice in all its purity, but we also isolate, and emphasize the importance of, another element which has been too much neglected. My criticism of the recent tendencies to make economic theory more and more formal is not that they have gone too far, but that they have not yet been carried far enough to complete the isolation of this branch of logic and to restore to its rightful place the

---

[3] I should like to make it clear from the outset that I use the term 'equilibrium analysis' throughout this paper in the narrower sense in which it is equivalent to what Professor Hans Mayer has christened the 'functional' (as distinguished from the 'causal-genetic') approach, and to what used to be loosely described as the 'mathematical school'. It is round this approach that most of the theoretical discussions of the past ten or fifteen years have taken place. It is true that Professor Mayer has held out before us the prospect of another, 'causal-genetic' approach, but it can hardly be denied that this is still largely a promise. It should, however, be mentioned here that some of the most stimulating suggestions on problems closely related to those treated here have come from this circle. Cf., H. Mayer, 'Der Erkenntniswert der funktionellen Preistheorien', *Die Wirtschaftstheorie der Gegenwart*, 2 (1931); P. N. Rosenstein-Rodan, 'Das Zeitmoment in der mathematischen Theorie des wirtschaftlichen Gleichgewichts', *Zeitschrift für Nationalökonomie*, 1, No. 1, and 'The Role of Time in Economic Theory', *Economica* N. S., 1 (1), (1934).

investigation of causal processes, using formal economic theory as a tool in the same way as mathematics.

II

But before I can prove my contention that the tautological propositions of pure-equilibrium analysis as such are not directly applicable to the explanation of social relations, I must first show that the concept of equilibrium *has* a clear meaning if applied to the actions of a single individual, and what this meaning is. Against my contention it might be argued that it is precisely here that the concept of equilibrium is of no significance, because, if one wanted to apply it, all one could say would be that an isolated person was always in equilibrium. But this last statement, although a truism, shows nothing but the way in which the concept of equilibrium is typically misused. What is relevant is not whether a person as such is or is not in equilibrium, but which of his actions stand in equilibrium relationships to each other. All propositions of equilibrium analysis, such as the proposition that relative values will correspond to relative costs, or that a person will equalize the marginal returns of any one factor in its different uses, are propositions about the relations between actions. Actions of a person can be said to be in equilibrium in so far as they can be understood as part of one plan. Only if this is the case, only if all these actions have been decided upon at one and the same moment, and in consideration of the same set of circumstances, have our statements about their interconnections, which we deduce from our assumptions about the knowledge and the preferences of the person, any application. It is important to remember that the so-called 'data', from which we set out in this sort of analysis, are (apart from his tastes) all facts given to the person in question, the things as they are known to (or believed by) him to exist, and not in any sense objective facts. It is only because of this that the propositions we deduce are necessarily *a priori* valid, and that we preserve the consistency of the argument.[4]

[4] Cf., on this point particularly L. Mises, *Grundprobleme der Nationalökonomie* (Jena 1933), pp. 22 ff., 160 ff.

The two main conclusions from these considerations are, *firstly*, that since equilibrium relations exist between the successive actions of a person only in so far as they are part of the execution of the same plan, any change in the relevant knowledge of the person, that is, any change which leads him to alter his plan, disrupts the equilibrium relation between his actions taken before and those taken after the change in his knowledge. In other words, the equilibrium relationship comprises only his actions during the period during which his anticipations prove correct. *Secondly*, that since equilibrium is a relationship between actions, and since the actions of one person must necessarily take place successively in time, it is obvious that the passage of time is essential to give the concept of equilibrium any meaning. This deserves mention since many economists appear to have been unable to find a place for time in equilibrium analysis and consequently have suggested that equilibrium must be conceived as timeless. This seems to me to be a meaningless statement.

III

Now, in spite of what I have said before about the doubtful meaning of equilibrium analysis in this sense if applied to the conditions of a competitive society, I do not of course want to deny that the concept was originally introduced precisely to describe the idea of some sort of balance between the actions of different individuals. All I have argued so far is that the sense in which we use the concept of equilibrium to describe the interdependence of the different actions of one person does not immediately admit of application to the relations between actions of different people. The question really is what use we make of it when we speak of equilibrium with reference to a competitive system.

The first answer which would seem to follow from our approach is that equilibrium in this connection exists if the actions of all members of the society over a period are all executions of their respective individual plans on which each decided at the beginning of the period. But when we inquire further what exactly this implies, it appears that this answer raises more difficulties than it solves. There is no special difficulty about the concept of an isolated person (or a group of persons directed by one of them) acting over a period according to a preconceived plan. In this case the execution of the plan need not satisfy any special criteria in order to be conceivable. It may of course be based on wrong assumptions concerning the external facts and on this account may have to be changed. But there will always be a conceivable set of external events which would make it possible for the plan to be executed as originally conceived.

The situation is, however, different with the plans determined upon simultaneously but independently by a number of persons. In the first instance, in order that all these plans can be carried out, it is necessary for them to be based on the expectation of the same set of external events, since, if different people were to base their plans on conflicting expectations, no set of external events could make the execution of all these plans possible. And, secondly, in a society based on exchange their plans will to a considerable extent refer to actions which require corresponding actions on the part of other individuals. This means that the plans of different individuals must in a special sense be compatible if it is to be even conceivable that they will be able to carry all of them out.[5] Or, to put the same thing in different words, since some of the 'data' on which any one person will base his plans will be the expectation that other people will act in a particular way, it is essential for the compatibility of the different plans that the plans

[5] It has long been a subject of wonder to me why there should, to my knowledge, have been no systematic attempts in sociology to analyse social relations in terms of correspondence and non-correspondence, or compatibility and non-compatibility, of individual aims and desires. It seems that the mathematical technique of *analysis situs* (topology) and particularly such concepts developed by it as that of *homeomorphism* might prove very useful in this connection, although it may appear doubtful whether even this technique, at any rate in the present state of its development, is adequate to the complexity of the structures with which we have to deal. A first attempt made recently in this direction by an eminent mathematician (Karl Menger, *Moral, Wille und Weltgestaltung*, [Vienna 1934]) has so far not yet led to very illuminating results. But we may look forward with interest to the treatise on exact sociological theory which Professor Menger has promised for the near future. (Cf., 'Einige neuere Fortschritte in der exakten Behandlung sozialwissenschaftlicher Probleme', in *Neuere Fortschritte in den exakten Wissenschaften* (Vienna 1936), p. 132.)

of the one contain exactly those actions which form the data for the plans of the other.

In the traditional treatment of equilibrium analysis part of this difficulty is apparently avoided by the assumption that the data, in the form of demand schedules representing individual tastes and technical facts, will be equally given to all individuals and that their acting on the same premises will somehow lead to their plans becoming adapted to each other. That this does not really overcome the difficulty created by the fact that one person's decisions are the other person's data, and that it involves to some degree circular reasoning, has often been pointed out. What, however, seems so far to have escaped notice is that this whole procedure involves a confusion of a much more general character, of which the point just mentioned is just a special instance, and which is due to an equivocation of the term 'datum'. The data which now are supposed to be objective facts and the same for all people are evidently no longer the same thing as the data which formed the starting point for the tautological transformations of the pure logic of choice. There 'data' meant all facts, and only the facts, which were present in the mind of the acting person, and only this subjective interpretation of the term datum made those propositions necessary truths. 'Datum' meant given, known, to the person under consideration. But in the transition from the analysis of the action of an individual to the analysis of the situation in a society the concept has undergone an insidious change of meaning.

IV

The confusion about the concept of a datum is at the bottom of so many of our difficulties in this field that it is necessary to consider it in somewhat more detail. Datum means of course something given, but the question which is left open, and which in the social sciences is capable of two different answers, is to whom the facts are supposed to be given. Economists appear subconsciously always to have been somewhat uneasy about this point, and to have reassured themselves against the feeling that they did not quite know to whom the facts were given by underlining the fact that they *were* given – even by using such pleonastic expressions as 'given data'. But this does not solve the question whether the facts referred to are supposed to be given to the observing economist, or to the persons whose actions he wants to explain, and if to the latter, whether it is assumed that the same facts are known to all the different persons in the system, or whether the 'data' for the different persons may be different.

There seems to be no possible doubt that these two concepts of 'data', on the one hand in the sense of the objective real facts, as the observing economist is supposed to know them, and on the other in the subjective sense, as things known to the persons whose behaviour we try to explain, are really fundamentally different and ought to be kept carefully apart. And, as we shall see, the question why the data in the subjective sense of the term should ever come to correspond to the objective data is one of the main problems we have to answer.

The usefulness of the distinction becomes immediately apparent when we apply it to the question of what we can mean by the concept of a society being at any one moment in a state of equilibrium. There are evidently two senses in which it can be said that the subjective data, given to the different persons, and the individual plans, which necessarily follow from them, are in agreement. We may merely mean that these plans are mutually compatible and that there is consequently a conceivable set of external events which will allow all people to carry out their plans and not cause any disappointments. If this mutual compatibility of intentions were not given, and if in consequence no set of external events could satisfy all expectations, we could clearly say that this is not a state of equilibrium. We have a situation where a revision of the plans on the part of at least some people is inevitable, or, to use a phrase which in the past has had a rather vague meaning, but which seems to fit this case perfectly, where endogenous disturbances are inevitable.

There is, however, still the other question of whether the individual subjective sets of data correspond to the objective data, and whether in consequence the expectations on which plans were based are borne out by the facts. If correspondence between data in this sense were required for equilibrium it would never be possible to decide otherwise than *ex post*, at the end of the period for which people have planned, whether at the beginning the society has been in equilibrium. It seems to be more in conformity with established usage to say in such a case that the equilibrium, as defined in the first sense, may be disturbed by an unforeseen development of the (objective) data, and to describe this as an exogenous disturbance. In fact it seems hardly possible to attach any definite meaning to the much-used concept of a change in the (objective) data unless we distinguish between external developments in conformity with, and those different from, general expectations, and define as a 'change' any divergence of the actual from the expected development, irrespective of whether it means a 'change' in some absolute sense. Surely if the alternations of the seasons suddenly ceased and the weather remained constant from a certain day onward, this would represent a change of data in our sense, that is a change relative to expectations, although in an absolute sense it would not represent a change but rather an absence of change. But all this means that we can speak of a change in data only if equilibrium in the first sense exists, that is, if expectations coincide. If they conflicted, any development of the external facts might bear out somebody's expectations and disappoint those of others, and there would be no possibility of deciding what was a change in the objective data.[6]

V

For a society then we *can* speak of a *state* of equilibrium at a point of time – but it means only that compatibility exists between the different plans which the individuals composing it have made for action in time. And equilibrium will continue, once it exists, so long as the external data correspond to the common expectations of all the members of the society. The continuance of a state of equilibrium in this sense is then not dependent on the objective data being constant in an absolute sense, and is not necessarily

[6] Cf. 'The Maintenance of Capital', *Economica* N. S., 2 (1935), p. 265.

confined to a stationary process. Equilibrium analysis becomes in principle applicable to a progressive society and to those inter-temporal price relationships which have given us so much trouble in recent times.[7]

These considerations seem to throw considerable light on the relationship between equilibrium and foresight, which has been somewhat hotly debated in recent times.[8] It appears that the concept of equilibrium merely means that the foresight of the different members of the society is in a special sense correct. It must be correct in the sense that every person's plan is based on the expectation of just those actions of other people which those other people intend to perform, and that all these plans are based on the expectation of the same set of external facts, so that under certain conditions nobody will have any reason to change his plans. Correct foresight is then not, as it has sometimes been understood, a precondition which must exist in order that equilibrium may be arrived at. It is rather the defining characteristic of a state of equilibrium. Nor need foresight for this purpose be perfect in the sense that it need extend into the indefinite future, or that everybody must foresee everything correctly. We should

---

[7] This separation of the concept of equilibrium from that of a stationary state seems to me to be no more than the necessary outcome of a process which has been going on for a fairly long time. That this association of the two concepts is not essential but only due to historical reasons is today probably generally felt. If complete separation has not yet been effected, it is apparently only because no alternative definition of a state of equilibrium had yet been suggested which has made it possible to state in a general form those propositions of equilibrium analysis which are essentially independent of the concept of a stationary state. Yet it is evident that most of the propositions of equilibrium analysis are not supposed to be applicable only in that stationary state which will probably never be reached. The process of separation seems to have begun with Marshall and his distinction between long and short run equilibria. (Cf. statements like this: 'For the nature of equilibrium itself, and that of the causes by which it is determined, depend on the length of the period over which the market is taken to extend'. *Principles*, 7th ed., 1, 6, p. 330.) The idea of a state of equilibrium which was not a stationary state was already inherent in my 'Das intertemporale Gleichgewichtssystem der Preise und die Bewegungen des Geldwerts' (*Weltwirtschaftliches Archiv*, 28 [1928]) and is of course essential if we want to use the equilibrium apparatus for the explanation of any of the phenomena connected with 'investment'. On the whole matter much historical information will be found in E. Schams, 'Komparative Statistik', *Zeitschrift für Nationalökonomie*, 2, No 1 (1930).

[8] Cf. particularly O. Morgenstern, 'Vollkommene Voraussicht und Wirtschaftliches Gleichgewicht', *Zeitschrift für Nationalökonomie*, 6, p. 3.

rather say that equilibrium will last so long as the anticipations prove correct, and that they need to be correct only on those points which are relevant for the decisions of the individuals. But on this question of what is relevant foresight or knowledge more later.

Before I proceed further I should probably stop for a moment to illustrate by a concrete example what I have just said about the meaning of a state of equilibrium and how it can be disturbed. Consider the preparations which will be going on at any moment for the production of houses. Brickmakers, plumbers and others will all be producing materials which in each case will correspond to a certain quantity of houses for which just this quantity of the particular material will be required. Similarly we may conceive of prospective buyers as accumulating savings which will enable them at certain dates to buy definite quantities of houses. If all these activities represent preparations for the production (and acquisition) of the same amount of houses we can say that there is equilibrium between them in the sense that all the people engaged in them may find that they can carry out their plans.[9] This need not be so, because other circumstances which are not part of their plan of action may turn out to be different from what they expected. Part of the materials may be destroyed by an accident, weather conditions may make building impossible, or an invention may alter the proportions in which the different factors are wanted. This is what we call a change in the (objective) data,

[9] Another example of more general importance would of course be the correspondence between 'investment' and 'saving' in the sense of the proportion (in terms of relative cost) in which entrepreneurs provide producers' goods and consumers' goods for a particular date, and the proportion in which consumers in general will at this date distribute their resources between producers' goods and consumers' goods. (Cf. my 'Preiserwartungen, monetäre Störungen und Fehlinvestitionen', *Ekonomisk Tidskrift*, 34, (1935) (French translation; 'Prévisions de prix, pertubations monétaires et paux investissments,' *Revue des Sciences Economiques* (October 1935) and 'The Maintenance of Capital', *Economica* N.S., 2, (1935), pp. 268-73.) It may be of interest in this connection to mention that in the course of investigations of the same field, which led me to these speculations, the theory of crises, the great French sociologist G. Tarde stressed the '*contradiction des croyances*' or '*contradiction de jugements*' or '*contradictions des espérances*' as the main cause of these phenomena (*Psychologie économique* (Paris 1902) 2, pp. 129-8; Cf. also N. Pinkus, *Das Problem des Normalen in der Nationalökonomie* (Leipzig, 1906), pp. 252 and 275.

which disturbs the equilibrium which has existed. But if the different plans were from the beginning incompatible, it is inevitable that somebody's plans will be upset and have to be altered, and that in consequence the whole complex of actions over the period will not show those characteristics which apply if all the actions of each individual can be understood as part of a single individual plan he has made at the beginning.[10]

VI

When in all this I emphasize the distinction between mere inter-compatibility of the individual plans[11] and the correspondence between them and the actual external facts or objective data, I do not of course mean to suggest that the subjective inter-agreement is not in some way brought about by the external facts. There would of course be no reason why the subjective data of different people should ever correspond unless they were due to the experience of the same objective facts. But the point is that pure-equilibrium analysis is not concerned with the way in which this correspondence is brought about. In the description of an existing state of equilibrium which it provides, it is simply assumed that the subjective data coincide with the objective facts. The equilibrium relationships cannot be deduced merely from the objective facts, since the analysis of what people will do can only start from what is known to them. Nor can equilibrium analysis start merely

---

[10] It is an interesting question, but one which I cannot discuss here, whether in order that we can speak of equilibrium, every single individual must be right, or whether it would not be sufficient if, in consequence of a compensation of errors in different directions, quantities of the different commodities coming on the market were the same as if every individual had been right. It seems to me as if equilibrium in the strict sense would require the first condition to be satisfied, but I can conceive that a wider concept, requiring only the second condition, might occasionally be useful. A fuller discussion of this problem would have to consider the whole question of the significance which some economists (including Pareto) attach to the law of great numbers in this connection. On the general point see P. N. Rosenstein-Rorlon, 'The Coordination of the General Theories of Money and Price', *Economica*, (August 1936).

[11] Or, since in view of the tautological character of the pure logic of choice, 'individual plans' and 'subjective data' can be used interchangeably, between the agreement between the subjective data of the different individuals.

from a given set of subjective data, since the subjective data of different people would be either compatible or incompatible, that is, they would already determine whether equilibrium did or did not exist.

We shall not get much further here unless we ask for the reasons for our concern with the admittedly fictitious state of equilibrium. Whatever may occasionally have been said by over-pure economists, there seems to be no possible doubt that the only justification for this is the supposed existence of a tendency towards equilibrium. It is only with this assertion that economics ceases to be an exercise in pure logic and becomes an empirical science; and it is to economics as an empirical science that we must now turn.

In the light of our analysis of the meaning of a state of equilibrium it should be easy to say what is the real content of the assertion that a tendency towards equilibrium exists. It can hardly mean anything but that under certain conditions the knowledge and intentions of the different members of society are supposed to come more and more into agreement, or, to put the same thing in less general and less exact but more concrete terms, that the expectations of the people and particularly of the entrepreneurs will become more and more correct. In this form the assertion of the existence of a tendency towards equilibrium is clearly an empirical proposition, that is, an assertion about what happens in the real world which ought, at least in principle, to be capable of verification. And it gives our somewhat abstract statement a rather plausible common-sense meaning. The only trouble is that we are still pretty much in the dark about 1) the *conditions* under which this tendency is supposed to exist, and 2) the nature of the *process* by which individual knowledge is changed.

VII

In the usual presentations of equilibrium analysis it is generally made to appear as if these questions of how the equilibrium comes about were solved. But if we look closer it soon becomes evident that these apparent demonstrations amount to no more than the apparent proof of what is already assumed.[12] The device generally adopted for this purpose is the assumption of a perfect market where every event becomes known instantaneously to every member. It is necessary to remember here that the perfect market which is required to satisfy the assumptions of equilibrium analysis must not be confined to the markets of all the individual commodities; the whole economic system must be assumed to be one perfect market in which everybody knows everything. The assumption of a perfect market then means nothing less than that all the members of the community, even if they are not supposed to be strictly omniscient, are at least supposed to know automatically all that is relevant for their decisions. It seems that that skeleton in our cupboard, the 'economic man', whom we have exorcised with prayer and fasting, has returned through the back door in the form of a quasi-omniscient individual.

The statement that, if people know everything, they are in equilibrium is true simply because that is how we define equilibrium. The assumption of a perfect market in this sense is just another way of saying that equilibrium exists, but does not get us any nearer an explanation of when and how such a state will come about. It is clear that if we want to make the assertion that under certain conditions people will approach that state we must explain by what process they will acquire the necessary knowledge. Of course any assumption about the actual acquisition of knowledge in the course of this process will also be of a hypothetical character. But this does not mean that all such assumptions are equally justified. We have to deal here with assumptions about causation, so that what we assume must not only be regarded as possible (which is certainly not the case if we just regard people as omniscient) but must also be regarded as likely to be true, and it must be possible, at least in principle, to demonstrate that it is true in particular cases.

---

[12] This seems to be implicitly admitted, although hardly consciously recognized, when in recent times it is frequently stressed that equilibrium analysis only describes the conditions of equilibrium without attempting to derive the position of equilibrium from the data. Equilibrium analysis in this sense would of course be pure logic and contain no assertions about the real world.

The essential point here is that it is these apparently subsidiary hypotheses or assumptions that people do learn from experience, and about how they acquire knowledge, which constitute the empirical content of our propositions about what happens in the real world. They usually appear disguised and incomplete as a description of the type of market to which our proposition refers; but this is only one, though perhaps the most important, aspect of the more general problem of how knowledge is acquired and communicated. The important thing of which economists frequently do not seem to be aware is that the nature of these hypotheses is in many respects rather different from the more general assumptions from which the Pure Logic of Choice starts. The main differences seem to me to be two.

Firstly, the assumptions from which the Pure Logic of Choice starts are facts which we know to be common to all human thought. They may be regarded as axioms which define or delimit the field within which we are able to understand or mentally to reconstruct the processes of thought of other people. They are therefore universally applicable to the field in which we are interested – although of course where *in concreto* the limits of this field are is an empirical question. They refer to a type of human action (what we commonly call rational, or even merely conscious, as distinguished from instinctive action) rather than to the particular conditions under which this action is undertaken. But the assumptions or hypotheses, which we have to introduce when we want to explain the social processes, concern the relation of the thought of an individual to the outside world, the question to what extent and how his hypotheses must necessarily run in terms of assertions about causal connections, about how experience creates knowledge.

Secondly, while in the field of the Pure Logic of Choice our analysis can be made exhaustive, that is, while we can here develop a formal apparatus which covers all conceivable situations, the supplementary hypotheses must of necessity be selective, that is, we must select from the infinite variety of possible situations such ideal types as for some reason we regard as specially relevant to conditions in the real world.[18] Of course we could also develop a separate science, the subject matter of which was *per definitionem* confined to a 'perfect market' or some similarly defined object, just as the Logic of Choice applies only to persons who have to allot limited means among a variety of ends. And for the field so defined our propositions would again become *a priori* true. But for such a procedure we should lack the justification which consists in the assumption that the situation in the real world is similar to what we assume it to be.

VIII

I must now turn to the question of what the concrete hypotheses are concerning the conditions under which people are supposed to acquire the relevant knowledge and the process by which they are supposed to acquire it. If it were at all clear what the hypotheses usually employed in this respect were, we should have to scrutinize them in two respects: we should have to investigate whether they were necessary and sufficient to explain a movement towards equilibrium, and we should have to show to what extent they were borne out by reality. But I am afraid I am now getting to a stage where it becomes exceedingly difficult to say what exactly are the assumptions on the basis of which we assert that there will be a tendency towards equilibrium, and to claim that our analysis has an application to the real world. I cannot pretend that I have as yet got much further on this point. Consequently all I can do is to ask a number of questions to which we shall have to find an answer if we want to be clear about the significance of our argument.

The only condition, about the necessity of which for the establishment of an equilibrium economists seem to be fairly

[18] The distinction drawn here may help to solve the old difference between economists and sociologists about the role which ideal types play in the reasoning of economic theory. The sociologists used to emphasize that the usual procedure of economic theory involved the assumption of particular ideal types, while the economic theorist pointed out that his reasoning was of such generality that he need not make use of any ideal types. The truth seems to be that within the field of the Pure Logic of Choice, in which the economist was largely interested, he was right in his assertion, but that as soon as he wanted to use it for the explanation of a social process he had to use ideal types of one sort or another.

agreed, is the 'constancy of the data'. But after what we have seen about the vagueness of the concept of 'datum' we shall suspect, and rightly, that this does not get us much further. Even if we assume – as we probably must – that here the term is used in its objective sense (which includes, it will be remembered, the preferences of the different individuals) it is by no means clear that this is either required or sufficient in order that people shall actually acquire the necessary knowledge, or that it was meant as a statement of the conditions under which they will do so. It is rather significant that at any rate some authors[14] feel it necessary to add 'perfect knowledge' as an additional and separate condition. And indeed we shall see that constancy of the objective data is neither a necessary nor a sufficient condition. That it cannot be a necessary condition follows from the facts, firstly, that nobody would want to interpret it in the absolute sense that nothing must ever happen in the world, and, secondly, that, as we have seen, as soon as we want to include changes which occur periodically or perhaps even changes which proceed at a constant rate, the only way in which we can define constancy is with reference to expectations. All that this condition amounts to then is that there must be some discernible regularity in the world which makes it possible to predict events correctly. But while this is clearly not sufficient to prove that people will learn to foresee events correctly, the same is true to a hardly less degree even about constancy of data in an absolute sense. For any one individual, constancy of the data does in no way mean constancy of all the facts independent of himself, since, of course, only the tastes and not the actions of the other people can in this sense be assumed to be constant. And as all those other people will change their decisions as they gain experience about the external facts and other people's action, there is no reason why these processes of successive changes should ever come to an end. These difficulties are well known[15] and I only mention them here to remind you how little we actually know about the conditions under which an equilibrium will ever be reached. But

---

[14] See N. Kaldor, 'A Classificatory Note on the Determinateness of Equilibrium', *Review of Economic Studies*, 1, No. 2, (1934), p. 123.

[15] On all this cf. Kaldor, 'A Classificatory Note. . . .', *passim*.

I do not propose to follow this line of approach further, though not because this question of the empirical probability that people will learn (that is, that their subjective data will come to correspond with each other and with the objective facts) is lacking in unsolved and highly interesting problems. The reason is rather that there seems to me to be another and more fruitful way of approach to the central problem.

IX

The questions I have just discussed concerning the conditions under which people are likely to acquire the necessary knowledge, and the process by which they will acquire it, has at least received some attention in past discussions. But there is a further question which seems to me to be at least equally important, but which appears to have received no attention at all, and that is how much knowledge and what sort of knowledge the different individuals must possess in order that we may be able to speak of equilibrium. It is clear that if the concept is to have any empirical significance it cannot presuppose that everybody knows everything. I have already had to use the undefined term 'relevant knowledge', that is, the knowledge which is relevant to a particular person. But what is this relevant knowledge? It can hardly mean simply the knowledge which actually influenced his actions, because his decisions might have been different not only if, for instance, the knowledge he possessed had been correct instead of incorrect, but also if he had possessed knowledge about altogether different fields.

Clearly there is here a problem of the *Division of Knowledge* which is quite analogous to, and at least as important as, the problem of the division of labour. But while the latter has been one of the main subjects of investigation ever since the beginning of our science, the former has been as completely neglected, although it seems to me to be the really central problem of economics as a social science.[16] The problem which we pretend to

---

[16] I am not certain, but I hope, that the distinction between the Pure Logic of Choice and economics as a social science is essentially the same distinction as that which Professor A. Ammon has in mind when he stresses again and again that a '*Theorie des Wirtschaftens*' is not yet a '*Theorie der Volkswirtschaft*'.

solve is how the spontaneous interaction of a number of people, each possessing only bits of knowledge, brings about a state of affairs in which prices correspond to costs, etc., and which could be brought about by deliberate direction only by somebody who possessed the combined knowledge of all those individuals. And experience shows us that something of this sort does happen, since the empirical observation that prices do tend to correspond to costs was the beginning of our science. But in our analysis, instead of showing what bits of information the different persons must possess in order to bring about that result, we fall in effect back on the assumption that everybody knows everything and so evade any real solution of the problem.

Before, however, we can proceed further, to consider this division of knowledge among different persons, it is necessary to become more specific about the sort of knowledge which is relevant in this connection. It has become customary among economists to stress only the need of knowledge of prices, apparently because – as a consequence of the confusions between objective and subjective data – the complete knowledge of the objective facts was taken for granted. In recent times even the knowledge of current prices has been taken so much for granted that the only connection in which the question of knowledge has been regarded as problematic has been the anticipation of future prices. But, as I have already indicated at the beginning, price expectations and even the knowledge of current prices are only a very small section of the problem of knowledge as I see it. The wider aspect of the problem of knowledge with which I am concerned is the knowledge of the basic fact of how the different commodities can be obtained and used,[17] and under what conditions they are actually obtained and used, that is, the general

---

[17] Knowledge in this sense is more than what is usually described as skill, and the division of knowledge of which we here speak more than is meant by the division of labour. To put it shortly, 'skill' refers only to the knowledge of which a person makes use in his trade, while the further knowledge, about which we must know something in order to be able to say anything about the processes in society, is the knowledge of alternative possibilities of action of which he makes no direct use. It may be added here that knowledge, in the sense in which the term is here used, is identical with foresight only in the sense in which all knowledge is capacity to predict.

question of why the subjective data to the different persons correspond to the objective facts. Our problem of knowledge here is just the existence of this correspondence which in much of current equilibrium analysis is simply assumed to exist, but which we have to explain if we want to show why the propositions, which are necessarily true about the attitude of a person towards things which he believes to have certain properties, should come to be true of the actions of society with regard to things which either do possess these properties, or which, for some reason we shall have to explain, are commonly believed by the members of society to possess these properties.[18]

But to revert to the special problem I have been discussing, the amount of knowledge different individuals must possess in order that equilibrium may prevail (or the 'relevant' knowledge they must possess), we shall get nearer to an answer if we remember how it can become apparent either that equilibrium did not exist or that it is being disturbed. We have seen that the equilibrium connections will be severed if any person changes his plans, either because his tastes change (which does not concern us here) or because new facts become known to him. But there are evidently two different ways in which he may learn of new facts which make him change his plans, which for our purposes are of altogether different significance. He may learn of the new facts as it were by accident, that is in a way which is not a necessary consequence of his attempt to execute his original plan, or it may be inevitable that in the course of his attempt he will find that the facts are

---

[18] That all propositions of economic theory refer to things which are defined in terms of human attitudes towards them, that is, that for instance the 'sugar' about which economic theory may occasionally speak, is not defined by its 'objective' qualities, but by the fact that people believe that it will serve certain needs of theirs in a certain way, is the source of all sorts of difficulties and confusions, particularly in connection with the problem of 'verification'. It is of course also in this connection that the contrast between the *verstehende* social science and the behaviourist approach becomes so glaring. I am not certain that the behaviourists in the social sciences are quite aware of *how* much of the traditional approach they would have to abandon if they wanted to be consistent, or that they would want to adhere to it consistently if they were aware of this. It would, for instance, imply that propositions of the theory of money would have to refer exclusively to, say, 'round discs of metal, bearing a certain stamp', or some similarly defined object or group of objects.

different from what he expected. It is obvious that, in order that he may proceed according to plan, his knowledge needs to be correct only on the points on which it will necessarily be confirmed or corrected in the course of the execution of the plan. But he may have no knowledge of things which, if he possessed it, would certainly affect his plan.

The conclusion then which we must draw is that the relevant knowledge which he must possess in order that equilibrium may prevail is the knowledge which he is bound to acquire in view of the position in which he originally is, and the plans which he then makes. It is certainly not all the knowledge which, if he acquired it by accident, would be useful to him, and lead to a change in his plan. And we may therefore very well have a position of equilibrium only because some people have no chance of learning about facts which, if they knew them, would induce them to alter their plans. Or, in other words, it is only relative to the knowledge which a person is bound to acquire in the course of the carrying out of his original plan and its successive alterations that an equilibrium is likely to be reached.

While such a position represents in one sense a position of equilibrium, it is however clear that it is not an equilibrium in the special sense in which equilibrium is regarded as a sort of optimum position. In order that the results of the combination of individual bits of knowledge should be comparable to the results of direction by an omniscient dictator, further conditions must apparently be introduced.[19] And while it seems quite clear that it is possible to define the amount of knowledge which individuals must possess in order that this result should be obtained, I know of no real attempt in this direction. One condition would probably be that each of the alternative uses of any sort of resources is known to the owner of some such resources actually used for another purpose and that in this way all the different uses of these resources are

[19] These conditions are usually described as absence of 'frictions'. In a recently published article ('Quantity of Capital and the Rate of Interest', *Journal of Political Economy*, 44, No. 5 (1936), p. 638) Professor F. H. Knight rightly points out that ' "error" is the usual meaning of friction in economic discussion'.

connected, either directly or indirectly.[20] But I mention this condition only as an instance of how it will in most cases be sufficient that in each field there is a certain margin of people who possess among them all the relevant knowledge. To elaborate this further would be an interesting and a very important task, but a task that would far exceed the limits of this paper.

But although what I have said on this point has been largely in the form of a criticism, I do not want to appear unduly despondent about what we have already achieved in this field. Even if we have jumped over an essential link in our argument, I still believe that by what is implicit in its reasoning, economics has come nearer than any other social science to an answer to that central question of all social sciences, how the combination of fragments of knowledge existing in different minds can bring about results which, if they were to be brought about deliberately, would require a knowledge on the part of the directing mind which no single person can possess. To show that in this sense the spontaneous actions of individuals will under conditions which we can define bring about a distribution of resources which can be understood as if it were made according to a single plan, although nobody has planned it, seems to me indeed an answer to the problem which has sometimes been metaphorically described as that of the 'social mind'. But we must not be surprised that such

[20] This would be one, but probably not yet a sufficient, condition to ensure that, with a given state of demand, the marginal productivity of the different factors of production in their different uses should be equalized and that in this sense an equilibrium of production should be brought about. That it is not necessary, as one might think, that every possible alternative use of any kind of resources should be known to at least one among the owners of each group of such resources which are used for one particular purpose is due to the fact that the alternatives known to the owners of the resources in a particular use are reflected in the prices of these resources. In this way it may be a sufficient distribution of knowledge of the alternative uses, $m, n, o, \ldots y, z$, of a commodity, if A, who uses the quantity of these resources in his possession for m, knows of n, and B, who uses his for n, knows of m, while C who uses his for o, knows of n, etc., etc., until we get to L, who uses his for z, but only knows of y. I am not clear to what extent in addition to this a particular distribution of the knowledge of the different proportions is required in which different factors can be combined in the production of any one commodity. For complete equilibrium additional assumptions will be required about the knowledge which consumers possess about the serviceability of the commodities for the satisfaction of their wants.

claims on our part have usually been rejected by sociologists, since we have not based them on the right grounds.

There is only one more point in this connection which I should like to mention. This is that if the tendency towards equilibrium, which we have reason to believe to exist on empirical grounds, is only towards an equilibrium relative to that knowledge which people will acquire in the course of their economic activity, and if any other change of knowledge must be regarded as a 'change in the data' in the usual sense of the term, which falls outside the sphere of equilibrium analysis, this would mean that equilibrium analysis can really tell us nothing about the significance of such changes in knowledge, and would go far to account for the fact that pure analysis seems to have so extraordinarily little to say about institutions, such as the press, the purpose of which is to communicate knowledge. And it might even explain why the pre-occupation with pure analysis should so frequently create a peculiar blindness to the role played in real life by such institutions as advertising.

x

With these rather desultory remarks on topics which would deserve much more careful examination I must conclude my survey of these problems. There are only one or two further remarks which I want to add.

One is that, in stressing the nature of the empirical propositions of which we must make use if the formal apparatus of equilibrium analysis is to serve for an explanation of the real world, and in emphasizing that the propositions about how people will learn, which are relevant in this connection, are of a fundamentally different nature from those of formal analysis, I do not mean to suggest that there opens here and now a wide field for empirical research. I very much doubt whether such investigation would teach us anything new. The important point is rather that we should become clear about what the questions of fact are on which the applicability of our argument to the real world depends, or, to put the same thing in other words, at what point our argument, when it is applied to phenomena of the real world, becomes subject to verification.

The second point is that I do not want of course to suggest that the sort of problems I have been discussing were foreign to the arguments of the economists of the older generations. The only objection that can be made against them is that they have so mixed up the two sorts of propositions, the *a priori* and the empirical, of which every realistic economist makes constant use, that it is frequently quite impossible to see what sort of validity they claimed for a particular statement. More recent work has been freer from this fault – but only at the price of leaving more and more obscure what sort of relevance their arguments had to the phenomena of the real world. All I have tried to do has been to find the way back to the common-sense meaning of our analysis, of which, I am afraid, we are apt to lose sight as our analysis becomes more elaborate. You may even feel that most of what I have said has been commonplace. But from time to time it is probably necessary to detach oneself from the technicalities of the argument and to ask quite naïvely what it is all about. If I have only shown that in some respects the answer to this question is not only not obvious, but that occasionally we do not even quite know what it is, I have succeeded in my purpose.

4

The rationale of cost accounting

R. S. EDWARDS

First published in *Some Modern Business Problems,*
ed. A. Plant (London 1937).

There is always a risk that a paper which deals with the general principles of a subject may be dubbed theoretical and on that account of little value to the businessman. It may be felt at the end of this lecture that I ought to be criticized on this score, and in anticipation I want to refer to the work of two of the earliest English writers on costing.

In 1887 Emile Garcke, an engineer, and F. M. Fells, an accountant, published jointly a work entitled *Factory Accounts*, and it would be generally admitted that the principles of costing which they set down remain largely unaltered to this day. Yet the review of the first edition in the *Accountant* was to the effect that the book was more theoretical than practical, that it was pedantic and involved 'in the nature of a work on political economy'. Moreover the claim that stock balances should be as readily ascertainable as cash balances was regarded as an unattainable ideal. Today the suggestions put forward in this book are regarded as commonplaces. I hope therefore that if anything I may say appears to be more academic than businesslike, it will not be condemned on those grounds *alone*, particularly in view of the fact that there is no time to develop practical applications.

Some familiarity with the general nature of cost accounting, as it is at present practised, will be taken for granted. No clear-cut definition is possible, and one can always point to borderline cases and ask 'Is this financial accounting or costing?' or again 'Is this statistics or accounting?' Little is gained by such discussions; in general we have come to look on costing as an elaboration of accounting used particularly in those cases where a number of factors of production are combined in manufacture.[1] The financial accounts disclose the total profit of a period, while costing systems normally aim at explaining this figure. An endeavour is made to analyse the past in order to avoid mistakes in the future. I think, however, that we must be quite clear that costing does not and is not intended to provide data for major changes in policy. For example, decisions whether to open a new department or close an old one would require special cost investigations which the ordinary cost-accounting system could not cover. It is the constantly recurring management problems on which costing is supposed to shed light.

The principle question we have to ask is this: out of the mass of interesting data which is available in any business, how much is worth collecting? The answer would appear to be: only that which can influence policy. Unless the information supplied enables the management to do something or refrain from doing something, its collection is not a business proposition.[2] Costing fails in its object unless it adds more to net profit than the expense of running the system.

In this connection experience in France is interesting. Throughout the nineteenth century French writers were producing interesting books on cost accounting for agriculture – they were far ahead of us in this direction. In the preface of most of these works there appeared a lamentable tale about the farmer's tardiness in improving his accounting methods. In spite of these admirable works the French farmer continued in his old ways. The probable reason is that, interesting as the information might have been, it would not have influenced policy sufficiently to add enough to profit to cover the expense of keeping the accounts.

It is not always easy to find out whether the collection of certain figures will pay. There is a wide range of cost data which might lead to small changes in policy, but the influence of which is of

---

[1] In recent years however, there have been attempts to apply the technique of costing to the problems of distributors.

[2] There may of course be people who like to have information out of pure curiosity, regardless of whether it can influence policy. There is nothing irrational in this provided it is remembered that it is merely a way of consuming income and not adding to it.

doubtful importance. There is another range of costing information in the nature of laboratory work which must be regarded as a long-run investment. In general, then, our method of attack will have to be: firstly to decide what information we should regard as necessary, if its collection were costless, and secondly to consider whether this information is of sufficient importance to warrant the expense of its collection.

What policy-influencing information would one like to have if it were supplied free? In answer to this question one can introduce a useful division into what I shall call, for convenience only, the entrepreneurial and the technical problems. The businessman's entrepreneurial problem is to decide on the size or rate of output which will yield maximum profit. The technical problem is to produce this flow of output at the lowest cost possible for the given scale of production, having regard to the facilities available. In other words, the technical problem belongs to the works manager – he is told what output to produce and must produce it at the lowest possible cost. The entrepreneurial problem *includes the technical ones*, and is the managing director's province.

II SOME DIFFICULTIES AND SUGGESTIONS REGARDING TERMINOLOGY

At this point we must stop to grapple with a few of the difficulties of accounting terminology. The main themes running through most books on costing concern firstly the difference between so-called 'direct' and 'indirect' cost and secondly the methods to be adopted in imputing the latter. That is to say, if aero engines are being produced, certain costs are traced to each engine or batch of engines and these are 'direct' costs. Raw material is the best example of this. But the great mass of overhead associated with the fixed equipment is regarded as 'indirect' cost and all sorts of ingenious attempts are made to allocate it. Broadly direct cost and prime cost are synonymous in accounting literature, and accountants would agree, I think, that either term includes those items which *it is worth while* to trace to the unit which is being costed.

For analysis this is unsatisfactory, because it brings us to a position in which prime cost as a concept depends on book-keeping difficulties and one can never be sure what any individual writer means. Prime cost normally includes the *relatively large* items of traceable cost, but in practice it may contain more besides, particularly, as we shall see later, if a loading rate is added for machine time or to cover stores costs. The line drawn by accountants between prime or direct cost and overhead or indirect cost is therefore arbitrary. If half-a-dozen accountants were asked to split up the debit side of a manufacturing and profit-and-loss account between prime cost, works oncost, office oncost and distribution oncost, and were then asked how the last three were to be allocated to the products, there would be very wide divergences of opinion. This is bound to be so because more explicit assumptions are necessary. Firstly, what period of time is to be considered? Many costs which are fixed for a day may become variable in a week – a great deal of labour supply is like this. Secondly, what unit is to be costed? Is it to be a department or just one unit of product in that department?

The following is a typical statement on the subject under consideration: 'The cost of labour (i.e. the amount of productive wages paid) plus the cost of raw materials, with all charges thereon, such as carriage inwards, freight, dock dues, etc., is called the Prime Cost.'[3] Such a categorical statement is quite useless for our purpose. What are productive wages – do they include the works manager's salary? Where are we to draw the line between wages and salaries generally or between productive and non-productive labour? Are we *never* to include expenditure other than so-called productive wages and raw materials? The definition leaves the major questions unanswered; instead of describing the characteristics of prime cost, we are told that certain items *are* prime cost.

Now the most important thing about costs is the extent to which they change with output. Whatever unit one decides to cost, whether it be a job or a department, it can be said that if the job were refused or the department closed, the total expenses of

[3] Carter, *Advanced Accounts* (1931), p. 851.

the business would be less by an amount which could be determined fairly accurately.

That is to say, in undertaking the job or continuing the department, the business is involved in additional expenses which could be avoided. As a result, to be worth while, the unit costed must generally add to the turnover of the firm, at least the amount of this additional cost. To make the position clearer, let us suppose we are costing the production of a machine in an engineering works. If the order for this machine were refused, we should not have to buy or take from stock the materials for the job; it might be possible to dispense with some labour, and some wear and tear of machine tools would be avoided; perhaps the bank overdraft could be reduced and interest saved. On the other hand, the rent of the factory would remain the same, the foremen would still have to be paid, the machinery would become obsolescent at the same rate.

Many other expenses are similarly unavoidable. If we call the additional expense incurred by producing the unit to be costed 'variable cost' and other expense 'fixed cost', then we shall have a useful distinction, as the production is worth while if it covers the variable cost and contributes something, however little, to the fixed cost. There is nothing absolute about the term 'variable cost'; the items composing it will differ with the change in the unit.

It will be conceded, I think, that given the unit there will be little difficulty in collecting fairly accurately prime costs interpreted as variable costs. No theoretical difficulties will arise, the problems are those of book-keeping only. But there are many variable expenses the separate allocation of which is regarded as too expensive if a continuous double-entry costing system is in operation. These items are lumped into the overhead so that this includes some directly variable, some partly variable and some absolutely fixed costs. The enormous drawback to a double-entry costing system 'tied in' to the financial accounts is that some arbitrary assumptions have to be set up to make it workable. As Professor Canning has said, 'Cost accounting procedure rests upon oversimplified and largely arbitrary fundamental analysis'.

III THE PROBLEM OF 'OVERHEAD'

All cost accountants will agree that their great difficulty is in the allocation of overhead or oncost. Naturally this is so, for a number of costs are being added together which have different degrees of variability.

First there are disputes as to what is manufacturing and what is distribution oncost, as it is assumed that these should be allocated on different bases; and whether certain expenses shall be left out altogether as being outside the scope of costing – cash discount and interest appear in this category. Then the expenses have to be split between departments; some are variable to the department and there is no difficulty, others are allocated arbitrarily on some basis considered 'fair'. Then comes the most difficult business of all – finding a way of 'tacking on' these departmental overhead costs to units of product which have gone through the departments. For example, overhead is allocated to the product variously as a percentage on so-called prime cost or on direct labour cost incurred or on the basis of direct labour hours or machine hours. Accountants condemn the 'prime cost' basis in most cases, and many of them object to 'direct labour cost', but on the whole they seem satisfied with the 'labour-hour' and 'machine-hour' rates. These are based on the generally implied assumption that overhead expenses vary with time. In the very long run this is probably true merely because in the long run most costs are prime costs; and practically everything wears out sooner or later. But in the relatively short period required for completion of a job or order it is not true.

To arrive at a percentage or rate for oncost distribution it is necessary to assume some output as a denominator. Given this estimated output and the estimated overhead for the period covered by the output, a rate can be established. We are usually told to use 'normal output' as the basis, though rarely informed how it is to be calculated. Presumably it is the average output which the firm expected to achieve, taking good and bad years together. Hence, if the oncost rates are calculated on this output and selling prices are based on the total cost including such oncost rates, the business would make the anticipated profit, provided the anticipated output could be sold at these prices. But if demand has changed there is no reason to assume that maximum profit will be made by charging a price to cover these fixed rates of oncost. Suppose a firm had anticipated a demand of 10,000 units per annum and had put down plant accordingly. Let us assume that the cost per unit, including overhead, on the basis of 10,000 units is £1; that demand, however, falls so that to market 10,000 we have to reduce price to 19s/95p per unit; that at £1 only 5,000 units will sell. In making its output decision it does not require to know that to cover overhead on 10,000 units it needs £1 per unit or that on 5,000 units it must get £2 per unit. What is required is information which in the *given circumstances* will help to fix prices or output at such a level as will maximize net profit. This is our entrepreneurial problem.

IV PRICE-FIXING AND OUTPUT DECISIONS

For the purpose of exposition let us assume a factory turns out only one product – what cost information would be required in price fixing? If the market is perfectly competitive, the producer has no choice as to price, all that can be varied is the output and this can be expanded profitably until the last additional unit involves additional costs just less than the revenue added by that unit, that is to say, its market price. To take a simplified example, assume the selling price of an article in perfect competition is £2 10s od (£2.50) per unit, and the monthly costs are as shown in Table 4.1.

The most profitable output is clearly round about 3,000 units; it may be below or above this figure, and to find it exactly the costing department would have to study how each additional unit produced adds to the cost, and the management should stop increasing output at that point where the last additional unit involves an addition to total costs of £2 10s od (£2.50). In going beyond this point we should be throwing money away. Long-run selling policy might make it necessary to throw money away for short periods, but this should not blind us to the fact that short-

Table 4.1

Output in units	2,000	3,000	4,000
	£	£	£
Materials	2,000	3,000	3,900
Labour	1,000	1,500	2,250
Overhead: variable	1,000	1,250	2,200
fixed	1,000	1,000	1,000
	5,000	6,750	9,350
Sales	5,000	7,500	10,000
Profit	*nil*	750	650

run profits are not being maximized. Moreover, if the market is not absolutely competitive, then additional units of output sold would after a time add less than the price to total revenue, as prices would have to be dropped to dispose of the supply. In this case the output at which profit is a maximum is not that at which price equals additional cost, but that at which the additional revenue obtained from producing and selling one more unit of output is equal to the addition to total costs incurred in producing that additional unit.

For example, a firm might dispose of 3,000 units at £2 10s od (£2.50) each, but we can suppose that to market 3,100 the price would have to be dropped to £2 9s od (£2.45). Therefore, 3,000 units yield £7,500 and 3,100 units produce £7,595, hence the additional revenue from the increase is £95, and we have to see whether the additional cost resulting from the increase in output is greater or less than this.[4] Therefore the management will always be asking two questions, and bringing the two answers together. Firstly how will price changes affect total revenue? (This will depend on the elasticity of demand for the product.) Secondly what will be the additional outlay in producing extra units, or conversely, what will be saved by reducing output? Incidentally,

---

[4] Thus we are not concerned with 100 units at £2 9s od (£2.45) but with £95 only which takes account of the reduction in price of the first 3,000 units.

additional costs are sometimes known as *differential* or *marginal* costs, and they are those costs which are variable.[5]

It is useful to inquire whether there are any cost figures usually collected and examined which cannot affect policy. For example, the rent of the factory is likely to be the same if production goes on for one hour a day or twenty-four. In every business there are some expenses which are unalterable over wide ranges of output or over considerable periods of time. Hence there is no reason to study these unless *major* changes in output are being considered. For example, it might pay to incur the costs of moving the plant and machinery to smaller premises if output is to be reduced to half *permanently*. But, as suggested earlier, cost accounting normally deals with the ordinary run of production, special statistical investigations being made for major operations.

Textbooks are prone to emphasize the fact that cost accounting analyses *past* costs not future estimates, but they often do not make clear the fact that this data is useful only in so far as it is a guide to future costs; it is future variable cost which is important. Therefore cost accountants can ignore expenses which are completely unchangeable, e.g. the preliminary expenses of setting up a business. Sometimes, however, expenditure is composite – partly fixed, partly variable. For example, depreciation of machinery includes obsolescence, that is to say, the loss due to changes in values which the business cannot control. There may also be an element of physical wear and tear which continues whether machinery is used or not. It is therefore important to find out how and to what extent variations in use affect the total wastage. Similarly every other expense must be examined in order to establish the relationship between changes in cost and output variations.

Admittedly it is not possible to establish such a relationship with absolute accuracy, nor would it be possible to bring additional cost and additional revenue to complete equality without much

[5] It may be that taking on additional work raises the price at which a firm can obtain its factors of production (e.g. labour). If this happens then the firm has to take account not only of the rise in price of the labour for the additional work but also of the higher cost of all other work which has to pay more for labour.

expense. It is easily possible for the cost of accuracy to outweigh the advantages.

Many problems melt away if the subject is approached in the way which has been outlined. For example, from about 1890 there has been a stream of literature repeating *ad nauseam* the arguments for and against the inclusion of interest as a cost. All we really need to ask is: will the additional output involve the tying-up of capital which could be used or invested elsewhere? If so, the interest that the capital could earn elsewhere is a cost. On the other hand, interest on capital tied up in machinery is not important because the capital is sunk and could not be invested elsewhere. But if major changes, like the closing of a department are under consideration, interest on the scrap value of the machinery is a cost, because the money could be invested in alternative uses. Another problem concerns the price to adopt in charging out raw materials; one school claims that materials should be issued at original cost, while the other side champions 'replacement' cost. The 'original' cost supporters quarrel among themselves as to the way in which cost price is to be arrived at. Some use the 'first in, first out principle', others 'the average price of stock on hand'. Surely what we have to decide is the additional cost which the use of the material imposes on the business. This additional cost is the replacement price of the materials if they have to be replaced; but if it is not intended to replace them, then scrap value would be more appropriate.

Let us now consider a more complicated case; a factory turning out two products, A and B, each of which goes through two processes, the first of which is common to both products. So far as the costing of the first process is concerned the position is the same as it is in the 'one-product' factory. The management will require to know the cost of additional units at various levels of output. Usually in a costing system the total expenditure of the business would be divided between the three processes carried on, that is to say, rent, rates, insurance, administration, and so on, would be allocated on various arbitrary bases considered 'fair'. So far as these costs are fixed and unavoidable, it does not matter how you allocate them; as long as the nature of the business remains the same these costs go on. But it is true that space and other available services used for one process in the business could possibly be employed on the others, so that between the products there is a degree of variability, the cost of keeping one process going being equal to the opportunity of net gain by using the resources in the other processes. Starting from a position of equilibrium (i.e. one in which the net profits cannot be increased by changing the output or price of either or both products) let us assume the demand for product A increases. In deciding what changes to make, the effect on costs of changed output would have to be examined. The sales department must provide data showing estimated changes in the quantity of sales as prices are varied. The cost department must estimate the variation in costs which would be brought about by changes in output. Normally it would be necessary to consider only the additional costs in the first process (which is common), and the second process for product A. But other changes may be envisaged; for example, it may pay to expand the premises and put down fresh plant, rather than face increasing unit cost. If so, depreciation and interest on the *additional* capital is a variable cost to be taken into account. Or factors of production may be borrowed from the department making product B. Suppose there is excess space in product B department which can be transferred, then only the cost of alterations such as knocking down partitions need be considered, but if by cutting down its space product B department is involved in higher costs to produce the same output as before, then these additional costs must be added in as part of the cost of increasing the output of product A.

It may be protested that unless arbitrary allocations of departmental expenses are made it is impossible to see which department is paying best and should be expanded. This is untrue, as we test the profitability of increased output by examining marginal variations in cost and revenue. In other words, we compare increments to cost with increments to revenue, rather than totals or averages. Such an examination may show that it will pay to increase the output of one product at the expense of the other, and the only way to tell how far the change should go is to compare the additional revenue from one product less the reduction in revenue from the other with the additional costs incurred by the business as a whole as a result of the change. One cannot decide which product to increase, and by how much, merely by looking at aggregate periodic departmental accounts in which fixed costs have been allocated in some way. If we cannot use the information why prepare it?

The job costing of an engineering works is a much more complicated affair than the simple examples we have taken. Job accounts are prepared to show the materials, labour, other direct expenses and overhead incurred on each job, in order to show what profit each job has yielded, to provide data for future estimates and to control efficiency and prevent waste. No job should be taken unless it covers the variable expenses it incurs, except for such special purposes as maintaining a labour force, holding a trade connection or forcing out a rival – even in such cases it is important to know the cost of the policy adopted. This cost will be the difference between the variable expense on the job and the price received for it, assuming that the latter is less than the former. Details of variable cost should therefore be collected. But the greater part of oncost which is added to the job for costing purposes is fixed and goes on regardless of changes in output. Hence as a general rule any job yielding more than its own variable cost adds to the revenue of the concern and should be accepted[6] unless it is believed that by taking it a more profitable one will have to be refused later. Variable cost marks a minimum to price but actual quotations will depend on market conditions.

Is it useful to add oncost to the job in the cost ledger? Will it help in policy? Let us examine the make up of, say, a machine-hour rate of oncost. Under this method of distributing overhead all the expenses of a department for a year are allocated to the machines in it – the latter are treated as production centres. Some 'normal' output is assumed, and on this basis the number of running hours for each machine is calculated. The cost of power,

[6] But see note 5 above.

superintendence, heat, light and rent of the department are allocated to machines (e.g. power is often metered out, and heat, light and rent charged on floor space). To this cost is added depreciation and repair of the machine and sometimes interest locked up therein. The total cost divided by the number of machine-hours gives the hourly rate on the basis of 'normal' output (which incidentally does not usually mean that rate of output at which cost is a minimum). Each job is charged with oncost according to the number of hours for which it uses the machine. Now, looking backwards on finished jobs, can the mangement derive any help from examining these figures of total cost? The machine-hour rate hides the distinction between fixed and variable costs and tends to convey a false impression of variability. It does not tell you whether you did right in taking on the job. Looking forward, it is necessary only to estimate the additional cost which will be incurred in taking on work – this is the minimum to be accepted and if anything above this can be obtained then the job is profitable. In tendering for orders knowledge of market conditions will govern the bids, not estimates of total cost. There is no reason to assume that it will be any easier to guess the prices of competitors by calculating one's own 'normal' cost. In fact the oncost rates are likely to be more hindrance than help, because they contain in a confused mass both variable expenses and fixed costs. Our conception of the total cost will be no guide to the bids of competitors for an order, as these latter will depend on the state of the competitors' order books, and in any case methods of computing oncost and estimates of normality vary so much between accountant and accountant that it would often be dangerous to suppose that one's competitors have allowed roughly for the same oncost as oneself.

V THE COSTING OF BY-PRODUCTS

Another very important problem dealt with in a most unsatisfactory way concerns the costing of by-products. There are several schools of thought among practitioners. For instance I think it is true to say that the American meat-packing industry regards dressed meat as the main product and all the other products such as hair, hides and wool are treated as by-products. The costs of handling the by-products are subtracted from the income derived from their sale. The net proceeds are then credited in the main manufacturing account, reducing the cost of meat accordingly. Thus all the profits are attributed to the main product. On the other hand, most firms in the oil-refining industry use the selling-prices of the products to determine the costs. For example, crude oil is split into five products. The account for that particular process is debited with the cost of crude oil together with the process costs and the total is divided among the five products in proportion to their market values. So by this method each product shows the same percentage of profit. A third method is to split the total in accordance with some chemical or other arbitrary formula, for example, on the basis of atomic weights.

In this connection there is a story told by an American economist, T. J. Kreps.[7] In a chemical works which was virtually controlled by a large bank the joint costs of a process were being allocated between the two products, caustic soda and chlorine. Owing to the method of allocation adopted fifty per cent to each product, the chlorine showed a loss. The absentee bankers wanted the chlorine foreman discharged, but the works manager, realizing that he would lose a good man, worked out a new cost allocation formula which was more favourable to chlorine; this product then showed a profit and the foreman kept his job. The new allocation was 56.73 to 43.27, and its pseudo-mathematical precision was the result of splitting costs in such a way that both products should show equal book profits. Obviously costing of this type is unsatisfactory and is no help in price policy or in controlling efficiency; the expense of allocation is money wasted. If the proportions in which two products come forward are absolutely fixed, then the joint costs of the process cannot be allocated between them, but if the proportions can be varied within limits and the variation alters the total cost, then it should be the job of the costing department to investigate *changes*

[7] T. J. Kreps, 'Joint Costs in the Chemical Industry', *Quarterly Journal of Economics* (1929-30).

in the cost arising out of changes in proportions, for to maximize net profit it will be necessary to watch price changes of raw materials and finished products and to vary the proportions of the two products to the point at which the added revenue from the last small variation is just balanced by the added cost.

VI COST ACCOUNTING AS A TOOL OF EFFICIENCY

So far we have considered a few points arising out of the entrepreneurial problem, but the technical problem has not been discussed. We hear a great deal about costing as an instrument for producing efficiency and cutting down waste to a minimum. But I think we should bear in mind that excess capacity does not necessarily imply inefficiency. Much is made of the statement that costing shows you the cost of idle capacity. What the management does want to know is whether the output it has agreed to produce could in any way be turned out more cheaply. Can it combine its resources in such a way as to lower the total resources required? Is there any waste it can avoid, which is greater than the expense of avoiding it? Many records at present in general use are valuable from this point of view; for instance, perpetual inventory usually pays because it imposes a control over waste and theft and helps to insure that production is not held up for lack of raw materials. Moreover it provides records which enable the management to reduce to a minimum the capital tied up and therefore prevents loss of interest and wastage due to obsolescence. Plant ledgers are useful because they afford a convenient way of collecting information as to the performance of machines and facilitate the calculation of depreciation.

It is not proposed to discuss the many ways of increasing efficiency which the textbook writers catalogue. Modern works on accounting have tended to give too much space to this aspect of management. Given that the rate of output is a settled question, then so long as relative prices of the factors of production remain unchanged, the efficiency question is not one for the cost department, it is just a matter of vigilance on the part of the works manager. But as soon as the proportionate prices of resources change it is the job of the cost office to see whether the combination of resources can be altered, in order to prevent a rise or bring about a fall in the cost of production by increasing the use of the relatively cheaper resources and decreasing the use of the relatively dearer ones.

One development of cost accounting which has received much publicity in connection with efficiency is known as standard costing. Studies are carried out for the purpose of finding either the cost to be expected under normal conditions or under ideal conditions at different levels of output and these are used as foot rules to measure actual performance; in this way the standards are to be a sort of incentive to greater effort. Some of the systems are exceedingly complicated and the standards are incorporated into the double-entry book-keeping – the hallmark of respectability. If the management can control slackness and create incentive by using these figures, then they may be justified, provided there is no cheaper way of doing the same job. For example one might work out that rate of output of a machine which could be produced at lowest cost. After calculation of the optimum capacity of each department from such computations, it might be possible to estimate the flow of output through the plant which would result in lowest unit costs. This would represent technical but not of course economic perfection (unless competition were perfect). In any case studies of the effect of different *rates* of flow of production would enable the management so to arrange its output within the budget period as to achieve the minimum cost possible for that output.

VII SOME CONCLUSIONS

I believe that cost accountants have spent too much effort in trying to arrive at total cost by building up complicated and delicate oncost structures which depend on arbitrary assumptions. But on the other hand in some industries long-period analysis can be helpful to the management and its estimating department. Although I consider it the cost accountant's main job to inform the management regarding the minimum at which additional work can be taken, this minimum will vary according to the extent to which capacity is being used, and will sometimes include capital costs. For example, if a firm is already working at full capacity, then any further output involves additional capital outlay and the revenue obtainable from the additional turnover must cover the amortization of the new capital outlay in order to be worth accepting. This, however, is not all; an engineering firm, for instance, has to estimate and tender for work. It does not know the estimates of other firms; the only information of which it is certain is its own minimum price, which will be different in periods of normal activity, in times of boom and in times of slackness; this minimum will in each case be the additional cost. But it should also know that *unless* it gets prices including overhead it will not be able to replace its fixed assets. This does not mean that it ought to charge these prices – to do so in some conditions would put it out of the market altogether; but the management should see that the firm is coming to an end. The cost department should say *definitely* at what figure a job is worth handling and *possibly* how much we ought to get if we are not to close down when our fixed equipment wears out. To do this overhead costs must be allocated over jobs in the least arbitrary manner possible. There is no time to go into this wide question, but I would like to emphasize that it is future costs we have to deal with not past ones. One has to provide in overhead the cost of replacing assets; the original cost is of no importance; the past is irrevocable. It is, however, of interest to a firm to know whether it is getting enough out of contracts to cover replacements costs. It may be argued, and with some point, that a detailed analysis of overhead is not worth while for this purpose and that the annual accounts will give sufficient warning. But in any case, if the future of costing lies principally in statistical examination of marginal variations, then it may be doubted whether it can be fitted into the framework of double-entry book-keeping.

Within the time remaining this evening it is impossible to make concrete suggestions as to how the analysis I have attempted to describe should be applied to individual cases, but I think that for each department the accountant should prepare, and continuously revise, schedules showing the additional cost of additional output. For this purpose, the cost accountant would need to be provided with details relating to market prices of materials; he would require a wealth of analysis concerning the expenditure of the business, and engineering data showing how, for example, the rate of wear and tear of machinery is affected by use. Overtime rates, fatigue studies and so on should be part of his stock-in-trade. He should, for example, be able to compute the additional cost of running nine hours per day instead of eight, or the cost of increasing the speed of machinery. He should be able to estimate the cost of an increase of output over and above the budget figure. In those cases where demand fluctuates it should be possible to decide on the cost accountant's evidence how far it is worth while to make for stock in the valley periods. Again the accountant's figures should show whether in a depression a smaller loss is made by selling at a known margin below variable cost than by closing down for a time.

Thus most of the cost accountant's data will come forward in the form of statistical statements, in the preparation of which little help can be derived from a 'tied-in' double-entry system. Of course certain information in individual cases may be wanted so often that it is cheaper to collect it continuously even though it may at times be useless, but this course can be carried too far. Many firms order the continuous collection of data, much of which is required only at infrequent intervals and some of which is never required at all. The cost of this continuous collection must be compared with the cost of a separate investigation each time the data is required, bearing in mind the fact that information to be of service, may be required at very short notice.

Although some criticisms of present methods of costing have been suggested, attempts to allocate fixed costs may be justified on grounds quite unconnected with the problems we have discussed. If time permitted it would be interesting to discuss the growth of uniform systems of costing advocated by many trade associations on the grounds that ignorance of manufacturing and selling costs induces unpleasant price competition. According to T. H. Sanders, Professor of Accounting at Harvard:

Some industries are especially characterized by the presence of large numbers of small manufacturers who are likely to pay little attention to costs, and as a result jeopardize the success of everybody in the business. The larger manufacturers have a genuine dread of competition originating in such sources, and one of their most effective means of combating it has been the development of cost-keeping methods which would tend to remove the prevailing ignorance.[8]

Thus systems of uniform costing are said to aim at preventing price competition due to ignorance. It is, however, doubtful whether a large proportion of goods are sold below total cost merely because the manufacturers know no better; it is more likely that most action of this sort is deliberate. But either way, if some manufacturers choose to make a present of part of their output, this does not reduce the price which other manufacturers are able to charge for their goods. As Professor Plant suggested to the writer, hospitals cannot usually buy bread more cheaply merely because some bakers on occasion give them free loaves. It may be true, however, that a uniform costing system can be used for fixing prices in order to bring about tacit monopoly. Whatever the long-run effect of this, e.g. in attracting new firms to the industry, it is certainly true that suppression of price competition usually leads to competition in quality or service, and the small firm should consider carefully its position in this respect, when opposed to large undertakings.

Sometimes in order to obtain contracts 'window dressing' is required, e.g. the 'cost-plus' basis may be in use or it may be necessary to satisfy a purchaser that the prices charged are 'fair' or 'reasonable'. For bargaining with the unsophisticated it may be very useful to point to fixed costs divided over normal output (output being calculated on the low side) and to say 'This is what it costs us'. This may be partly cost accounting and partly salesmanship. But, of course, in so far as buyers are dependent on the continued existence of supplies from certain firms they must be prepared to pay long-period costs, including sufficient to replace assets as they wear out.

[8] T. H. Sanders, *Cost Accounting for Control*, p. 454.

It may be pointed out that finished stock and work in progress have to be valued for balance-sheet purposes and that current methods of costing are useful for this. The basis generally adopted for finished stock is 'cost or replacement value, whichever is the lower', and this method is accepted by the Inland Revenue for income tax purposes. These valuations generally include a proportion of oncost, the amount of which depends on the views of the accountants concerned. One of the practical objections to treating interest as a cost has been that to do so would 'anticipate profit' on unsold stock and work in progress and, incidentally, income tax would be attracted sooner than need be. Some firms in valuing work in progress exclude all oncost to be on the safe side. But the Revenue authorities object to this on the ground that tax collection is delayed thereby. It might be claimed by the tax payer that the value of unfinished goods is so problematic that nothing should be added to the variable cost, but on the other hand the Revenue authorities might well contend that to a going concern the value of the work in progress is equal to the net selling price of finished stock, less the additional costs required to complete the work in progress. In practice compromise is reached by adding an arbitrary proportion of fixed costs. The whole procedure is unsatisfactory and the principles of valuation require re-examination by accountants; it is unlikely that a costing system allocating fixed cost is justified on these grounds alone.

If I may be allowed to summarize my views, I should say that we can distinguish three lines of approach to the costing problem.

Firstly, information is necessary to enable the most profitable output to be decided. This depends on marginal revenue and marginal cost. We have called this the entrepreneurial problem.

Secondly, information is necessary to ensure that the proposed output is produced at the lowest cost possible for that output having regard to the facilities available. This is the technical problem of combining factors of production and avoiding waste.

Lastly, there is the book-keeping problem of deciding how best to deal with the first two questions having in mind that collecting information costs money.

5

Business organization and the accountant

R. H. COASE

I INTRODUCTORY NOTE

What follows is a shortened version of a series of twelve articles published in the *Accountant* from 1 October to 17 December 1938 under the title 'Business Organization and the Accountant'. The omissions largely consist of illustrations of the argument and a discussion of the problems of estimating costs in practice. The suggestion for writing this series of articles came from R. S. (now Sir Ronald) Edwards. Originally the intention was to take a number of problems of business administration and to show how such problems should be tackled. It was on this basis that I began writing in the summer of 1938. However, comments from Edwards on the draft of a section dealing with vertical integration suggested that readers of the *Accountant* would find my discussion hard to follow without some account of the approach I was using. I therefore decided to write an introductory section in which I explained the basic concepts being employed. In the event the introductory section took up the whole of the series. This explains why the title of the series is not wholly appropriate to its contents.

The articles were written and typed each week during Wednesday night and were taken to the office of the *Accountant* by my wife on Thursday (while I slept). They appeared in print on Saturday. They could be written in this way because I thought of my articles simply as an exposition of views which were generally accepted by economists. The application of these views to business problems was the special interest of a group of economists at L.S.E. working under Professor (now Sir Arnold)

Plant of which I was a member along with Edwards and R. F. Fowler, the two others with whom I worked most closely. That these articles proved to have more than transitory interest, and were reprinted and often referred to, was a great surprise to me. Perhaps because the outbreak of the war diverted economists from their academic studies, these articles came to represent the only extended statement in print of the approach to costs, particularly as applied to business problems, which was the common property of economists at l.s.e. in the 1930s. If Professor Buchanan's thesis about the special character of the l.s.e. approach to costs is correct, it is the fact that these articles do not represent a personal view which gives them their historical significance.

II SOME BASIC CONCEPTS

The method of approach which will be employed is probably best indicated by explaining certain basic concepts. These basic concepts are of general application and find a prominent place in modern discussions on the subject of cost accounting. The first point that needs to be made and strongly emphasized is that attention must be concentrated on the variations which will result if a particular decision is taken, and the variations that are relevant to business decisions are those in costs and/or receipts. This reasoning applies to every business decision, whether it is concerned with the opening or closing of a department, the manufacture of a new product, the introduction of more frequent style changes or an alteration in the volume of production. Whatever the character of the decision, one has to inquire into the variations in costs and receipts which will follow. Costs and receipts which will remain unchanged whatever decision is taken can be ignored. All this sounds very simple and obvious, and it may seem to certain readers that I am flogging a dead horse. Unfortunately, it would appear that this is not entirely the case. Not only is it true that businessmen do not always follow this simple method of reasoning, but in one branch of accounting, namely cost control, it seems that the consequences of this type of reasoning are ignored.

It is clear that if the information regarding costs is to be of use in facilitating business decisions it must ultimately be presented in a form which enables variations in costs to be obtained. But it seems improbable that any accounting system could continuously produce cost information which might be required for every business decision; it is certainly doubtful whether it would be profitable to do so. The problem then arises as to what cost variations are to be considered. If we are to judge by the following quotations from Mr Edwards's paper on the 'Rationale of Cost Accounting'[1] the aim of a cost-accounting system is to discover variations in costs with changes in output. Mr Edwards says that '... the most important thing about costs is the extent to which they change with output',[2] and 'I consider it the cost accountant's main job to inform the management regarding the minimum at which additional work can be taken'.[3] Many writers seem to take a wider view of the nature of cost accounting. At times, however, writers on this subject appear to consider that cost variation is no part of the job of cost accounting; they suggest, for example, that the aim is merely to find out the total cost of a unit of output in the past. It is doubtful whether this phrase can have any real meaning, and the highly arbitrary calculations which are necessary to arrive at a figure seem to support this view. But whatever the view held of the scope of present-day cost accounting it will surely be agreed that information on cost variations is essential for the making of correct business decisions and that the accountant is probably the man who is in the best position to give the required information. Those who believe that it is part of the function of a cost-accounting system to give information relating to variations in costs might well consider how far the information given should relate merely to the variations in cost through changes in output and whether it should also embrace questions such as the opening and closing of departments and the introduction or discontinuance of a product. How far the information required can be provided by the employment of the traditional accounting

[1] R. S. Edwards, 'The Rationale of Cost Accounting', reprinted here, pp. 71-92.
[2] Edwards, 'The Rationale of Cost Accounting', p. 76.
[3] Edwards, 'The Rationale of Cost Accounting', p. 88.

technique is a still wider question. As Mr Edwards says '. . . if the future of costing lies principally in statistical examination of marginal variations, then it may be doubted whether it can be fitted into the framework of double-entry book-keeping'.[4] It should be noted that accounting records merely disclose figures relating to past operations. Business decisions depend on estimates of the future. Accounting records cannot therefore be used as a guide for future action without considering how far the conditions which have existed in the past will continue in the future.

Our purpose will be served if attention is confined to the simple case of variations in costs through variations in output. It is possible to set out the estimated variations in costs which will result from altering output. Certain points, however, should be noted. First there is no need to distinguish between 'fixed' and 'variable' costs. By concentrating on what cost variations will occur, one avoids the necessity of dividing costs up into the categories of 'fixed' and 'variable' costs; there is indeed good reason for thinking that categories of cost which vary for some changes in output do not vary for all changes of output. Secondly it is worth noticing that variations in cost will also depend on the notice which is given of the proposed output change. The variation in costs associated with changes in output will be very different if the variations are to occur next week from what they would be if they were to be carried out next year. A third point is that these costs will also depend on the proposed output for the period after the one under consideration.

Now let us assume that a businessman is examining the variations in costs which he estimates would occur if output varied at some future date. The businessman might produce nothing. If he produces some output certain additional costs will be incurred. These we may term the avoidable costs of that output because they can be avoided by not producing it. Table 5.1 sets out hypothetical figures. In the first column is shown the number of units which might be produced in that unit period of time; in the second column is shown the avoidable costs of producing each size of output.

[4] Edwards, 'The Rationale of Cost Accounting', p. 89.

Table 5.1

Output (*No. of units*)	Avoidable costs of that output £
1	10
2	19
3	27
4	30
5	35
6	44
7	54
8	65
9	77
10	90

Unless receipts to be received from the sale of the output are more than these avoidable costs, it will not be profitable to produce that output. So far we have only considered the total avoidable costs of an output. In economic literature another concept is often employed, that of marginal cost, which may be defined as the avoidable cost of an additional unit. If one considers the figures in the table, this avoidable cost of an additional unit is the increase in the total avoidable costs when the output is increased by one. The avoidable cost of producing one unit is £10, the avoidable costs of producing an output of two units are £19; it follows that the marginal cost of the second unit is £9. Similarly, since the avoidable costs of an output of two units are £19 and of three units £27, it follows that the marginal cost of the third unit is £8. Table 5.2 sets out the marginal costs of the various units.

It should be observed that the multiplication of the marginal cost by the number of units produced does not necessarily give the total avoidable costs of that output. If one takes the output of five units, the marginal cost of the fifth unit is £5. Multiplying this by five gives a figure of £25; the avoidable costs of the total output are in fact £35. Similarly the marginal cost of the tenth unit is £13 and multiplying this by ten gives the figure £130; in fact the avoidable costs of the total output are £90. A consideration of marginal costs indicates that a further condition has to be fulfilled if the most profitable output is to be produced. Not

Table 5.2

Unit of output	Marginal cost
	£
1	10
2	9
3	8
4	3
5	5
6	9
7	10
8	11
9	12
10	13

only must the total receipts cover the total avoidable costs, but the additional receipts obtained by the sale of the marginal unit must also be greater than marginal cost. In the case of perfect competition, since the variations in the output of a single producer have no effect on price, it follows that the additional revenue from the sale of an additional unit of output (which we may term marginal revenue) is equal to the price. If, however, to sell additional units of the product, the price has to be lowered, marginal revenue will be less than the price since to sell those additional units the receipts on those units which could have been sold at a higher price are reduced. Marginal revenue is thus less than price and may even be negative. We may, however, lay down as a general rule that it will pay to expand production so long as marginal revenue is expected to be greater than marginal cost and the avoidable costs of the total output less than the total receipts.

It would be Utopian to imagine that a businessman, except by luck, could manage to attain this position of maximum profit. Indeed it may cost more to discover this point than the additional profits that would be earned. It is to be hoped, however, that the cost accountant may so refine his technique to take account of variations in cost and thus facilitate the task of the businessman.[5]

[5] There followed a section in the original articles which illustrated the use of the concepts of marginal cost and opportunity cost by considering an electricity-supply undertaking which owned a coal mine and which discussed when the undertaking should buy coal on the open market [footnote added].

R. H. Coase

Up to the present my chief aim has been to emphasize the importance to business policy of concentrating on variations in costs and/or receipts. It goes without saying that within the business organization information must be made available which enables these variations to be estimated. Before tackling the practical problem of how this information is to be obtained and presented, there are certain analytical difficulties which need to be faced. These difficulties centre around the fact that costs and receipts cannot be expressed unambiguously in money terms since courses of action may have advantages and disadvantages which are not monetary in character, because of the existence of uncertainty and also because of differences in the point of time at which payments are made and receipts obtained.

The fact that there may be non-monetary advantages and disadvantages attaching to different business policies is a difficulty which need only be dealt with briefly since it may be assumed that in most joint-stock companies and in many other businesses, this factor is of little or no significance. None the less it may at times be important. A businessman may wish at the present time not to buy German or Japanese goods quite apart from any considerations relating to their price or quality; or his views on the problems of national defence may make him desirous of, or averse from, supplying firms in the armament industries. Some attempt might be made to measure the strength of these preferences in money terms, but little benefit would seem to be gained by so doing.[6] To this extent the figures of costs and receipts produced by the accountant are incomplete, and without a knowledge of the preferences of the businessman no decisions on questions of business policy can be reached. This factor makes, for example, the computing of income in money terms more and more unreal, the more personal the entity that is considered. The increased-net-worth concept of income, discussed at length in a series of

---

[6] A manufacturer of pig iron, who prefers to supply armament firms, might reckon his preference in money terms at 10s (50p) per ton. He would therefore add 10s (50p) per ton to his receipts when his pig iron is sold for this purpose.

articles by Mr Edwards,[7] is essentially a monetary concept and fails to describe the situation in a realistic manner as soon as non-monetary costs and receipts have to be considered.

It can be claimed that the non-monetary factors which have just been discussed are of no importance in most businesses and can be ignored. Exactly the same analytical difficulties arise, however, in the case of a factor which cannot possibly be ignored. This factor is the existence of uncertainty. When one is estimating costs or receipts, the figures of the estimate by themselves do not show anything near the whole truth. There is the further question of how likely it is that these figures will be achieved. The figures have to be considered in relation to the probability of this result actually coming about. There is yet another difficulty, because even if the figures which are produced relate to the most probable result, it may not be this result which is of vital significance in determining the decision. A person who buys a lottery ticket is not interested in the most probable result! And all business has to some extent the characteristics of a lottery, the direction of investment being influenced by possibilities other than the most probable result. A businessman considering what will be the effect on costs and receipts of a particular decision will no doubt be contemplating a whole series of possibilities, some highly improbable, some by no means improbable and others quite likely. No single figure (even if it were considered the most likely one) would be adequate. Consider now a businessman trying to decide between alternative courses of action, each of which might produce so many different results. It is clear that the choice will depend partially on the attitude to risk-taking of the person deciding. Some businessmen will be influenced much more by possibilities of high profits which are not very probable than will others. There is no one decision which can be considered to maximize profits independently of the attitude of risk-taking of the businessman. A further point is that the correctness of the decision cannot be determined by subsequent events. If a businessman undertakes to do something which entails certain risks, he

---

[7] Originally published in the *Accountant* (2 July–24 September 1938) and reprinted in *Studies in Accounting*, ed. W. T. Baxter, pp. 227-320.

considers that the chance of gain is worth the risks he runs, and whether ultimately he succeeds or fails has no relevance to this preference.

This lack of objectivity must necessarily be disturbing to those who wish to employ the normal technique of accounting for the solution of many business problems. However a vital factor is apparently being ignored if estimates of costs and receipts make no reference to the probability of these estimates being correct. There is, of course, the extremely difficult problem of whether any *numerical* value can be given to the probability of the forecast being correct. If it cannot, and it would surely not be denied that in most cases this is so, the most useful way of presenting information is probably to produce several different sets of figures, each one relating to a particular group of assumptions about the course of events in the future. Just as monetary calculations become less realistic as they are applied to a more personal entity, so it is that we find that the single-figure costs and receipts of the cost-accounting textbooks become less significant the more uncertain is the future.

IV THE TIME FACTOR

The third difficulty in expressing costs and receipts in money terms is due to the time element. Payments and receipts at different times have to be summated and compared. This can, I think, be made clear by means of an example. Let us assume that an engineering concern is offered two contracts, both of which will employ the full resources of its organization and will take a considerable period of time to complete, one for the construction of a bridge and the other for the construction of an oil refinery. It is obvious that in the case of such jobs as these payments will be made continuously over a long period. It is possible to imagine cases in which receipts come when the job is completed at one particular time, but it is more realistic to consider a case in which the clients pay for the job by instalments, the times when the payments are made possibly being related to the completion of the various sections of the work. To decide whether it is worth while to undertake either of these jobs, and also which of them is the most profitable, it is necessary to take into account the fact that payments are made and receipts obtained at many different points of time. How is this to be done? In order to add payments or receipts or to make comparisons it is necessary to transform these sums into their value at a given date. The time chosen by those who have considered this problem has usually been the present.[8] The *present value* of the sums accruing or being disbursed at each point of time has first to be discovered. Then these sums, which will be positive for accruals and negative for disbursements, when added together represent the present value of the income which would be obtained from undertaking this particular activity. We have therefore to consider how the present value of a future payment or receipt is determined. We shall assume that estimates are made of future payments and receipts and that these estimates are treated as if they were certain. The present value is obtained by discounting the future sums accruing to or being disbursed by the business by a rate of interest. This procedure, which is of course bound up with the choice of the rate of interest, has now to be investigated. Suppose one has to make a payment now instead of at some future date. What sum would leave one in exactly the same position from the point of view of profits as if one had made the payment at the later date? Clearly it is the sum which, at the rate of interest one could obtain if one did not make the payment now, or the rate of interest one would have to pay if one were forced to borrow in order to be able to make the payment now, would amount to the future sum at the later date. Similarly, if one received a sum in the present instead of at some future date, the sum in the future to which it is equivalent is that sum plus the interest it enabled one to earn or the interest it enabled one to avoid if previously one were borrowing. The rate of interest therefore that one uses for purposes of discounting is quite determinate.[9] It is indeed unfortunate that this process is usually

[8] There is of course no reason why some other date should not be chosen if it is thought that this will prove more convenient.

[9] In practice, since the interest rate would probably vary with the amount one lent or borrowed, there would not necessarily be a single rate.

known as discounting. The problem is to transfer the date of a payment or receipt without altering one's profit position. This can be done if one subtracts (when a receipt is brought nearer in time or a payment is moved further off) any interest it enables one to receive or avoid paying, or adds (when a payment is brought nearer in time or a receipt is moved further off) any interest one has to forgo or interest payment one is forced to incur. The addition or subtraction of interest – the discounting – is thus merely a means of ensuring that the transfer of payments or receipts through time does not alter the profits earned.

It cannot be too strongly emphasized that calculations of present values such as have just been made depend on the assumption that the estimates of payments, receipts and the rate of interest can be treated as if they were certain. In fact, however, the introduction of the time element also brings into play the factor whose influence was discussed earlier in this article, the factor of uncertainty. The figures for payments, receipts and the rate of interest are mere estimates. Before coming to any decision, a businessman will have to consider the probability of these estimates actually proving to be accurate. When the satisfaction of a particular contract involves payments and receipts which extend over a period of time, the businessman's attitude to risk-taking, which, as I have said, is purely subjective, will be an important factor determining the decision actually taken. Since no method of accounting can reproduce on paper the mental processes of a businessman, the decision to be taken is one which no mechanical process of discounting can disclose. The only procedure which seems likely to be helpful is apparently the one which was previously suggested, namely, the preparation of several estimates based on different sets of assumptions about the future. We noted previously that the greater the uncertainty, the less significant are single-figure costs and receipts for the solution of business problems. Although the element of time by itself raises no insuperable difficulties, the fact that a lengthening of the period over which forecasts are made will tend to be associated with an increase in the uncertainty with which these forecasts are regarded presents a formidable difficulty for those who wish to present information in a useful way for businessmen.

V THE NATURE OF COSTS

The difficulties which have been examined up to this stage have been common both to the measurement of costs and receipts. Some attention must now be paid to the nature of costs, since their derived and indirect character is liable to cause difficulty. In this article the notion of costs which will be used is that of 'opportunity' or 'alternative' cost. The cost of doing anything consists of the receipts which could have been obtained if that particular decision had not been taken. When someone says that a particular course of action is 'not worth the cost', this merely means that he prefers some other course – the receipts of the individual, whether monetary or non-monetary, will be greater if he does not do it. This particular concept of costs would seem to be the only one which is of use in the solution of business problems, since it concentrates attention on the alternative courses of action which are open to the businessman. Costs will only be covered if he chooses, out of the various courses of action which seem open to him, that one which maximizes his profits. To cover costs and to maximize profits are essentially two ways of expressing the same phenomenon. In practice it is probably better to regard the cost of doing anything as the highest alternative receipts that might have been obtained rather than vaguely as all the alternatives that are open.

Some characteristics of cost when it is interpreted in this way should be noted. First of all costs are not necessarily the same as payments. It is this fact that makes the 'costs' disclosed by cost accountants something quite different from 'opportunity cost', for cost accounting methods would seem to be designed to 'recover' all payments that have been made for purposes of production. This point can be illustrated by considering the cost of using a particular machine for a certain purpose. Cost accountants would presumably give different answers according to the particular method of depreciation which they employ; but if cost is interpreted as opportunity cost the answer is quite simple and definite. The cost of using the machine is the highest receipts that could be obtained by some alternative employment of the machine. This may be any figure and may be unrelated to the cost of the machine. The other point that must be mentioned is the forward-looking character of the opportunity-cost concept where business decisions are concerned. It is useless to look back at the past, except as an object lesson. Of course one can say that one might have made a wiser decision and that in this sense costs were not covered. But to employ the term in this way does not seem to be very helpful, for, as Jevons reminded us, 'Bygones are forever bygones'. The only course which is open to a businessman is to make the best choice given the knowledge at his disposal, and in this task I hope to show that the concept of opportunity cost can be of considerable assistance.

Having explained the meaning of the concept of 'opportunity' or 'alternative' cost, I now turn to the question of its application to the solution of business problems. It will be assumed that an attempt is being made to calculate the minimum price at which it pays to accept a particular job. This minimum price is, of course, the total avoidable cost of that job. In working out this total avoidable cost, the calculation of the cost items, materials, depreciation, and interest on capital will be considered as examples of the use of the 'opportunity'-cost concept in the solution of such a problem. Much that I have to say may appear obvious, but it is necessary to secure agreement on simple matters before proceeding to consider more complex questions.

VI COST OF MATERIALS

The determination of the cost of materials for a job for which the materials have not yet been bought is simple. It is the estimated amount of money to be spent on their purchase. This accords exactly with the 'opportunity'-cost concept since, if the materials were not purchased, that amount of money would be available for the business. A more difficult problem arises, however, if the materials which are to be used have to be drawn from stock. What is the cost of using them? In the ordinary cost-accounting text-books are to be found a multiplicity of methods of calculating the cost of materials. There is the method by which this is taken to be the amount paid for the oldest part of the stock; another way of making this calculation is to discover the average amount paid for the existing stock; apparently at times the market price of the materials when they are issued is used, while yet another method is to take as one's basis the amount paid for the highest-priced stock. And, as readers will know, this list is not exhaustive. Some writers expressly point out that their figures are not to be used for estimating. It is not, however, always quite clear whether what is meant is that the price one quotes must to some extent depend on demand conditions, or whether these cost-accounting methods do not give one the minimum price at which it pays a business to take a job. Some writers – those, for example, who claim that cost-accounting methods enable one to eliminate unprofitable lines – seem to imply that it is the minimum price which is achieved, and it is therefore necessary to consider whether or not these methods do give one the figure that is required.

Our aim is to discover what allowance has to be made for the cost of materials when a calculation of total avoidable cost is being made. If the 'opportunity'-cost concept is employed, the question that has to be asked is what one would do with the material if it were not used on this job. It could either be sold or used on some other job. The cost of using the material is therefore either 1) the price if sold minus the costs of selling, or 2) the expense that would be avoided if the material were used on some other job; that is, the payment that would have been made for materials minus the cost of holding the existing materials until they are required.[10] Whichever of these two amounts is the greater may be regarded as the cost of using the material.

I shall now illustrate the proposition which has just been developed by means of an example. First of all let us suppose that

[10] The other job may be a similar one at a later date or of quite a different character. The material displaced may actually be a less expensive one. Another cost that may have to be deducted is the expense of transforming the material into the form in which it is required for the other job.

a company has entered into a long-term contract for the supply of a certain raw material at £10 per ton, it being agreed that a minimum quantity of 1,000 tons will be taken each year. Let us also assume that the amount of material which is consumed is in fact slightly less than 1,000 tons. What will be the cost of using the material? Since, as I have said, the amount consumed is less than 1,000 tons, it follows that there is in fact always material which is available for production. The possibility of using material on another job if it is not used for this one does not therefore arise. The 'opportunity' cost of the material must therefore be the price in the open market less the costs of selling, or possibly, if this were higher, £10 minus the sum the suppliers would accept or plus the sum they would pay to set aside the contract.

The idea that entering into a long-term contract at a fixed price for a material in some sense avoids fluctuations in the cost of that raw material (a notion which would certainly be derived from a study of many of the usual cost-accounting methods) is one which I believe to be erroneous. The main result of entering into such a contract is to make profits higher than they would be if the price during the period is on balance greater than £10, and lower if the price is on balance less than £10. 'Opportunity'-costs, however, will continue in such a case to fluctuate with price movements on the open market.[11] The vigilance of those concerned with seeing that the best use is made of the firm's resources must not be relaxed because of the existence of such a contract. A numerical example will, I think, make this perfectly clear. Let us reconsider the policy of the company which we had supposed to have entered into a long-term contract for the supply of a material at £10 per ton. Suppose that the market price of the material is £18 per ton, and that the costs of selling are £1 per ton. The receipts from selling a ton of the material would be £17 per ton.

Now let us suppose that a contract is offered which will entail avoidable costs of £150 and will also require ten tons of the

---

[11] The absolute movements in cost, assuming that selling expenses are unchanged, will be the same. But since in this case 'opportunity' cost is equal to the price minus the selling expense, the percentage variation in cost will be greater than the percentage variation in the price.

material. If one reckons the cost of the materials at £10 per ton, which is the amount actually paid for the material, the total avoidable cost would come to £250. Suppose that the price which is offered for the job is £300. It would appear on the basis of this calculation that the business concerned would earn a profit of £50 from carrying out this contract. On the other hand, if the calculations were made, using as the basis for the material cost £17 per ton, the total avoidable cost would have amounted to £320. The job would then have appeared unprofitable, since the receipts from the jobs would not have covered the total avoidable cost. My view is that this calculation gives a correct result and in fact it would be more profitable for the firm to refuse the contract. It can, I think, be demonstrated that it would have been in a better position through doing so. If the job were actually carried out, the receipts and payments would be as shown in Table 5.3.

Table 5.3

	£
Receipts	300
Payments: for labour, power, etc.	150
for material	100
Total payments	250
Receipts less payments	£50

If the contract were not carried out and the materials were sold, the figures of receipts and payments would then be as shown in Table 5.4.

Table 5.4

	£
Receipts from sale of material	170
Payment for material	100
Receipts less payments	£70

It should be noted that since the payment of £100 for materials would remain the same whatever decision is taken, there is really no need to include this sum in the calculations.

A point that does not need much emphasizing is that the cost-accounting methods for the pricing of materials which were discussed earlier do not give one the 'opportunity' cost of materials. Most of the methods – for example, the use of the price of the oldest stock or of an average price paid for materials in stock – are determined by past payments or payments which have been agreed upon in the past. As we have seen, there is no reason for supposing that the price one has paid for materials, or a figure derived from a calculation based on the prices one has paid, will give one the 'opportunity' cost of using materials. Even the method by which materials are charged out at market prices, and which implies a break with the idea that cost calculation must be linked up with payments, is unsatisfactory. On the one hand it ignores the expenses involved in reselling materials one has purchased – expenses which may be quite considerable; on the other hand it does not take into account the value of the materials if used for some other job. I do not wish to suggest that there may not be many purposes which are served admirably by modern cost-accounting methods. My sole aim in this section is to point out that these methods do not give one 'opportunity' costs and do not enable one to calculate avoidable costs. This being so, it seems to me that any claim that modern cost accounting (at any rate in the form in which it is to be found in the textbooks) enables unprofitable lines to be discovered and eliminated is misleading. It is only possible to discover whether or not a particular activity is profitable by comparing the avoidable costs with the receipts. And this, as I understand it, is a task which modern cost-accounting methods do not enable one to perform.

VII DEPRECIATION

This subject is one which it is difficult to treat, if only for the reason given by Professor Hatfield when he said that 'accountants are not of one voice on the subject, nor have they all learned to make satisfactory exposition'.[12] I do not, however, propose to put forward a precise definition of depreciation and I shall content

---

[12] H. R. Hatfield, 'What they say about Depreciation', *Accounting Review* (March 1936). Reprinted in *Studies in Accounting*, ed. W. T. Baxter, pp. 337-50.

myself with saying, and I believe there can be little doubt about this, that the problem of depreciation arises from the fact that assets may fall in value. As I understand it, much of the accounting literature on the subject considers depreciation from one of two points of view. The first is concerned with the problem of valuation for the purpose of measuring profits, and the second with determining the amount of reinvestment which is necessary if capital is to be 'maintained intact'. These are, however, problems of financial and investment policy and need not, I think, be considered by those who are concerned with the ordinary run of business decisions.

The reason why depreciation has to be considered when the notion of 'opportunity' cost is being examined is that the value of an asset is sometimes affected by the use to which it is put. At this stage some reference is necessary to the meaning which I attach to the phrase 'the value of an asset'. By this phrase I mean the present value of the net receipts which it is estimated will be obtained from ownership of that asset. If future receipts and/or payments may be altered by the way in which an asset is used in the present, it is clear that the value of the asset, in my sense, depends to some extent on how it is used. It is this fact that I wish to take into account. If the value of an asset, as this phrase is used by accountants, has no relation to future payments and receipts, but is equal to the original cost of the asset reduced by the application of some mechanical rule, then changes in that value clearly have no connection with the cost which I am examining. It should be noted that, even if the value of an asset is calculated in the way I have suggested, it is only those changes in value which result from use that are relevant when one is deciding whether or not to take on a particular job. Let us assume that if a machine is not used, its value will fall from £100 to £80 and that, if it is used, its value will fall from £100 to £75. In this case *depreciation through use* is £5 and it is this figure with which we are concerned when we are discussing depreciation as an 'opportunity' cost. What I have termed 'depreciation through use' Mr Keynes calls user cost.[13]

[13] See *The General Theory of Employment, Interest and Money*, p. 53.

Let us now return to our problem. The choice between using or not using a machine, or between using a machine for one purpose and using it for another, will be influenced by the effect such uses have on future payments and receipts. It is possible to calculate the present value of future receipts and payments by discounting them by a rate of interest, a process that I have already described. The cost which we are considering is measured by the change in the present value of an asset which results from use. Examples of this cost can easily be found. If a machine is used in the present instead of leaving it idle, it may well be that its life is shortened. This means that profits that would have been earned at the end of its life will now no longer be received. This loss of profits in the future through the use of a machine in the present is a cost of using the machine which must be taken into account. Similarly the increased use of a machine may imply higher costs of maintenance in the future, or may render the machine unsuitable for purposes which otherwise it would have served and thus raise costs and/or lower receipts on jobs on which it is employed. These are examples of depreciation through use. It is clear that this cost is dependent on estimates of the future. Since, however, the future is uncertain, the allowance that will be made for this factor will be partially dependent on the attitude to risk-taking of the businessman. Although it will to some extent depend on subjective factors, depreciation through use is a cost which will have to be taken into account in calculating 'opportunity' cost.

I shall endeavour to show, by means of an example, the significance of what I have termed 'depreciation through use' and others call 'user cost'. In the case of many industrial concerns it may be that depreciation through use is of little importance; the same, however, cannot be said of mining companies or other concerns with assets of a similar character. This is very clearly brought out by Mr F. W. Paish in an article on 'Causes of Changes in Gold Supply',[14] He says:

In most types of production we have to consider the problem of the optimum rate of application of variable factors, including raw materials, to certain fixed equipment of which the useful life does

[14] *Economica* (November 1938), p. 384.

not greatly vary with the intensity of utilization. In other words, the proportion of marginal cost, which consists of user cost, is relatively small, and even substantial differences in estimates of user cost would have very little effect on total marginal costs and on the rate of output. In the case of a mine, however, the position is the exact opposite. There is a given stock of raw material of which the rate of output, and therefore the length of life, is almost infinitely variable according to the amount of fixed capital and other resources which are applied to its exploitation. In this case every ton of ore extracted means a ton of ore less to be extracted at some future date; and if the deposit is a valuable one, which is expected to show a large profit over costs of extraction, the greater proportion of marginal cost may be the user cost of the deposit.

The fact which Mr Paish brings out, namely that in the case of a mine an increase in output will reduce future receipts, is one which has to be taken into account when output policy is being considered. A numerical example is bound to be somewhat of a simplification, but it may clarify the argument. We shall suppose that we are considering the output to be produced from a given mine. One assumption that will be made is that each additional ton produced in the current year reduces the output that can be produced in the tenth year by one ton. The net receipts from production in the tenth year accrue at the end of that year. We shall also assume that the estimates that are made are regarded with certainty. Marginal cost may be taken to be the cost of an additional ton and marginal receipts the receipts from the sale of an additional ton (see Table 5.5).

Let us suppose that producing 197 tons instead of 196 tons in the current year means that it is only possible to produce 199 tons in the tenth year and not 200 tons. Similarly let us suppose that producing 198 tons in the present year, instead of 197 tons, means that it is impossible to produce 199 tons in the tenth year, but only 198 tons; and similarly with other changes in output. If 197 tons are produced instead of 196 tons, £50 that would have been received at the end of ten years will not now be obtained. If 198 tons are produced in the current year instead of 197 tons, £90 that would have become available at the end of the tenth year will

Table 5.5

Costs and Receipts in the Tenth Year

Output (tons)	Marginal cost £	Marginal receipts £	Marginal net receipts £
197	100	250	150
198	140	250	110
199	160	250	90
200	200	250	50

Costs and Receipts in the First year

Output (tons)	Marginal cost (excluding user cost) £	Marginal receipts £
197	80	250
198	100	250
199	140	250
200	180	250

now not do so. If we assume that the interest rate that we have to use for discounting is five per cent per annum, the user cost is in these cases the present value of £50 and £90 in ten years at five per cent per annum. The costs-and-receipts position for the first year may be set out once again including depreciation through use or user cost (see Table 5.6).

It can be seen by looking at Table 5.6 that it will not pay to

Table 5.6

Costs and Receipts in the First Year

Output (tons)	Marginal cost (excluding user cost) £	User cost £	Total marginal cost £	Marginal receipts £
197	80	31	111	250
198	100	54	154	250
199	140	68	208	250
200	180	92	272	250

produce an output greater than 199 tons, because marginal cost (including user cost) for a larger output is greater than marginal receipts. Had depreciation through use been ignored, it would have appeared as if an output of at least 200 tons would have been profitable. But to ignore depreciation through use would mean ignoring the effect changes in output have on future receipts. Depreciation through use is part of 'opportunity' cost, because if that output were not produced, certain other receipts would accrue – although in the future. The fact that these receipts accrue in the future involves the difficulty which was discussed earlier, the comparison of receipts at different points of time. The method by which this difficulty can be overcome is to compute the present value of these future receipts by discounting, although, as I said, this makes the process seem too mechanical and obscures the reasons why this process produces significant results. There is a further point to which I have continually drawn attention. Since estimates of future receipts and future rates of interest cannot be made with certainty, all that it is possible to do on paper is to produce for the guidance of the businessman different estimates of what depreciation through use would be if various groups of assumptions about the future were realized. The actual choice that the businessman makes will then depend to some extent on subjective factors.

VIII INTEREST ON CAPITAL

The problem of whether or not to include interest on capital in the calculation of cost is one of the most controversial in cost accounting. The usual method of approach is, however, a somewhat peculiar one. Instead of treating the problem directly, writers on cost accounting commonly list the advantages and disadvantages of considering interest as a cost and then give their own opinion as to whether or not the advantages outweigh the disadvantages. As a result, several quite distinct questions are discussed at the same time. There is not only the question of whether interest is a cost, there is also the problem of whether it can be easily calculated or whether, even if it is calculated, it is of sufficient importance to be worth bothering about. It is thus possible for a conclusion to be reached that interest on capital should not be included in the cost accounts without thorough discussion as to whether it is a cost. The conclusion may be reached because, for example, the author thinks that even if it is a cost, it would be much too complicated a matter to calculate it. In this way the main question is avoided. Although this procedure is no doubt quite adequate for the purpose these writers have in mind, it seems to me unfortunate, since a concentration on the fundamental question of whether interest is a cost would have indicated the characteristics of the 'actual cost' which modern cost accounting aims at disclosing.

Before proceeding to consider the more fundamental question, we must take account of those technical problems which have made many writers on cost accounting decide on the exclusion of interest from their calculations. First of all there is the belief that if interest is to be included it will not be possible to do so within the framework afforded by double-entry book-keeping. This if I understand him right, is the view of Mr W. W. Bigg. He says:

... there is no reason why the cost accounts should be encumbered with a mass of calculations which merely tend to complicate the results achieved thereby. The result of including interest may be ascertained with the minimum of difficulty by the preparation of statistical statements quite apart from the cost accounts and from such statements the necessary information can be obtained to enable an economic price to be fixed. To this treatment the majority of the objections to the inclusion of interest in the cost accounts do not apply.[15]

It may well be that double-entry book-keeping has its limitations, but it would seem to be quite another matter to argue – and Mr Bigg does not argue – that because double-entry book-keeping cannot handle a particular problem, it is therefore no concern of the accountant. The problem we are discussing may still be a matter of lively interest to accountants, even if it cannot be solved within the confines of modern cost accounts.

[15] W. W. Bigg, *Cost Accounts* (1932), pp. 84-5. A similar point is made in Wheldon, *Cost Accounting and Costing Methods*, pp. 128-9.

A subsidiary objection to the inclusion of interest as a cost, which seems connected with the point we have just discussed, is that cost accounts should deal with actual money payments. It may, of course, be true that cost accounts in fact only deal with actual money payments; it may even be true that the particular technique employed is incapable of any modification to enable interest to be included. What it does not determine is whether interest is a cost. It is also said that to include interest on capital (when this is not paid to someone outside the business) would mean anticipating profits in the valuation of stocks. There seems, however, to be no reason why the procedure adopted for the valuation of stocks should in any way depend on the answer given to the question we are examining.

The arguments which are used to support the inclusion of interest in cost calculations are fairly straightforward. It is pointed out that capital is just as much a factor of production as labour and that if labour costs are included so should interest on capital. It would obviously be foolish to decide whether to substitute machinery for labour in production without taking into account interest. As it is said in Mr Bigg's book, 'if £2,000 is expended upon the purchase of a machine, it must be remembered that in the first year of its life it has cost, at five per cent, £100 in respect of interest lost on the money expended....'[16]

Similarly, when the profitability of different operations is being compared, the argument is used that quite erroneous results would be reached if account were not taken of the fact that some jobs require more capital equipment or take longer and tie up more money in work in progress. It is difficult to find in the literature counter arguments to these views. Assertions such as 'interest is the reward of capital as much as wages are of labour is one of economics, not of costing,' and 'to include interest paid on borrowed capital only cannot be accepted, because it has no more connection with manufacturing than all the capital invested in the business. Interest in both cases is a matter of finance, not of manufacturing',[17] are hardly to be taken seriously. There is, how-

[16] Bigg, *Cost Accounts*, p. 82.
[17] Both are to be found in Wheldon, *Cost Accounting and Costing Methods*, p. 128.

ever, one answer to these arguments which is of some substance. It is to be found in Professor T. H. Sanders's *Cost Accounting for Control*. He says that interest 'is not really a cost, but only an opportunity forgone; and the capital in buildings and equipment for a certain industry having been once invested, that capital is no longer free for investment elsewhere'. There would seem to be little doubt that if one were considering whether or not to take on a particular contract which involved the actual purchase of capital equipment, that interest on the amount expended would reckon as a cost. Professor Sanders's objection applies, however, once the machinery has been installed. First of all it is clear that the net receipts contributed by the machinery must be estimated to be greater than the interest that could be obtained on the amount of money represented by the secondhand value of the equipment minus the costs of selling it. But if it is decided that the machinery is not to be sold, this factor is of no relevance when the cost of using the equipment for a particular job is being calculated. Nor is any allowance for interest on the original cost of the machinery. All that need be considered is the alternative net receipts that would be obtained if the machine were employed on some other job. If there is no other job on which the equipment could be used, the cost of using the machine (if we exclude depreciation through use) will be nil. It is not therefore possible to say whether any allowance should be made for the use of the capital; this depends on the facts of the case. It is, however, somewhat misleading to talk about this cost as interest on capital. It is merely the highest alternative net receipts that could be obtained if the particular job under consideration were not taken. The problems of how one determines the value of the capital and the interest rate to employ if one is to include interest on capital in one's cost calculation are avoided. Similarly it is shown to be a matter of no importance for our problem whether the money which was spent on the purchase of the equipment was obtained by the issue of debentures or was money provided by the business itself. It is also clear that in those cases where an allowance is made for interest on capital, in, for example, the uniform cost systems of trade associations, it is most improbable that the 'opportunity' cost of using capital is obtained.

I stated earlier that I would illustrate the 'opportunity'-cost concept by considering the three items of cost, materials, depreciation and interest on capital. The 'opportunity' cost of using materials in stock we found to be either the price if sold minus the cost of selling, or the expense that would be avoided if the material were used on some other job. Depreciation considered as an 'opportunty' cost could be taken to be depreciation through use or the present value of the future profits lost through use. Interest on capital, if it is to be interpreted as 'opportunity' cost, must be regarded as the alternative net receipts that could be obtained by the use of the machinery.

IX SOME CRITICS ANSWERED[18]

I now propose to pause, and review the theory which I have been discussing. A pause will at the same time present an opportunity for examining certain criticisms which have been made of the theory.

It has been suggested that I was 'confusing charges against profit with costs'. It was further stated that : 'One of the great advantages to be derived from cost accounts is the explanations which they afford of the financial results disclosed by the normal trading and profit-and-loss account'.[19] I trust I have not misunderstood the point, but judging from the rest of the letter, it seems that the argument is that we must allocate 'oncosts' to departments in order to discover the profits contributed by each of them. My answer to this is that it is not possible (except in most unlikely circumstances) to divide up total profits and to decide how much is to be attributed to each department. Of course the methods which involve allocation of 'oncosts' do result in a figure for profits being associated with each department, but it is suggested that if a logical method is adopted for discovering the

---

[18] What follows was an attempt to answer criticisms of my approach which had been made in correspondence printed in the *Accountant* (footnote added).

[19] In a letter written by Mr W. W. Bigg, the *Accountant* (15 October 1938).

profits which result from the existence of each department, it will in general be found that adding together the profits contributed by each department separately does not give a figure equal to the total profits of the business. To explain this point, I shall work in some detail through an example. I shall assume that we are investigating the affairs of a department store with four departments: piece goods, men's and women's wear, furniture and a restaurant. Table 5.7 gives particulars relating to this business. The departmental expenses for materials and sales assistants would cease if that department were closed down.

Table 5.7

Costs and Sales

	Materials	*Wages of sales assistants*	*Sales*
	£	£	£
Piece goods	200	100	750
Men's and women's wear	300	160	1,200
Furniture	300	100	900
Restaurant	300	110	700
All departments	£1,100	£470	£3,550

	£
Other expenses: advertising	300
general and other miscellaneous expenses	960
rent	200
Total of other expenses	£1,460

The total sales for the period were £3,550 while the total expenses were £3,030. We may therefore assume that the profits were £520. The problem we are considering is whether it is possible to divide up this sum and say how much was contributed by each department. It would seem logical to define the contribution to profits of a particular department as the addition to profits due to having it. We have seen that profits with all four departments were £520; if the withdrawal of a particular department would have caused profits to fall to £400, it would seem reasonable to say that the profits contributed by that department are £120. If we assume that this is the basis for calculating the profits of each department, we have to estimate the effect of closing each one in turn. We shall also suppose that there is no possibility of leasing the space that is freed.

Let us start with the piece-goods department. In the case of the particular department store we are considering, we may assume that it is one which attracts many customers to the store and that a most important result of closing down the piece-goods department would be that fewer customers come to the store. The effect of this is so great that in spite of the additional room that is available for display, it is estimated that the sales of all the remaining departments would fall. The estimated operating results if the piece-goods department were closed down are shown in Table 5.8.

Table 5.8

Costs and Sales

	Materials	*Wages of sales assistants*	*Sales*
	£	£	£
Men's and women's wear	290	150	1,000
Furniture	280	90	880
Restaurant	270	90	600

	£
Other expenses: advertising	250
general and other miscellaneous expenses	800
rent	200

It will be seen that the total sales would be £2,480 and the total expenses £2,420. The profits would therefore be £60. As the profits including the piece-goods department were £520, the profits resulting from having that department are £460.

Now let us suppose that it is the department selling men's and women's wear that is closed down. Piece-goods require a great deal of space and the additional room can be used by that department. It is estimated that there would be an increase in sales by the piece-goods department, but a fall in the sales of the others. These results are set out in Table 5.9.

Table 5.9

Costs and Sales

	Materials £	Wages of sales assistants £	Sales £
Piece goods	300	130	1,050
Furniture	290	90	890
Restaurant	290	100	650

	£
Other expenses: advertising	260
general and other miscellaneous expenses	840
rent	200

The total expenses would be £2,500, while sales would amount to £2,590; a profit of £90 would be shown. The profits contributed by the men's and women's wear department would therefore seem to be £430.

We can now consider the effect of closing down the furniture

Table 5.10

Costs and Sales

	Materials £	Wages of sales assistants £	Sales £
Piece goods	205	105	800
Men's and women's wear	300	160	1,075
Restaurant	295	105	670

	£
Other expenses: advertising	280
general and other miscellaneous expenses	860
rent	200

department. The space that it occupies could be used to some extent by the piece-goods department which, it is estimated, would result in a rise in sales; the other departments, however, would show slight falls. Table 5.10 shows the estimated operating results had the furniture department been closed down.

The profit under these circumstances would be £35, since sales are estimated at £2,545 and expenses at £2,510. The furniture department therefore adds to profits a sum of £485.

And now we come to a consideration of the last department, the restaurant. The loss of this department would mean, it is estimated, a slight fall in the sales of the others. But it would also result in a large fall in general and miscellaneous expenses. The estimated figures after the close of the restaurant are set out in Table 5.11.

Table 5.11

Costs and Sales

	Materials £	Wages of sales assistants £	Sales £
Piece goods	200	100	730
Men's and women's wear	295	155	1,000
Furniture	290	100	850

	£
Other expenses: advertising	250
general and other miscellaneous expenses	780
rent	200

The profits in this case would be much higher; actually they would be £210. Sales would be £2,580 and expenses £2,370. The amount of the profits that seem to be attributable to the existence of the restaurant is £310.

Thus it is that if we calculate the profits contributed by each department on what seems to me to be the only basis on which this can be done, the individual profits of the departments work out at £460, £430, £485 and £310. The total of these figures is £1,685. The actual profits were £520. It seems clear that it is not

possible to divide up total profits among the different departments and to say how much each one contributes. The only case
in which it is possible to do this is that in which there are no
economies in having one particular combination of departments.
The point that I am making is not dependent on the fact that
possessing certain departments affects the sales of others (as it does
in a department store), but applies equally well to a manufacturing business in which this factor might be of no importance.

A final example (Table 5.12) will, I hope, make this quite clear.
Suppose that we are examining a manufacturing business which
is producing unbranded radios and refrigerators. We may also
assume that sales would remain the same whether the production
of these two products is combined or not.

Table 5.12

Costs and Sales

	Departmental expenses £	Sales £
Radio	3,000	5,000
Refrigerator	1,000	3,000

The total of other expenses may be taken to be £2,500 if the
manufacture of these two products is combined but £2,000 for
each product if either of them is produced separately. Thus
profits are £1,500 if manufacture is combined, but no profits at
all would be earned if production were separate. How is it
possible to say how much of the profits are contributed by each
department? Without either of them there would be no profits.
As will be seen from this example, the mere fact that one could
discover the profits of a department if it were run as a separate
business does not enable one, if there are economies in having
several departments, to say how much is contributed to profits by
each department if in fact they are combined within a single
business.

X COSTS IN RELATION TO DECISIONS

It will perhaps indicate most clearly the nature of the approach to business problems discussed if emphasis is placed on its close connection with the making of decisions. The technique which has been examined is one which aims at aiding businessmen in making decisions. One can discuss the meaning of the term 'avoidable costs' but what costs *are* avoidable and their actual measurement can only be determined with reference to a particular decision. It is for this reason that I dislike a classification of costs which divides them into 'fixed' and 'variable' costs – depreciation, interest on capital and the managing director's salary being, for example, regarded as fixed costs while wages and the cost of materials are regarded as variable costs. Instead of speaking of fixed and variable costs, some writers use the terms overhead and prime costs while others distinguish between indirect and direct costs. The difficulty of using such a rigid classification is that whether a particular category of cost is likely to vary depends solely on the decision which is being taken. If the effect of enlarging a certain department is being considered, the costs that will prove to be variable are likely to be quite different from those that would vary if the introduction of a new product is being contemplated. It seems best therefore not to make any attempt to segregate costs into the classes 'fixed' and 'variable' but merely to try to discover what costs would be avoidable if a particular course of action were taken or, looking at the problem the other way round, what additional costs would be incurred if that action were carried out. The same procedure applies of course to receipts.

This linking of cost analysis to particular decisions makes any mechanical classification of costs almost impossible. The costs whose variations are of significance for one decision will be of no significance for others. There are innumerable decisions and each one may require a different classification. In fact this difficulty has not been very apparent in modern cost accounting, partly because its function has been taken to be the ascertainment of 'actual cost' in the past without reference to the use to be made of this figure, but also because, in so far as these results were thought to have relevance to business decisions, it was a particular set of decisions that cost accountants had in mind. It would seem that the figures produced were thought to be of use in such decisions as those relating to output changes, or in deciding whether to accept a certain contract or close a department. Other decisions – and possibly even these – would require special investigations to provide the information on which the decision is to be based. The problem of what information is to be collected, how far it is to be presented regularly and how far it is to be collected as part of a special investigation are practical points of obvious importance but about which little can be learnt in the cost-accounting textbooks.

XI MARGINAL COSTS

I have already pointed out that if we are to judge from writers on cost accounting the business decision for which the figures disclosed in the cost accounts are of most significance is that relating to the output to be produced. It is, of course, a general criticism of modern cost control that it does not concern itself with calculating avoidable costs. When, however, information is prepared for the purpose of determining output, a further criticism must be added, since the figures provided relate to *average* rather than *marginal* cost. Marginal cost I defined as the avoidable cost of an additional unit of output. Some attempt must be made to estimate marginal cost if the output which yields the greatest profits is to be chosen. As an example of the use of the marginal-cost concept, we may examine the case of an electricity-supply undertaking which owns a coal mine and which has to determine how much to produce in its own mine.[20] The most profitable policy for this undertaking would be to produce coal in its own mine so long as total avoidable costs were covered and marginal cost was not greater than the cost of purchasing the coal on the open market. There are then two questions which the management would have to ask con-

[20] This example had been discussed earlier in the original articles but this section has been omitted in this condensation [footnote added].

stantly. First of all it would have to consider whether the expenses that it would save by not producing anything (the avoidable cost) are greater or less than the amount it would have to pay for the same quantity. The other question is whether the cost of producing one more unit is greater or less than the expense of buying it. If it is less, then it would pay to increase production from the mine; if greater, it might be profitable to contract. To serve as an example, Table 5.13 gives the costs.

Table 5.13

Output (tons)	Total avoidable costs £	Marginal cost (avoidable costs of an additional 100 tons) £
1000	674	113
1100	799	125
1200	946	147
1300	1115	169

If the price of a 100-ton lot is £150, it is clear that for all amounts shown in the table, the total avoidable costs are less than the expense involved in buying these quantities on the open market. On the other hand, it would not be profitable to produce more than 1,200 tons, since, if 1,300 tons were produced, the extra 100 tons would have involved the business in additional expenses of £169 whereas the same quantity could be obtained for £150 by purchase on the open market.

The marginal-cost table shows the costs of producing further units of output from the undertaking's own mine, and it seems clear that this has to be compared with the costs of purchasing coal if the economical level of production is to be reached. A real difficulty arises, however, if marginal costs do not move regularly as in my table but, after rising with every increase in output, start to fall and then recommence rising. In such a case a mechanical application of the rule I gave would suggest that there are several outputs at which profits are a maximum. When this is so, it is necessary to choose out of these outputs that one which is most profitable for the undertaking. Let us consider a case in which the marginal costs have this characteristic. Assume that the cost figures for the coal mine have been as they are set in Table 5.14.

Table 5.14

Output (tons)	Total avoidable costs £	Marginal cost (avoidable costs of an additional 100 tons) £
100	50	50
200	146	96
300	256	110
400	400	144
500	560	160
600	760	200
700	935	175
800	1075	140
900	1175	100
1000	1255	80
1100	1375	120
1200	1550	175
1300	1800	250
1400	2100	300
1500	2300	200
1600	2420	120
1700	2560	140
1800	2780	220

We may assume that the consumption of coal is estimated at 1,800 tons. If the price of coal is £150 per 100-ton lot, how much of the 1,800 tons required will be produced in the mine? It would seem to be either 400 or 1,100 tons or 1,700 tons. If the output is increased from 400 to 1,100 tons, total avoidable costs rise from £400 to £1,375. The additional 700 tons will therefore cost £975. To purchase this amount on the open market at a price of £150 per 100-ton lot would cost £1,050. It is therefore more profitable for the undertaking to produce 1,100 rather than 400 tons. If, however, 1,700 tons are produced instead of 1,100 tons, total avoidable costs will increase by £1,185. To purchase 600 tons on the open market would cost £900. It follows that of the three outputs mentioned, it would be most profitable to produce 1,100 tons.

One correspondent suggested that it would be preferable for the undertaking to produce that output at which average costs are at a minimum. If, however, the cost of purchasing additional units of output on the open market is greater than the costs of producing these units from the undertaking's own mine, it seems clear that it will pay to expand production whatever happens to average costs.

It is worth while emphasizing that the concept of marginal cost can only be employed when decisions relating to output are under consideration; the notion of avoidable costs is, however, of universal application.

6

The subjective theory of value and accounting 'cost'

G. F. THIRLBY

A paper read to the Cape Town Branch of the
Economic Society of South Africa on 13 April 1945.
First published in *Economica* (February 1946).

In a recent article[1] in the *Economic Journal*, Mr Harry Norris (an accountant) puts out certain 'feelers' into the overlap of the provinces of economists and accountants, hoping thereby to 'stimulate economists into thinking about accounting procedures in the light of economic science'. Mr Norris tells us that a comparison of ideas is something of which accountants, and perhaps economists, stand in need, though economists may find difficulty in discovering exactly what accountants mean by certain terms which they use. Speaking of the subject in which he is particularly interested – income – he acknowledges the substantial truth of Professor Canning's view that accountants have not developed, and probably have never put their minds to the task of developing, any complete philosophical system of thought about it. It is only fair to add that Mr Norris is 'not able to find any great clarity of thought among economists as to what constitutes income'.

Some time ago, having suggested that 'economic science has not yet become integrated into the philosophy of accounting teachers and writers', I ventured to recommend that the results of such a study as Mr Norris desires should form part of the curriculum of university students of commerce, saying that 'the ubiquity of accounting and the need for its reconciliation with economics rather suggests that part of a second course in accounting in the commerce curriculum should be called "Accounting in the Light of Economic Analysis" '.[2] It is natural therefore that

[1] Harry Norris. 'Notes on the Relationship between Economists and Accountants', *Economic Journal* 54, Nos. 215-16 (December 1944).
[2] G. F. Thirlby, 'The University Commerce Curriculum', *Sociological Review*, 34, Nos. 3 and 4 (July-October 1942).

I should welcome, and even try to respond to, Mr Norris's invitation.

My subject, however, is not income, but a term which Mr Norris uses incidentally, namely, cost. And I must confess that the main stimulus prompting me to discuss it was, not Mr Norris's article, but one written by Professor C. S. Richards.[3] In his article, in which he emphatically recommends the practice of cost accounting, Professor Richards himself deplores the use of 'vague phrases and undefined terms ... which lack clarity and the implications of which are seldom analysed nor their consequences appreciated'. But, although perhaps no term is used more loosely nowadays than 'cost', and although Professor Richards in his frequent uses of the term is traversing ground covered by both economists and accountants, he offers no discussion of the different meanings attached to the term in economics and accounting. The difference is fundamental.

The task that I have set myself is, not to deal exhaustively with all details of cost-accounting practice, but to suggest 1) the meaning of cost to a person – whom I shall refer to as the subjectivist – whose thought is conditioned or disciplined by the subjective theory of value; 2) the place and significance of cost in this sense in a philosophy of business administration; 3) the different meaning that the term has to an accountant; 4) the relationship of cost in this accounting sense to the subjectivist's philosophy of business administration.

I THE MEANING OF COST TO THE SUBJECTIVIST

To the subjectivist cost would be understood to refer to the prospective opportunity displaced by the administrative decision to take one course of action rather than another.[4] Cost is

---

[3] C. S. Richards, 'The Task before Us: with special reference to Industry', *South African Journal of Economics*, 12, No. 3 (September 1944).

[4] 'The conception of real costs as displaced alternatives is now accepted by the majority of theoretical economists'. L. Robbins, Introduction to Wicksteed, *The Common Sense of Political Economy* (London, 1933), p. xviii. It is significant that Professor Robbins adds to these words 'but ... we are still a long way from making it part and parcel of our daily speculations on those problems to which it is most

inevitably related to the behaviour of a person. The person is faced with the possibility of taking one or other of (at least) two courses of action, but not both. He considers the relative significance to him of the two courses of action, and finds that one course is of higher significance than the other. He 'prefers' one course to the other. His prospective opportunity of taking the less-preferred course becomes the prospective cost of his taking the more-preferred course. By deciding to take the preferred course, he incurs the cost – he displaces the alternative opportunity. The cost is not the *things* – e.g., *money – which will flow along certain channels* as a result of the decision; it is the loss, prospective or realized, to the person making the decision, of the opportunity of using those things in the alternative course of action. *A fortiori*, this cost *cannot be discovered by another person who eventually watches and records the flow of those things along those channels.* Cost is not something which is objectively discoverable in this manner; it is something which existed in the mind of the decision-maker before the flow began, and something which may quite likely have been but vaguely apprehended.

The alternatives between which the final selection is made are themselves a result of personal discovery and selection. The available alternatives cannot be said to exist unless the person making the decision is aware of them.[5] If they could, their number would be infinite and their consideration by the decision-maker intractable. 'Any number of potential applications "compete" for the use of the productive services.'[6] But the human being is not omniscient. It is obvious that the very limitation upon human capacity necessitates the selection for consideration of only a few of the alternatives, and that the selection might easily be a

relevant', and that on a previous page (p. xv) he has stated that 'since the war [1914-18], there has appeared a great mass of literature on the cost question which, for all the awareness it displays of the essential problem at issue, might for the most part have been the same if Wicksteed had never written'.

[5] Cf. 'Resources and needs exist for practical purposes only through somebody knowing about them and there will always be infinitely more known to all the people together than can be known to the most competent authority'. Hayek, 'Scientism and the Study of Society', *Economica* N. S., 11, No. 41 (February 1944), p. 37.

[6] Fritz Machlup, 'Competition, Pliopoly and Profit', parts I and II, *Economica* N. S., 9, Nos. 33 and 34 (February and May 1942), part I, p. 9.

different one, either if the particular administrator (decision-maker) happened to notice different alternatives, and make a different selection, or if a different administrator made the selection.

The act of discovering cost, which really means discovering which of the considered alternatives is to be rejected, inevitably involves valuation. The decision-maker, in arranging the opportunities in order of preference or significance, is performing what is essentially an act of valuation, valuing the preferred opportunity higher than the alternative to be rejected.

This valuation necessarily involves estimates of happenings in the future about which the decision-maker can never be certain. The decision is based upon *ex ante* reckonings, or advance calculations, which involve looking into the future, and consequently must, even for this reason, be matters of opinion. Yet 'such advance calculations are made every day by scores of businessmen, either for themselves when they are making up their minds about the prospects of a contemplated business venture, or for potential partners or lenders when such are invited to consider participation in the enterprise'.[7] This statement was intended to refer to plans for new industrial undertakings, but its reference can be legitimately extended to cover plans preceding all business decisions.

Cost is ephemeral. The cost involved in a particular decision loses its significance with the making of a decision because the decision displaces the alternative course of action. *If* the accepted course of action *were completely* planned at the time of the decision and *if* the course of action *were* taken and *actually carried out* in accordance with the plan, no new decision – choice between alternatives – occurring in the interim, then no cost – no cost of 'production' – could be said to occur in the interim, however many times money was converted into goods by purchase or hire, and however many times goods were converted into other goods and sold. In the meantime production would have been *proceeding according to plan* – the plan accepted by the decision and put into

[7] Machlup, 'Competition, Pliopoly and Profit', part II, p. 156.

operation as a result of it – or, in other words, it would have been proceeding under *standing orders*.

But usually new decisions will be made before the first one is completely implemented. And cost occurs every time a business decision is made, however large or small the matter under consideration, whether the decision is upon such a matter as to delay the execution of a small order for goods so that a previously unexpected rush order may be accepted, or whether it is to set up and carry on a large industrial enterprise.

The decision is the *primum mobile* of production, without which nothing that occurs can be regarded as production. It is the logical starting point for any investigation which seeks an explanation of why production or the industrial structure is what it is.

II THE PLACE AND SIGNIFICANCE OF COST IN A PHILOSOPHY OF BUSINESS ADMINISTRATION

The subjectivist sees 'the whole direction of resources to ends as a continuous selection between alternatives, guided throughout by a weighing of the significance of the anticipated results, in which the "cost" of adopting any alternative is simply the relinquishing of some other alternative; reward and sacrifice alike being measured and determined by the ultimate significance of the respective products, as anticipated by the producers'.[8]

By discussing an aspect of the functioning of an imaginary firm,[9] I shall try to explain how this must be presumed to apply to the internal workings of a modern departmentalized firm, with divided administration. But first I must refer to the coordination process in a firm in which administration is *not* divided – i.e. in a one-man business.

We can imagine a man in a small retail business deliberating upon the question of how much money to retain (or acquire) for

[8] Wicksteed, *The Common-sense of Political Economy*, p. 820.

[9] I propose to confine my discussion in this section to a single coordinated decision *ex ante*. It is my hope that this will be adequate to suggest that an understanding of this coordinated decision *ex ante* is the appropriate starting point for the development of a philosophy of modern large-scale business organization.

the purpose of investment in stock which is to be bought and sold over a (relatively short) forthcoming period. We will suppose that he is already in the middle of his deliberations. He has already considered a certain sum to be worth while investing in this manner. He has decided that he could do better with it there than elsewhere: the cost would be worth while incurring. If now the man is thinking of the advantage of using £50 more than that sum, he will be comparing 1) the significance of the alternative opportunity of using (or not acquiring) that increment of money, with 2) the significance of the result of investing it in stock and realizing the stock. And obviously he cannot consider 2) without considering 3) what extra stock he would buy at what extra price, and how much extra its sale would be likely to realize. Further, if he allows himself to consider different kinds of stock, he cannot consider 3) unless he considers 4) to which kind of stock to allot the £50, or in what proportion to allot it to different kinds. In other words, *there must be* ex ante *coordination of* 1) *the significance of the alternative opportunity of using (or not acquiring) the increment of money with* 2) *the significance of the eventual returns from the investment of the increment in stock; and this coordination incidentally involves other acts of co-ordination, namely* 3) *the coordination of the prospects of buying goods with the prospects of selling them, and* 4) *the coordination of the relative significance of the prospective returns from investment in alternative kinds of goods.*

We may now suppose that the man considers the retention (or acquisition) and investment of this extra £50 to be advantageous, that he then considers, in the same way, the advantage of using a further £50, and so on until eventually he thinks that the invest-ment of another £50 would not be worth while – and that consequently he decides that the best sum to retain (or acquire) and invest is the total sum of money which does not include this last increment.

The description of the man's deliberations up to this point is sufficient to illustrate the nature of the coordinated decision *ex ante* which it is necessary to comprehend before a satisfactory approach can be made to the understanding of the conduct of business under divided administration. But it will be convenient for my later discussion to assume that a contractual rent payment is made during 'the forthcoming period'. So I am obliged to elaborate a little.

The deliberations cannot be said to be fully coordinated and completed at this point. The man's calculations have led him to the conclusion that, in so far as he has calculated, it will be advantageous to him to continue business for 'the forthcoming period'. But it is possible that this advantage would disappear if he considered the possibility of otherwise disposing of, not only the money, but also other factors (e.g. his premises or the lease of them) which he will use for the business in 'the forthcoming period' if he does decide to carry it on.

To avoid a long and complicated discussion concerning the extent to which these other factors can be varied in quantity, and the effect of varying them (e.g. the effect of letting off portions of the premises, or extending them, or allotting different portions to different portions of the business), I shall assume that the man does not at this time allow such variations to enter into his calculations. This seems to be a reasonable assumption to make, because, as the objective possibilities are infinite, a person must impose some rules ('standing orders') upon himself, intuitively or otherwise, to limit the number which he considers and the times at which he considers them. But I shall allow him to consider the *complete* disposal of the business for a period or permanently.

I shall assume also that the man has a lease of the premises for a period longer than what I referred to as 'the forthcoming period'. The coordination of the result of the calculations (or budgeting) already considered with the question of whether it would be advantageous to dispose of the business must therefore be considered to be a problem of coordinating the result of the calculations (or budgeting) already considered with a wider budgeting ('wider' here referring to a longer time period). It must be so regarded because the significance of the opportunities of disposing of the business for 'the forthcoming [relatively short] period' are not likely to be considered without taking into account what would happen in the more distant future. Why? For the simple reason that to close down in the meantime would affect subsequent prospects – e.g. some contractual rent might be saved by subletting the premises for 'the forthcoming period', but some regular customers might not return after their enforced absence.

We may now suppose that the prospective advantage shown by the narrower calculation is either so great that the man is not prompted to consider this wider budgeting, or that, if it is small enough to prompt him to do so, his wider budgeting has led him to the conclusion that to close down temporarily or permanently would be to his disadvantage. Obviously he might come to this conclusion although his prospective net money returns for 'the forthcoming period' were lower than the contractual rent payment to be made for 'the forthcoming period', and although he might consider it possible to reduce the difference by subletting for 'the forthcoming period': his decision would depend partly upon what he thought of his more distant prospects. But whether the contractual rent payment is expected to be covered out of net money returns will not affect the issue to be discussed.

The language in which I have described this illustration of the coordination process of the small business man at the street-corner shop would perhaps be quite unintelligible to him; but the description is, I suggest, one that the subjectivist would give of a process that he supposes not only the small man at the street-corner shop, but also all firms, trading or manufacturing, to be continually performing.[10] The subjectivist supposes the equilibration of which he speaks, and the functioning of industry and commerce to which this equilibration really refers, to depend upon the performance of the process, the decision based upon it, and the acceptance by the firm of the consequences of the decision. *The acceptance of the consequences* includes the acceptance of the 'automatic sanction'[11] for error. The coordination process and the supervision of the execution of the decision may be loosely or negligently performed, or, on the other hand, they may be rigorously or carefully performed. They may be per-

[10] The process would, I suppose, be commonly referred to as the planning of the acquisition (or retention) and use of short-term funds, or short-term capital, or working capital.

[11] This term is used by Brutzkus in *Economic Planning in Soviet Russia*.

formed according to any limiting rules that the firm chooses to impose upon itself. Different aspects of the process and execution may be delegated to different people. But, however this may be, the firm is supposed to accept the consequences of what it does. If, for example, a firm relapses into and works upon an unjustified assumption that the events of 'yesterday' will be repeated 'today', and tacitly issues standing orders based on such an assumption, it is presumed to do so on its own responsibility.

The process, decision and framing of orders for the execution of the decision constitute an act of business administration. In modern undertakings this act of business administration is often divided among a number of people (administrators). The lines of fracture of the act of business administration might be different in different cases. One man might be responsible for estimating the market for goods on the buying side and for the actual buying, another for estimating the market for goods on the selling side and for the actual selling. This could well be the arrangement in a firm in which purchases were made abroad and sales made locally. One or other of these men might be responsible for estimating the market for short-term funds and actually negotiating loans; or a third person might attend to this. The work on the buying side, or on the selling side, might be split, each of several men being responsible for the market for a particular type or range of goods. Or each of several men might be responsible for both the buying and the selling market for one of several types or ranges of goods. In one or other of these situations there might be a person who accepted responsibility for the estimates and actions of those amongst whom part of the work was so divided, and for the coordination of their estimates. This man, responsible to a higher authority, would be giving advice and criticism to those responsible to him, without usurping their initiative and discretion as administrators. Clearly he would be a man of broad knowledge of men and probably of the markets in which his sub-administrators were operating: the judgement of people's behaviour in advance is of the essence of administration – a matter which tends rather to be obscured when one speaks of judging of what people are going to do as 'estimating the future market conditions'.

Whatever the lines of fracture are, *the complementary activities of the people (administrators) amongst whom the act of business administration is divided must be presumed to be coordinated, for the purpose of making the* ex ante *decision, by one, or by a committee,*[12] *of all or several, of the administrators.* At the same time the very division of function gives rise to the danger of loose coordination, with the firm's left hand not knowing what its right hand is doing.

The arrangements, or rules, laid down by itself, which the firm adopts to determine this division of function and coordination, together with other regulations, might be called the 'standing orders' of the firm; and a tree describing the division of the administrative function and coordination 'the administration chart' of the firm. The way in which administrative authority – authority to make decisions which *ex definitione* involve cost – is divided and distributed through the organization, and how it is circumscribed, this arrangement is itself a matter for administrative decision. It is a matter of choice between this structure and some other. It involves subjective judgement; consequently no 'right' way can be objectively determined.

The organization that I have chosen to illustrate the coordinated decision *ex ante* is one in which there are several (two) people, each responsible for the buying and selling market for a particular range of goods. Another man accepts responsibility for their activities. A third is responsible for estimating the market for short-term funds and actually obtaining them. This arrangement enables me to confine my discussion, in the main, to the aspect of the process of coordination relating to the linking of the market for short-term funds with the market for the goods into which the money is to be converted, without discussing in detail the coordination of the buying and selling markets for goods.[13]

[12] On the limitations of committee management, see Hayek 'Scientism and the Study of Society', p. 31, footnote 2.

[13] My abstract discussion is founded upon a section of a concrete discussion of Budgetary Control in Department Stores given some years ago by Professor Arnold Plant in his lectures on Business Administration.

Let us suppose that, instead of being the small man at the street-corner shop, our firm is a mercantile firm, e.g. a department store, working under divided administration. Each of two department managers (buyers) A and B has discretion as to what varieties of goods he acquires for sale, and is responsible for making and coordinating the forecasts of the buying and selling markets for those goods. A higher authority, whom we will call the merchandise manager, is responsible for settling the *proportions* in which money is alloted to the buyers for investment in stock. A still higher authority, whom we will call the highest authority, settles the total amount to be allotted to the merchandise manager for this purpose. All are planning their operations for 'the forthcoming period'. The highest authority will carry out the process of determining the optimum amount of money to invest in the stock in the same way as the man at the street-corner shop did, except that its study of variations in anticipated results inside the business will not go further than considering the significance of variations of revenue which the merchandise manager offers to try to get from the buyers if one quantity of money or another is allotted to him. When it is eventually made, the decision of this highest authority, which will be the coordinated decision *ex ante,* will finally settle the total amount of money, and incidentally any contractual payments for its use, planned to be invested in stock in the forthcoming period, and may be considered to be reserved to the highest authority by standing orders which require the merchandise manager to submit his offers to it.

But before the merchandise manager can do this, he will need to obtain offers from the buyers. He will require from A estimates of the variations in revenue which A expects to make with variations in the quantity of money allotted. to him, and he will require from B estimates of the variations in revenue which B expects to make with variations in the quantity of money allotted to him, so that he – the merchandise manager – can choose whether to allot to A, or whether to allot to B, each successive increment of money which may be allotted to him by the highest authority, and so decide what increment of revenue to offer the highest authority for each increment of money which may be allotted. The decision required of the merchandise manager is how to distribute the allotment of money, whatever it may be, between the buyers. This decision may be considered as being reserved to him by standing orders which require the buyers to submit their offers to him.

But before A (or B) can do what the merchandise manager requires of him, he will need to consider how to distribute his allotment of money from the merchandise manager, whatever that may turn out to be, amongst the purchases of the different kinds of goods that he contemplates buying, $a_1, a_2 \ldots$ (or $b_1, b_2 \ldots$). Just as the merchandise manager is conceived to be dosing prospective increments of money between A and B, so that he may decide what increment of revenue to offer the highest authority for each increment of money that may be allotted, so A (or B) is conceived to be dosing prospective increments of money between $a_1, a_2 \ldots$ (or $b_1, b_2 \ldots$), so that he may decide what increment of revenue to offer to the merchandise manager for each increment of money that may be allotted. The decision required of A (or B) is how to invest the allotment of money, whatever it may be, in the various kinds of goods. This decision may be considered to be reserved to him by standing orders. (Obviously the decision requires simultaneous coordination of buying and selling prospects.)

So A (B) coordinates the prospects of investment in different channels in his own field (department); the merchandise manager coordinates A's and B's investment prospects; the highest authority coordinates the merchandise manager's investment prospects with the advantages of using money outside the business (or of not acquiring money). After choosing the optimum sum for investment in the business, it makes the coordinated decision *ex ante*. The coordinated decision *ex ante* settles the amount of money to be acquired by (or retained in) the business and allotted to the merchandise manager, the proportions of it to be allotted by the merchandise manager to A and B, and the proportions which A (or B) intends to allot to the purchase of $a_1, a_2 \ldots$ (or $b_1, b_2 \ldots$). At the same time, it settles any contractual obligations by the firm for the use of the money, the amount of revenue that the highest authority expects to receive eventually from the merchandise manager, the amount of revenue that the merchandise manager expects to receive from A and from B, the amount A expects from the sale of a_1 and from the sale of a_2 ..., and the amount B expects from the sale of b_1 and from the sale of b_2. ... The amount of money to be used by the firm, plus any contractual obligations for the use of the money, on the one side, and the revenue expected from the merchandise manager on the other side, might be referred to as the budget of the highest authority and be thought of as a wider budget than that of the merchandise manager. The allotments of money to be made to A and B, and the revenue expected from them by the merchandise manager, might be referred to as the merchandise manager's budget and be thought of as a wider budget than that of A and B. Its details are not a matter concerning the highest authority directly. The amounts of money to be spent by, and the revenues expected by, A (or B) might be referred to as A's (or B's) budget and be thought of as a narrower budget than that of the merchandise manager. Its details are not a matter concerning the merchandise manager directly. The term 'estimated profit calculation'[14] might be used throughout as an alternative expression for 'budget'. The contents of the budgets are anticipated results (of the coordinated decision *ex ante*) which are expected to become objective. They do not disclose costs in the subjectivist's sense of the word.

What costs do occur in this process? Cost to the highest administrator is the opportunity of disposing, outside the business, of money in its possession and money that it might acquire. This is not a cost to the merchandise manager. That is to say, the question of whether to allot money to the merchandise manager instead of using it outside the business (or instead of not acquiring it from outside the business) is excluded from consideration by the merchandise manager by standing orders which reserve the question for consideration by the highest authority. Cost to the merchandise manager is the sacrifice that he incurs, in deciding to allot (any particular increment in) the quantity of money to A, by displacing the opportunity of allotting it to B instead (or vice versa). But this is not a cost to A (or B). That is to say, the question

---

[14] A term used by Machlup, 'Competition, Pliopoly and Profit', part II.

of allotting money to B instead of to A (or vice versa) is excluded from consideration by A (or B) by standing orders which reserve the question for the consideration of the merchandise manager. Cost to A (or B) is the sacrifice that he incurs, in deciding to allot (any particular increment in) the quantity of money to goods a_1 (or b_1), by displacing the opportunity of allotting it to a_2 . . . (or b_2 . . .) instead (or vice versa). Cost occurs whenever, and only when, an administrator makes a decision, choosing between prospective alternative courses which appear to be open to him, between which he has discretion to choose. Under divided administration, the action open to a particular administrator is dependent upon the action to be taken simultaneously by other administrators. Consequently coordination of his plans with those of the other administrators must occur before his final decision can be made.

We may assume, without elaborate discussion, that the highest administrator has coordinated the result of this narrower budgeting process with the wider question of whether the result justified the use of the premises for the forthcoming period – in the same way as the man at the street-corner shop did – and that the highest administrator has decided that the business shall continue for the forthcoming period. A contractual rent payment will fall due during that period.

III THE DIFFERENT MEANING THAT COST HAS TO AN ACCOUNTANT

'Cost' to the accountant means something quite different. What he refers to as cost would, but for a trick, or imaginary conversion, that he performs, be an objective result which emerges 1) after all the decision-making which has involved cost has been done; 2) as a result of the decision-making; 3) – which, of course, follows from 2) – as part of the *ex post* events which are described or implied in the *ex ante* plan to which the anticipated profit calculation belongs.

The trick, or imaginary conversion, which he performs is this. He assumes (implicitly) that when money has been spent or contracted to be spent to acquire things, the money has not necessarily and inevitably been spent or contracted to be spent as it has, leaving the business with the things acquired, but that the things acquired carry the money with them, and that bits of the things flowing into different departments or products of the business carry bits of money with them, or that bits of the life period or assumed life period of the things acquired carry bits of the money with them; and that the money in question has not been wholly spent so long as any of the things acquired and still possessed has one of the bits of money attached to it. The bits of money are 'costs'. These 'costs' are carefully distinguished from values: 'It is costs we deal in, not values'. (Mr Norris, below).

This description of the accountant's behaviour and attitude seems to be confirmed in the following statement appearing in Mr Norris's article.

Earnings to an accountant are simply money revenues from operations minus the cost of performing those operations. There is an outflow of money costs to be classified (the labels used in the classification tree are wages, power, materials, components, finished articles, and so on) and linked up with the inflow of money revenues. The product flows out to the customer; a legal claim for money flows into the business as revenue. It is costs we deal in, not values. Some costs we attach to bits of material, writing them off when the material is sold, others we attach to the calendar and write off according to lapse of time. There are complications in this; and there are, in my view, some illogicalities and errors in common accounting practice; but what we *aim* to do is simply what I have stated, to find the surplus of revenue over expired costs. To do this one may have occasion to *refer* to the incidence of values – of raw materials for instance – but figures of value are not used *as such*; they are merely an aid in cost apportionment.[15]

Mr Norris refers to the 'cost of performing ... operations'. To the subjectivist the cost of performing an operation is the administrator's alternative opportunity displaced by that administrator's decision to have the operation performed. The displaced oppor-

[15] Norris, 'Notes on the Relationship between Economists and Accountants' p. 376.

tunity might be the performance of the operation in some other way, or the following of some entirely different course of action. Not so to the accountant. The accountant thinks first of an observable (objective) 'outflow of money costs'; something which can be computed objectively by observing and recording. It is clear that this 'outflow of money costs' is primarily understood to be the money flowing out of the business in exchange for things to be used in the business.

Subsequently, however, the accountant shifts his attention from the money outflow to the *inflow*, of the things received in exchange for the money outflow, into the business and thence into the operation and the product. It might be thought that, if the accountant rigorously pursued his objective study of flows, he would record these inflows of factors into the product in quantities of things, without attaching figures of the money paid for them. It is perhaps not quite clear from Mr Norris's statement that the accountant does attach the money figures; but it is well known that such is his practice. That is what is meant or implied by saying that 'some costs we attach to bits of material ... others we attach to the calendar ...'. The 'costs' are then 'expired' by writing off in the manner indicated. Clearly the accountant is here tacitly assuming that, or behaving as if, the money which is spent, or contracted to be spent, on the purchase of factors is not spent, or contracted to be spent, at the time when it is actually spent, or contracted to be spent, but remains attached to the factors, to be spent subsequently according to whatever arbitrary or 'conventional' method of 'expiring' the money ('cost') is adopted by the accountant.[16]

IV ACCOUNTING 'COST' RELATED TO THE
SUBJECTIVIST'S PHILOSOPHY OF BUSINESS
ADMINISTRATION

In section II, the discussion of the coordinated decision *ex ante* had proceeded to the point at which the decision had been made

[16] That economists sometimes tacitly adopt the same sort of assumption is apparent in a definition of depreciation cost by Mr. Hawtrey which is criticised in G. F. Thirlby, 'Permanent Resources', *Economica*, N. S., 10, No. 39 (August 1943), pp. 247 ff.

and the budgets or estimated profit calculations of the various administrators had come into existence. The place of accounting 'cost' can now be discovered by discussing subsequent events.

It follows from the opening quotation of section II that, in the subjectivist's philosophy, everything that can be regarded as part of the firm's business operations ('production') must be the result of one administrative decision or another.[17] Some of these results, occurring subsequently to the coordinated decision *ex ante* which is under discussion, will or may be the results of earlier decisions which had not yet been fully implemented: such, for example, as the contractual rent payment accruing due during 'the forthcoming period'. Any other results must, *unless and until a further administrative decision is made,* be results of the particular coordinated decision *ex ante* which is under discussion. If no new decision *did* occur, and if the coordinated decision *ex ante* were completely implemented – a supposition which implies that all anticipations proved to be sufficiently correct to allow complete implementation – objective results would occur which would correspond exactly with the plans of the several administrators. Eventually *accounts* could be produced, correctly recording results, which would correspond exactly with the budgets or estimated profit calculations.

None of these budgets or accounts would include cost in the subjectivist's sense. To what extent would they include 'cost' in the accountant's sense?

The contents of the several budgets (of which the subsequent accounts are replicas) have already been described. If the money used were borrowed money, the account of the highest administrator would include any objective payment ('interest') for the use of money. This appears to be an 'outflow of money costs', that is to say, 'cost' in the accountant's sense before he shifts his attention from the money outflow to the *inflow* of things acquired by the expenditure of money. The item does not appear in the account – as I have envisaged it – of the merchandise manager or of A or B: it is no concern of these people. If the accountant chose to

---

[17] This implies that results of breaches of standing orders issued to executives and other people, and results of 'acts of God', are excluded from 'production'.

'attach' the item, or shares of it, to the money resources which its payment brought into the business – i.e. to the money flowing to the merchandise manager and thence to the buyers – and subsequently to the goods into which the money was converted, 'expiring' it as sales of goods were made, his doing so would have no apparent significance to any of the administrators. The item, as a *prospective* payment in the original planning stage, appeared only in the budget (estimated profit calculation) of the *highest authority*. It was the objective payment (at that time *prospective*) necessary to achieve the optimum (prospective) revenue. The marginal increment of revenue having been considered worth the cost of the marginal increment of money to be invested, the item in question became one whose expenditure was expected to be justified by the whole activity of the business in the forthcoming period as planned by the coordinated decision *ex ante*. The 'efficiency' of the subordinate administrators remains to be tested, not by whether they contribute the money allotted to them plus an 'attachment' of the item in question, but by whether they contribute the revenue which they offered.

Similar remarks apply to the contractual rent payment arising out of the earlier decision. To 'attach' this item to the flow of things through the business would appear to have no administrative significance.

But this does not exhaust the matter. The accountant would, I presume, say that so far I have referred only to 'fixed cost', or 'overhead cost', or 'oncost', or whatever he chooses to call the 'interest' and 'rent'. There is still the outflow of money upon the purchase of stock to be dealt with. A, for example, will be spending his allotment of money. The accountant will see the outflow of money and the inflow of goods, and may wish to 'attach' bits of the money to bits of the goods, and 'expire' the money in the manner indicated by Mr Norris. His doing so appears again to have no administrative significance. A offered a certain revenue in return for being granted a certain allotment of money. It can be understood that an account should be kept of the actual allotment of money and the actual revenue, and used by the merchandise manager as a check upon A's performance. And if A had offered to absorb the allotment of money and return the revenue at certain rates during the period, it can be understood that interim accounts should be kept with the same object. But A was not asked to disclose what goods he would buy with the money, or what prices he proposed to pay and charge for the goods: such matters were left within his administrative discretion. A was not asked to supply the merchandise manager with a budget in respect of each line of goods, although he prepared one for himself. If an *account* in respect of each line of goods were sent to the merchandise manager he would have no budget with which to compare it. The scope of accounting, as an administrative check upon A's performance, appears to be limited to rendering an account in the same form as the budget approved by the merchandise manager. It is easy to construct simple cases to suggest the abortiveness for this purpose of further independent accounting.

Let us suppose, for example, that A's mark-up on stock ranged between twenty and forty per cent on buying prices, and that he achieved his anticipations in all respects except one. In one line of goods he expected to make forty per cent, but, after ordering the goods and before making any sales, decided that he had over-estimated the selling market. In order to clear the stock, he put on a mark-up of only thirty per cent, and realized this. His failure will be shown in the account, by a shortfall in his actual revenue below the anticipated revenue in his original budget. But this comparison will not show wherein his failure lay. Neither apparently will the pursuance by the accountant of the practice of 'attaching' and 'expiring' and linking divisions of revenue to the divisions of 'cost', for obviously the thirty per cent result, in the achievement of which the failure occurred, appears to be a better result than others, in the achievement of which no failure occurred. Only if A had submitted his corresponding budget, showing that the result ought to have been forty per cent, would the account have significance. It is easy, too, to construct simple cases to suggest that, if formal budgets were submitted for the purpose of making such comparisons, the accountant would, in his accounts, have to accommodate his methods of 'attaching' and 'expiring' to the discretion allowed by the firm's administrative arrangements, and not proceed with his own independent methods of 'attaching' and 'expiring'. Suppose, for example, that A, acting within his administrative discretion, planned to buy fifty homogeneous raincoats for £50 and to sell forty-eight of them upstairs for 30s (£1.50) each, and the other two in a bargain basement for 18s (90p) each, and actually achieved the results anticipated. Clearly there is here one piece of business which is indivisible: one venture which has to be read as a whole. To 'attach', for example, £2 to the two raincoats going to the bargain basement and £48 to the others, and to 'expire' £48 against the sales upstairs, leaving £2 to be 'expired' against the 36s (£1.80) revenue in the bargain basement, showing a 'loss' of 4s (20p) in a separate account, would be meaningless if not misleading. It would certainly be misleading to suppose that accounts incorporating 'attachments' and 'expirings' according to independent methods of the kind indicated could operate as a criterion of A's efficiency in exercising his discretion to budget and act as he did.

Nothing that I have said should be regarded as suggesting that no separate accounts should be kept of sales of separate products. Obviously, if A issues goods to salesmen – whom I assume here to have no discretion to vary the prices which A puts on the goods – he is likely to want reports upon which products are producing his incoming revenue: he will want to know whether particular goods are being sold at the rate he expected. The collection of this information does not, however, require any 'attachment' and 'expiring' of bits of money. Invoice analysis, or some other method, could yield the required information either in physical units of stock or in resale prices. For A to receive reports as to how the raincoats were selling, it would not be necessary to 'attach' and 'expire' bits of the amount of money spent on them.

There is still another matter. I have suggested that the extended independent accounting could not in the circumstances be regarded as having the function of being a report to the merchandise manager on A's performance. Could it have the function of informing A what he ought to charge for the goods in stock? Could the 'unexpired' bit of money 'attached' to the bit of material be regarded as any criterion of what A ought to charge the public? The answer that the subjectivist must give is that it could not – emphatically not. To assume that it could would be to make an assumption which belongs to the category of 'cost-of-production fallacies'.[18] It must be added, again with emphasis, that the irrelevance of the 'unexpired' bits of money for price-fixing does not depend in any way upon the accountant's method of 'attaching' and 'expiring'. It is not a matter of petty illogicalities in particular methods. The irrelevance and the 'cost-of-production fallacy' lie in the very 'attaching' itself. The money 'attached' has already been spent. It appears only by the trick of 'attaching'. A has the goods, not the money 'attached' to them.[19] The money 'attached' is not a cost although the accountant gives it that name. The only cost which is significant for the purpose is the cost – in the subjectivist's sense – which occurs if a new decision happens to be made.[20] Under what circumstances *will* a new decision be made? Selling prices are tentatively planned *ex ante*, that is to say, before the goods are bought.[21] But it is likely that often, as time passes and the relatively obscure future approaches nearer to the present, the administrator will revise his appreciation of the selling market conditions, and consequently revise the selling prices that he had in mind when he bought the goods. One of the simple examples that I gave suggested as much. In that case A decided that he had overestimated the selling market. He cut his expected selling price. The subjectivist argument is that the money spent on the goods has no relevance for fixing a limit to the extent of this cut. Is there then no limit *on the cost side* to the extent of the cut? The answer

[18] I presume that Marx would have 'expired' units of 'labour' instead of units of money.

[19] 'The value of what you have got is not affected by the value of what you have relinquished or forgone in order to get it . . . You have the thing you bought, not the price you paid for it'. Wicksteed, *The Common-sense of Political Economy*, pp. 88-9.

[20] This cost might be of higher or lower significance to A than an amount of money – if he had it – equal to the amount 'attached' to the goods.

[21] I find that students under the accounting influence sometimes find it a little difficult to understand this, particularly if the goods are bought in one country and sold in another. I have taken to asking them the question 'If this is not so – if there is no *ex ante* coordination of the buying and selling markets – how does the buyer of a commodity know how much to buy? Is he indifferent as to whether he buys a collar-box full, enough to fill a fleet of ships, or a quantity given by a number drawn out of a hat?'

is that the limit has to be found in the contemporaneous and intertemporal opportunities which I have discussed elsewhere.[22]

The problem before A here would be whether he would be better off eventually by cutting the price at once and realizing over a shorter period, or by hanging on for the higher price (and perhaps having to cut it eventually). This is not merely a question of choosing between two alternative total revenues; it involves also the question of money being available earlier or later – perhaps for reinvestment. The course of action (alternative opportunity) rejected by A would be his cost of taking the course which he chose.

In spite of this association of the practice of 'attaching' and 'expiring' with 'cost-of-production fallacies', it cannot be pretended that in the modern world firms do not adopt, as part of their standing orders, the convention of assuming that the 'bit of material' is to be regarded as having a cost equivalent in significance to the sum of money so 'attached' to it – in spite also of Mr Norris's contention that the 'costs' are to be distinguished from values. It is well known that they do.[23] Seeing this, the subjectivist, without questioning the business administrator's freedom to do what he liked (providing that he accepted responsibility for what he did, and the 'automatic sanction' for error) would associate such firms with Wicksteed's businessman whose 'temper is expensive'.[24] He might enlarge upon the dangers inherent in its practice to the

[22] See Thirlby, 'Permanent Resources'.

[23] Some evidence, if any is needed, is contained in the following extract from an article by Mr K. Lacey: 'There are many . . . types of business (e.g. those producing proprietary lines), the selling prices of whose products lag very far behind the movement of raw material prices, and tend rather to be based upon the average cost of their stocks on hand. The profits of such businesses on the first-in–first-out basis do not vary quite so greatly over the Trade Cycle, and the adoption of the last-in–first-out basis might have the unusual effect in some instances of making their profits more unstable from year to year than they are at present. There is a fallacy here however, and it must not be assumed that the earning of a reasonably stable profit is evidence that no self-deception exists and that no alteration in method is desirable. The position here is that sales are made at too low a price relative to replacement costs when market values are rising, and at too high a price relative to replacement costs when market values are falling' ('Commodity Stocks and the Trade Cycle', *Economica* N. S., 11), No 41 (February 1944), (Mr Norris joined issue with Mr Lacey in the following August issue of *Economica*.) This article is further welcome evidence that accountants are becoming concerned about the effects of accounting practice.

[24] Wicksteed, *The Common-sense of Political Economy*, p. 387.

firm itself,[25] and, where the practice was common to a large number of firms,[26] or where the application of the 'automatic sanction' was modified,[27] to society. But this is not the place to raise these discussions.

VII APPENDIX

My discussion of 'The subjective theory of value and accounting "cost" ' is intended to throw out some suggestions which may not be immediately apparent on the face of it.

1 If economics is to be useful to assist discussion of the problems of internal organization of the firm and the explanation of the industrial structure and its weaknesses, the aspect of economics that should be developed is that which deals with people's behaviour when they are deciding what to do next with their resources. It is not sufficient, however, to assume that the decision-making is performed by individual people whose decisions are co-ordinated with those of other people *only through the medium of the market. Within* the 'large-scale undertaking' decision-making is shared. Coordination occurs through other means than the market. The relationship between the buyer of factors and the seller of the product, for example, is *not a market* relationship. What is required from economics is the presentation of models showing how the decision-making might be split up (shared or delegated) and coordinated, together with models of 'standing orders' determining the channels and timing of coordination. Energy might then be diverted from the impotent condemnation of monopolistic institutions to a critical examination of internal organization with a view to discovering its weaknesses, which incidentally lead to the formation of such monopolistic institutions.

2 If accountants studied a theory of administration, working from the Subjective Theory of Value, through the coordinated decision *ex ante*, towards a set of theoretical models of administration charts, standing orders and budgets, they would discover

[25] See twelve articles by R. H. Coase in the English *Accountant*, 99.

[26] See Lacey, 'Commodity Stocks and the Trade Cycle'.

[27] E.g. where there is compulsory cartellization. On the association of cost-accounting with cartellization, *see* Burn, *Economic History of Steel Making* (Cambridge 1940), pp. 494-5.

that both the orientation of accounts and the methods of accounting ought to be accommodated to the particular administrative arrangements of the particular firm or organization. Accounts would always be related to administrators' budgets and would always be of a form corresponding to those budgets, instead of being prepared independently of them. There would be no pretence that money was attached to things when it had already been spent, or contracted to be spent, upon those things. All the pseudo-problems of 'allocating', 'burdening' or 'charging' would disappear.

The following comment is offered after a first reading of Mr Harry Norris's article on 'Profit: Accounting Theory and Economics' in the August issue of *Economica*.

Mr Norris states: 'We accountants grant the attribute of objectivity to "profit" if not to "income" ...' (p. 132). The difficulty of conceding that accountants are right in doing this will never be understood until it is recognized that the objective results upon which accountants work can be explained only by reference back to, and in the light of, the opinion of the decision-maker whose decision gave rise to those objective results. Out of his process of decision-making emerges the decision-maker's budget relating to the course of action which he decides to take. This may or may not be recorded. Such a budget, without an analysis of the opinion of the decision-maker attached to it, would not disclose the subjective acts of valuation which determined that his planned course of action was in his opinion the most advantageous or 'profitable'. For example, at a particular time and in a particular situation the budget might contain on its 'expenditure' side merely an enumeration of diverse non-monetary resources already in the ownership or control of the decision-maker, which he had decided to use for a particular job because he contemplated no better use for them. On the 'revenue' side might be a sum of money which he expected to achieve by selling the results of the job. The expected 'profitability' of the job would reside in his valuing his contemplated returns from this job higher than his contemplated returns from any (or the best) alternative use of his resources. This subjective valuation would not appear in the budget of anticipated objective results. Neither would it, nor ought it to, apear in the subsequent account of actual objective results. Autonomous accounting which, without reference to the decision-maker's opinion, but in order to make up an account of 'profit' in monetary terms, subsequently introduced an assesment of 'cost' into the record of objective results, would apparently be substituting (*ex post*) a simulated objective result for the decision-maker's subjective act of valuation (*ex ante*).

Mr Norris perhaps makes his best approach to recognition of the link between the decision (and budget) and the objective results (and account) in his discussion of 'fashion' goods on p. 130. His remarks might be compared with my own reference to homogeneous raincoats (above).

7

The Ruler

G. F. THIRLBY

A paper read, in part, to the Cape Town branch of the Economic Society of South Africa on 11 October 1946. First published in full in the *South African Journal of Economics* (December 1946).

Introduction

This is a paper[1] concerning rules based upon the idea that the output of an industrial unit ought to be adjusted so as to secure that revenue bears a certain relationship to cost: so that marginal revenue is equal to marginal cost: or that price is equal to marginal cost; or that total revenue is equal to total cost. It is *not* intended to raise the question whether there is theoretical justification for saying that one or other of these relationships is the one that ought to be achieved. The question that it *does* raise is whether the actual cost–revenue relationship is an objective something in the sense that it can be scrutinized, in order to discover whether it conforms to the desired relationship, by an *ad hoc* authority external to the industrial unit concerned.[2] Somewhere or other I have seen the suggestion that, for failing to carry out instructions to achieve the desired relationship, the 'manager' of the unit should be dismissed. It is obviously implied that somebody can look and see whether the relationship is being, or has been, achieved. Throughout my paper I shall refer to the *ad hoc* authority as 'the Ruler'.[3] The expression 'the rule' will refer to these rules in general unless I say that I am discussing a particular one.

[1] Read, in part, to the Cape Town branch of the Economic Society of South Africa on 11 October 1946. The final stimulus prompting me to write the paper was Mr T. Wilson's 'Price and Outlay Policy of State Enterprise' *Economic Journal*, 55, No. 220 (December 1945). Originally it was a running commentary upon that note, elaborating criticism which Mr Wilson himself put forward, but eventually joining issue with him upon his own proposals.

[2] Accordingly, the paper has relevance to the prevalent idea that the efficiency of industries can somehow be judged by measuring their costs.

[3] Because his function is to measure.

This then is the suggestion emerging from my paper: that the relationship has not the objectivity that is by implication attributed to it; consequently that the application of the rule is impracticable. It follows too that the proposal to apply the rule betrays a grievous failure to allow for the nature of the administrative task. This is a remarkable conclusion, because, whatever else the rule advocates wish to do, their main object seems to be to secure the appropriate administration of resources: they seem to want to get things in the right places so as to satisfy everybody as much as possible in the best way.

I shall first discuss and illustrate at length the nature of the administrative task and how the cost–revenue relationship emerges with the performance of that task and then consider the application of the rule on the supposition that the terms 'cost' and 'revenue' are to be taken to have the meaning implied in the opening discussion, and also on the supposition that they are to be taken to have other meanings.

Administration in planning stages. Location, layout and choice of equipment
Administration occurs in planning stages. The cost–revenue relationship and the final budget relating to intended operations emerge in planning stages. Important aspects of planning are the choice of the location, layout and technical equipment of the plant. The most efficient structure is not given technically, but depends upon an administrative judgement about the forthcoming market conditions. The choice and the cost–revenue relationship are inextricably interconnected. The choices are a matter of selection from alternative combinations of resources: an infinite number of variations from which the administrator selects a few for more deliberate consideration before he makes a final choice. A contemplated variation to achieve revenue in one way may involve contemplated losses of revenue that might be achieved if the variation did not occur: the sacrifice of potential alternative revenue appears as cost. A rule purporting to secure a certain cost–revenue relationship could have no claim to secure the optimum combination and spatial distribution of resources

unless it took account of opportunities to be displaced. But alternative opportunities are elusive even to the person whose job it is to look for them, and are never susceptible to precise measurement even by him.

Illustration[4]

During the deliberations concerning the planning and running of the Cape Town and Wellington Railway, much discussion and dispute arose over the question of how to connect the line with a place called Stellenbosch, which lay south of the direct route between the terminii. One of the alternative methods proposed was to allow the trunk to deviate in order to take in Stellenbosch. But it was pointed out that this deviation would be likely to cause the loss of traffic which a direct trunk would obtain from important corn-growing districts north of the line. In other words, at this level of deliberation, *one element in the cost of this variation in structure* in the sense of layout (or, alternatively, location) *would be the anticipated loss of revenue* from this traffic from the north, a cost which would have to be set against the expected revenue from the Stellenbosch traffic. There was an opportunity of earning certain revenue – from the corn traffic – by one variation of structure. That opportunity would be lost by adopting the other variation instead.

To prevent this loss of traffic from the corn-growing districts, it was suggested that the line should follow the direct route for a certain distance from Cape Town (so making it unnecessary for people in the north to cross some shifting sands in order to get to the line), and then make the deviation. But, as this arrangement would add somewhat to the total length of journey by rail from Wellington to Cape Town, an objection to it was raised on the ground that people near to the Wellington terminus would prefer to send their goods direct by road. At this stage of the discussion, the anticipated loss of revenue from the Wellington traffic can be

---

[4] The fragments of information about the Cape Town and Wellington Railway are derived from minutes of evidence taken before Select Committees and other official documents. (See Votes and Proceedings of Parliament of the Cape of Good Hope from 1854 onwards, particularly two Reports of 1859, Appendix 2 [C.1 and A.6).]

regarded as an element in the cost of retaining the corn traffic by a projected modification of the technical structure in the sense of layout (or location).

Another method of providing for Stellenbosch which was calculated to avoid losing either of these traffics was that of constructing a short branch from about the middle of a direct trunk. This proposal again introduced the question of reduced traffic – e.g. from people south of the line who would have a further distance to travel to Cape Town via the branch should they use it. However, I have sufficiently indicated how such influences must be presumed to be interrelated with the choice of structure in one sense of the expression, namely, in the sense of layout or location, and at this point only wish to suggest how they are interrelated with it in the other sense of choice of technical equipment. It was proposed that, if a branch were substituted for the deviation, it might take the form of a tramway (presumably a horse-tramway) instead of being equipped to the standard intended for the trunk line. Obviously, the point of the proposal was that revenue might not be adequate to justify the introduction of resources of higher cost than those required for the tramway.

The decisions reached need not concern us: all that is necessary is that we should see the influences at work, and understand their meaning in relation to the problem of the appropriate distribution of resources; in particular, the meaning of the omission of lost opportunities from 'cost'.

The omission of lost opportunities from 'cost'

I know the thoughts that will be in some minds as I say this: 'But it is not this aspect of cost that we are interested in. What we are interested in is cost in the sense of the amount of liquid resources which it is finally decided to bring into the enterprise: the money which will flow in'. I must at this point be brief in attempting to allay this impatience. I shall simply assume (pretend) that whoever it was who had the disposal of the liquid resources for the railway undertaking was at the same time considering as an alternative investment the disposal of exactly the same liquid resources by erecting and running a chain of saloon bars. Then the cost of bringing the liquid resources into the railway undertaking must be related to the yield in revenue expected to accrue from this alternative opportunity. But to confine one's attention to this level of deliberation allows to escape from notice all the fallible judgements connected with the planning of location, layout and technical equipment which it was my purpose to bring to the fore.

It seems fairly obvious that, even if, at any particular level of deliberation, the rule could be, and was being, observed, its observance would not imply that people's preferences were not to be defeated through inappropriate combination or spatial distribution of factors of production, *unless into 'cost' were added lost opportunities which the decision-maker had never observed, or, having observed, had ignored.* For example, if the application of the same factors and money in one manner or place A were expected to yield 100, in another manner or place B 100, and in another manner or place C 150, but if C were ignored or not noticed, A being chosen (for no apparent reason!) instead of B, cost (in the sense of anticipated alternative revenue) would be 100 and cost equal to revenue. If, however, C were taken into account in considering A, cost would be 150, i.e. higher than revenue 100; if the relative strength of anticipated money demand were taken as the criterion, the factors and money would be more 'efficiently' used not at A but at C, where cost would be 100 and revenue 150. It is not suggested, of course, that the 'inefficiency' involved in ignoring opportunities would be confined to undertakings subject to the rule; only that the rule may not be able to ensure that it does not occur. It no doubt occurs anyway, because nobody is omniscient. As a safeguard against it, one relies, within limits, upon somebody else's taking advantage of one man's oversight.

The railway illustration is not an exceptional case
It may be suggested that the problem of settling the railway route to which I have referred is one special to railway undertakings and has little relevance to other undertakings. This is certainly not true. The connection will be more obvious if the problem is thought of as analogous to that of settling the location, rather than the layout, of a different kind of industrial plant: the

location problem is one of judging the strength of conflicting pulls, some of them different factor supply prices, some of them different product demand prices, at different geographical points and – when changes over time are being forecasted – at different points of time. The other matter – choice of equipment – is a question which in many industrial plants is likely to be constantly recurring, not only when new (or renewed) equipment is required, but also when projected changes in kind or quantity of output raise the question of what old or new equipment to use.

The propensity to avoid the issue
It may be sought to avoid the issue by saying that anyway this matter of planning the technical structure is one which would be settled by somebody other than 'the manager' whose cost–revenue relationship is to be scrutinized; that for him the plant would be a technical datum, outside the range of his responsibility. This might in some cases and to some extent be true; but to make it so would be merely to shift the burden of cost–revenue calculation[5] on to the shoulders of a higher authority, and leave his activities, and the relations between him and 'the manager', still to be discussed. The economist who abstracts from these questions abstracts to the same extent from business administration.

There *is* a tendency for economists to avoid or ignore the problem of choice of structure.[6] Some of them regard case discussion of deliberations upon such matters as being of technical rather than of economic importance.[7] In 'short-run' theoretical cost–revenue discussions, the choice of structure tends to be hidden behind a vague something termed 'the entrepreneur's fixed costs'. The mere assumption, for 'long-run' discussion, that the 'firm' or 'entrepreneur' selects, or has selected, an optimum structure, does not carry us far in the direction of understanding the issues rendering the choice, and the cost–revenue relationship

---

[5] And the liability to be dismissed – by whom?

[6] Cf. Mr Wilson's suggestion that Mr Lerner has no time to spare, in his *Economics of Control*, for the 'other problem, which is also partly economic, of ensuring technical efficiency in the use of resources'. (T. Wilson, 'Price and Outlay Policy of State Enterprise'.)

[7] This statement is prompted by my own experience.

bound up with it, highly subjective, indefinite and fallible. I shall refer to these concepts of 'fixed costs', 'short run' and 'long run' again. But I must first call attention to another 'inefficiency' factor which might preclude the application of the rule : that arising out of loose coordination of the diffused administrative elements inside a large-scale industrial undertaking – i.e. an undertaking in which administration is split among a number of people and has to be coordinated somehow.[8]

Loose coordination

This appears as failure to bring one man's knowledge to bear upon the activities of another so as to influence a decision which is supposed to be made by them jointly.[9]

Illustrations

Let us suppose that in a certain undertaking the buying of a raw material, manufacture and the selling of the product are controlled by three different people, who are heads of separate purchasing, production and sales departments respectively, the activities of the three people being coordinated by a committee of the three, the committee being superordinate to its subordinate members. Purchasing (at a definite price, or within certain price variations), manufacture per unit of time and sales (at a certain price) have been planned, and are proceeding under standing orders laid down by the committee to implement the plan. But for some reason sales are likely to fall below the level anticipated by the committee.

Now it is possible that the sales department, negligently or otherwise, remains unaware of the impending fall until it actually occurs. Or the sales department may be in various senses aware of

---

[8] It may be argued that the same, or a similar, lack of coordination can occur in a single mind. But I prefer to treat the matter as it appears in the form of the elusive 'diseconomy' of divided administration which 'budgetary' control may to some extent offset. Cf. G. F. Thirlby, 'The Subjective Theory of Value and Accounting "Cost" ', reprinted here, pages 135-61.

[9] I suppose every spouse can recall some occasion on which he (or she) would have done something different had the other spouse told him (or her) something which she (or he) ought to have told him (or her). I doubt whether Wicksteed adequately treated this aspect of human affairs.

it, although its awareness is not appropriately coordinated. Salesmen may know but not report. They may report, while their reports are left unread. The reports may be read by somebody, while the information is not communicated to the head of the sales department. The information may be communicated to the department head, but he may fail to report to the committee. For concision, let us suppose that the knowledge resides in the head of the sales department, but that for some reason it does not get communicated to the committee; and let us abstract from the possibility that the committee had, as a deliberate act of administrative judgement in laying down standing orders, decided not to consider changes in the selling market until an actual fall in sales occurred. Purchase of the raw material and manufacture continue under the existing standing orders, yielding a product which will not fetch the planned price.

Loose coordination failing to reflect impending market changes in the production plan

The illustration that I have chosen is one in which there is a failure to communicate a knowledge of impending changes in market conditions, and cause it to be reflected in the production plan. Where production is for 'the market', production must in any case precede sale: a risk that market conditions will change unexpectedly in the interim is always present. The expression 'efficient administration' might be said to imply the acquisition and use of knowledge of impending changes – to reflect, as it were, in the plan of operations, the changes which will have occurred by the time of sale. The best-administered organization is not omniscient: it is possible for market conditions to change against its latest anticipations. But it is possible to think of an organization being more or less lax or weak in revising its anticipations and securing the reflection of the changes in its production arrangements,[10] although we may not be able to devise a measure of the degree of its laxity or weakness. Possibly the test of efficiency here

[10] It is difficult to believe that the railways could not have been more administratively effective in forecasting and appropriately responding to the effects of road motor competition.

would consist of a comparison of an *ex post* account of operations with an *ex ante* plan of operations. In the illustration which I have given the weakness would be shown up by a falling short of realized below anticipated revenue – unless a sufficient safety margin had been allowed in the plan, a possibility which might hide the weakness, if weakness it would be when a safety margin had allowed for it.

Can the rule control the weakness?

It is difficult to see how the mere application of the rule could in this respect either add strength to the administration or operate as a test of its weakness. The conditions of the rule might well have been satisfied in the *ex ante* calculations, although the administration failed then and subsequently to allow for the change in the market conditions. That is to say, the administration might have planned, and begun to produce, that output which appeared to observe the approved cost–revenue relationship, and failed to adjust for the market change before receiving its impact. Weakness of coordination is something not susceptible to measurement, though it would have its effect upon the capacity of the enterprise to stand on its own feet and, in so far as it was not allowed for by safety margins in forecasted results, upon the eventual divergence of results from the original forecast. I should perhaps say here, parenthetically, that if *realized* revenue has to be equal to expected revenue, it seems to me that the rule is being widened to accord (in respect of revenue) with a test that assumes that accounts ought to correspond with budgets.

It was consciousness of the importance of the acquisition of knowledge of impending changes, and of the importance of replanning to secure the reflection of changed anticipations in production operations, which led me to stress loose coordination as a possible inefficiency factor, and which now leads me to point out that replanning following changed anticipations involves a recalculation of cost; that at this replanning stage the cost of using acquired assets really depends upon the opinion of the administration of the undertaking about the alternative markets which it forecasts.

Replanning. Recalculation of cost. Cost dependent upon the opinion of the administration
If a market change which was not anticipated by the existing standing orders has occurred, or is now expected to occur, whether the late anticipation or non-anticipation of it is attributable to loose administrative arrangements or not, and whether the rule has been applied or not, it is apparent that replanning is called for: cost has to be recalculated. In the circumstances in which the firm finds itself with accumulated stock which it cannot sell at the planned price, the *cost* of getting rid of the stock immediately in the intended market is determined by the opportunities which the administration foresees for its disposal immediately in different markets or later on in the same or different markets. Very similar remarks apply to the equipment used in production. It is fairly apparent that what *cost* will be is a matter of the opinion of the administration of the firm. This opinion is dependent upon their forecasts of their market opportunities.

The problem of structure-variation recurs
At this replanning stage the administration is faced with choices similar to those between alternative combinations (or spatial distribution) of factors with which it was faced at the original planning stage. The choice might for example be one between continuing production at a reduced level with the same equipment or (if the equipment had sufficiently important competing uses) switching to other equipment. Clearly cost and revenue calculation may again be interconnected with opinion about appropriate structure-variation.

The rule is concerned with planning stages or it is not concerned with cost. To discover cost of production continuing under standing orders, it is necessary to trace back to planning stages. The terms 'fixed costs' and 'variable costs' should be reconsidered. If those who advocate the enforcement of the rule plead that they are not concerned with these planning stages, but only with interim periods between planning stages, it must be replied that then they are not concerned with cost. Cost occurs only when decisions are made, that is, in planning stages. In the interim periods resources (including money) flow under standing orders, but the cost involved in the flow was incurred by the decisions which settled those standing orders. Machlup has extended the familiar saying 'All costs are variable in the long run' to 'All costs are variable in the long run, that is, in a planning stage'.[11] My remarks go a little further: costs occur only in planning stages. To discover what the cost of the flow of production occurring between two planning stages had been (and, *a fortiori*, what the cost of its intra- or extra-marginal unit had been)[12] it would be necessary to trace back to, and inquire into, the decision which started or changed the flow – i.e. to trace back to the planning stage and to the administrator's mind. It might be necessary to trace back to several planning stages. In doing this we should discover that if the distinction between 'fixed' and 'variable' costs is a distinction between what occurs in a planning stage and what occurs in an interim during which no planning occurs; the distinction is a false one.

Illustration

Suppose that in January it had been decided to use certain plant for the production of a certain commodity throughout the year, without considering further the cost of using the plant, irrespective of whether output was changed during the year; and that in March the output (and quantity of materials, etc. applied to the plant) was changed by a new decision which, as arranged in January, was reached without reconsidering whether to transfer the plant to another use. Examination of the flow of resources in April would show certain quantities of factors being applied to the plant, and possibly certain money being paid for the factors – even for the use of the plant. But these would be merely objective flows (with, incidentally, no distinguishable marginal unit of product).[12] They ought to correspond with the anticipated objective flows embodied in the budget of January, subject to the revision of March; but to discover the costs which had been

---

[11] Fritz Machlup, 'Competition, Pliopoly and Profit', part II, *Economica*, N. S., 9, No. 34, (May 1942).
[12] See Appendix I.

involved in settling these flows (and, incidentally, the cost which had been involved in the production of the marginal unit of product)[13] it would be necessary to trace back and do two things: 1) in order to discover the alternative opportunities of using the materials, etc. applied to the plant, and/or money paid for such things, to examine the narrower budgeting *process* and decision of March which had determined the volume of April production, and 2) in order to discover the alternative opportunities of using the plant throughout the year (or of using the money required for its hire), to examine the wider budgeting *process* and decision of January which had determined the use of the plant in April as well as the volume of production before March. In doing the second thing we should be looking for what are called 'fixed costs', which are supposed to be 'variable in the long run',[14] that is (as Machlup puts it) 'in a planning stage'. In doing the first thing, we should be looking for what are called the 'variable costs'. But to find them too it would be necessary to go to a 'planning stage' : *March was a planning stage.*

The use of 'fixed' equipment. 'Bygones', user cost and renewals. The qualifications of the person(s) reckoning user cost
In an earlier part of my paper I referred to the propensity to avoid the issue concerning the administrative act of choice involved in planning. The avoidance of the issue occurs if it is assumed that plant has already been erected and its cost is therefore a 'bygone'.[15] A matter which requires elucidation here is the nature of the 'bygone'.

It is of course true, as I have indicated, that the administration of a firm may by an earlier decision, whose implementation becomes part of the firm's standing orders, rule out the cost of using 'fixed' equipment from consideration at later planning stages.

[13] See Appendix I.
[14] The 'long run' is precisely as long as a piece of string which is longer than a shorter piece.
[15] Mr Wilson queries this behaviour. In referring to the propensity to consider 'the operation of increasing returns industries . . . from a short-period point of view when a certain amount of fixed equipment is in existence . . .' he says that, 'in discussing this situation economists are able to make full use of their intriguing discovery that "bygones are bygones" . . . .' 'Price and Outlay Policy of State Enterprise', (third section).

But where the cost of using it has not been ruled out of consideration, or where the period during which it was so ruled out (but not the 'life' of the equipment itself) has expired, and a new decision as to the equipment's use is about to be made, the (anticipated) use will usually or often[16] have a cost which comes up for consideration in the deliberations preceding the impending decision: the cost dependent upon the administration's contemplation of contemporaneous or intertemporal alternative opportunities of using the equipment. In what seems to me to be alternative terminology coming from Keynes via Mr Bauer: 'The user cost of a unit of output in the short period is the reduction in the discounted value of expected future quasi-rents of a piece of equipment through using it for the production of that unit of output rather than leaving it unused.'[17]

The same remarks apply not only to 'fixed' equipment but also to materials, unexpired labour contracts, other factors and money within the ownership of the firm at the planning stage. It is then not admissible to assume that the cost of using 'fixed' equipment and other owned resources is a 'bygone' that does not have to be taken into account in planning. What *is* a 'bygone' that has become irrelevant is the loss of whatever has already been given up (or contracted to be given up) – usually money – in exchange for those things.

It follows from what I have just said that the 'long period' at the end of which 'fixed' equipment cost reappears does not necessarily run until the time comes for *renewal* of equipment.[18] It is not

[16] For circumstances under which it will not have such a cost, see Hayek, *The Pure Theory of Capital*, (London 1941), and G. F. Thirlby, 'Permanent Resources', *Economica*, N. S., 10, No. 39 (August 1943).

[17] P. T. Bauer, 'Notes on Cost', *Economica*, N. S., 12 No. 46, (May 1945), p. 96. All uses, including the use for the unit of output under consideration, that are contemplated at any planning stage must, to a greater or lesser extent, be future uses. Some of them – uses for alternative purposes – may be contemporaneous with the use for the unit of output under consideration. Later uses also may be for alternative purposes. With these adjustments the expression quoted seems to be in order.

[18] It appeared to be necessary to make this matter quite clear because Mr Wilson ('Price and Outlay Policy of State Enterprise'), does not seem to have done so. Distinguishing it from the 'short-period' reckoning in which he more or less concedes that 'fixed' equipment cost is an irrelevant 'bygone', he conceives of the longer-period reckoning, that is to say, a reckoning in which 'fixed' equipment cost appears, as occurring when a decision is taken to *instal* equipment.

admissible to assume that the consideration of equipment cost is restricted to occasions when decisions are taken to *instal* equipment, even if these occasions include those upon which renewals or extensions are contemplated: the consideration of the cost of *using* equipment occurs at other times. The process of settling what this cost is consists in an administrative judgement upon whether it is better to use the equipment for this or for that product, to use it immediately or to reserve its use for the more distant future. Obviously this is a judgement upon what is going to happen in the selling market, and one which might be expected to be made by somebody who is operating in the market and who probably spends his life there. It is a judgement upon what people (the consuming public) are likely to be willing to do with their future incomes. There seems to be quite inadequate allowance in academic discussion for the fact that this sort of thing has to be done – an inadequate allowance for the fact that the selling prices of the product and the quantities saleable are not *known*, but have to be *judged*,[19] at the earlier point of time when the decision to produce is made, and that the judgement has to go on continuously, or at least constantly, if appropriate rebudgeting and readjustment of production is to occur subsequently.[20]

[19] It is quite irrelevant to the present issue to point out that many businessmen do in fact judge that they will be the same tomorrow as they have been today. The relevant point is that somebody has to be presumed to be *responsible* for forecasting or for not bothering to forecast.

[20] There is implicit recognition of this fact in the discussion following Mr Wilson's suggestion that 'probably the only way to get at any sort of approximate answer [to the question whether a large "widening" of the capital structure should occur] would be to consider whether it would be possible to cover the total costs of the undertaking if it were run monopolistically'. ('Price and Outlay Policy of State Enterprise', p. 458). The force of his subsequent remarks upon the relative incompetence of 'socialist managers' of an 'undertaking run according to the rule' to pronounce upon 'what consumers would give for the product', and to determine investment policy, really depends upon the fact that the monopolist of whom he is thinking is, unlike the 'socialist managers', a person operating in the market with a constantly developing and revised understanding of the behaviour of the consuming public in the sphere in which he is operating. (I do not wish this remark to convey the impression that I think that 'socialist managers' could not be such persons – much less that I think that it would not be their function to employ this competence. The indispensability of business administration does not of course depend upon whether the industrial organization is 'socialistic' or 'capitalistic'. That this truth was discovered in Russia very soon after the 1917 revolution is apparent from the literature (e.g. Hubbard's *Soviet Labour and Industry*.)

The conjuncture out of which the cost–revenue relationship emerges. Its indefiniteness and fallibility. Competent administration more important than the rule?

The cost–revenue relationship will vary over a period of time as often as acts of administration occur. It is as indefinite and fallible as the opinion of the administration about the forthcoming market conditions and their significance, and as the laxity of the administrative coordination allows it to be. This is still more apparent when it is seen that at any point of time at which one of the acts of administration occurs, that particular act which determines the input and output *of the firm as a whole,* and incidentally the marginal unit of output,[21] is a *coordinated decision* dependent upon a number of simultaneous subordinate acts of administration (decisions) which are equally indefinite and fallible in the sense of being personal opinions about future conditions. In an abstract model which I have used elsewhere[22] the subordinate decisions in the particular undertaking and in reference to the particular coordinated decision *ex ante* appear in as many different places as spikes on a porcupine. Each of these subordinate decisions, and its fallibility, has its effect upon total output, and upon the total and marginal[21] cost of that output, settled by the final coordinated decision *ex ante.* It seems to be seriously open to question whether the result of this highly subjective and constantly modified conjuncture could be externally controlled by enforcement of the rule; and, from the point of view of getting output appropriate to the market environment, it might seem to be more important to secure that administrative positions were occupied by competent administrators than to try to doctor the cost–revenue relationship by issuing a rule to the effect that it must be this and not that.

[21] See Appendix I.

[22] 'The Subjective Theory of Value and Accounting "Cost" ', reprinted here, pages 135-61, *passim.* If the fact that this model relates to a mercantile rather than to an industrial undertaking is disliked, the term 'buyer' may be changed to 'product-line superintendent', and the term 'merchandise manager' to 'general superintendent'. The *administrative* structure is then similar in the two cases. But in the industrial case it would be hard, with a clear conscience, to abstract from discussion of the disposal of the use of plant – e.g. the use of a common foundry disposed of by the general superintendent between the two product-line superintendents.

An attempt to apply the rule might conceivably lead to the transformation of the Ruler into the administrator. This being so, it is as well to emphasize what his becoming administrator would mean.

The Ruler turned administrator

I suggested earlier that the advocates of the enforcement of the rule might deny that they were concerned with planning stages. Alternatively and oppositely they might conceivably say that the Ruler would be *responsible* for all planning, not only at each point of time at which planning occurred, but at each administrative point in the organization at which planning was occurring at any point of time. This could mean either of two things. It might mean that the Ruler would make all the subordinate, as well as all the coordinating, planning or budgeting (cost, revenue and output) calculations, leaving no administrative responsibility to any other person in the undertaking, all of whom would in the execution of the plan become executives or operatives functioning under standing orders (the plan) laid down by the Ruler (the sole administrator). In this case, even if the Ruler (as a sworn member of the Rule Party) could be relied upon always to apply the rule to his subordinate and coordinative calculations, it is obvious that (unless membership of the party also implied a particularly high degree of omniscience) the sphere of activity (size of undertaking) of any particular Ruler would have to be fairly restricted, to avoid the undertaking's becoming top-heavy. In this case all the personal (administrative) judgement would reside in the Ruler, but that personal judgement with all its limitations and weaknesses would not be escaped.

Alternatively responsibility for all planning might mean responsibility for coordination and overriding responsibility for subordinate acts performed by others – in the manner indicated in the abstract model of the mercantile organization.[23] Here his immediately subordinate administrators (subordinate Rulers) would be telling the Ruler what results they intended to achieve, but he would be relying largely upon his judgement of men to tell

[23] See my 'The Subjective Theory of Value and Accounting "Cost" '.

him how far they were likely to be right. (In the mercantile organization the highest authority *might* well have been relying largely upon an incentive to efficiency given to the subordinates by the promise of a commission varying with results.)

In considering the application of the rule I hope by implication to suggest why an attempt to apply it might lead to the transformation of the Ruler into the administrator.

The application of the rule, on the assumption that what is required is that total cost and total revenue should be equal. The nature of the cost-revenue relationship

From now onwards I must for the sake of clarity distinguish the different rules from one another, and for the sake of brevity confine my discussion to one of them: the rule that requires total cost and total revenue to be equal to each other.[24]

What is to be the nature of the cost–revenue relationship that is to be the subject of examination by the Ruler? Is the expression to refer to

1 cost and revenue in the sense implied in my discussion so far,[25] or

2 the anticipated objective results in the budget, or 'estimated-profit calculation', which inevitably depend for what they are upon the deliberations leading to 1, and which consequently may be different according to who is the administrator, or

3 the realized objective results in the account, which ought, subject to certain exceptions, to agree with the (revised) budget?

1 The application when the relationship refers to cost and revenue in the sense so far implied

In this sense revenue must refer to the revenue expected by the

---

[24] In Appendix I, however, there is some deliberation on the margin.

[25] I should perhaps say here, what is implicit in the earlier part of my paper, that if the cost–revenue relationship that is to be scrutinized is the cost–revenue relationship of economics (or ought I to say of the Subjective Theory of Value?), it is the *ex ante* deliberations which have to be investigated, for only in them is there any indication of the displaced opportunities, the effect of the marginal variations from the proposed level of operations (see Appendix I) and the safety margins (allowances for uncertainty) which have to be understood if the decision is to be understood.

administrator to accrue from the contemplated investment of certain resources in a particular way (say the investment of liquid resources and the administrator's own services in a railway undertaking); cost must refer to the revenue[26] that he would expect to accrue if the same resources were invested otherwise (in what he thought to be the best alternative way – say in a chain of saloon bars). I should say at once that it seems to me that to require that these two figures should be equal requires that the administrator should discover two avenues of investment between which he cannot choose without resorting to a toss-up. There is also the other difficulty that the cost figure will never become objective, i.e. it will never be possible to check whether the forecast of the alternative revenue was correct, because the alternative undertaking will never come into existence to produce the *actual* alternative revenue. Both these difficulties occur not only at this highest level of deliberation – i.e. where the total revenue from the contemplated undertaking is being compared with the total revenue of the potential undertaking proposed to be rejected – but at all other levels of deliberation where a choice has to be made, e.g. where two alternative variations in structure are being compared with each other. I pass over the two difficulties as such, but ask the further question whether the Ruler would be expected to be content with nothing but two bare alternative revenue figures relating to the highest level of deliberation, or whether he would be required to look deeper into the two conjunctures throwing up the two figures. Going to the extreme, let us suppose that the administrator is to make a full statement concerning all the alternative outputs (and their variations over time) and technical structures that he has thought fit to consider as possibly being suitable to meet the demand conditions that he thinks likely to mature in the particular situation of the enterprise contemplated, and an appropriately incorporated statement (required to determine the *cost* of his proposed activities) relating to the alternative opportunities, for investment in other situations, to be displaced by investment in this particular one, and also a full

[26] Strictly, to the significance of the revenue. Revenue from saloon bars *may* not be as significant as an equal amount from railways.

confession of his doubts and fears concerning the accuracy of his judgements and the appropriateness of his tentative decisions.[27] Let us suppose further that both the administrator and the Ruler are agreed that as many relevant factual data (obtained e.g. by market surveys) as can be procured have been procured, and have been equally available to and considered by both, but that on some significant question which such data cannot completely answer, but which is a question for administrative judgement and decision (e.g. one relating to the probable strength and continuity of future demand), the administrator and the Ruler disagree. For example, suppose the case were similar to the railway case which I cited earlier, the administrator being of the opinion that a horse-tramway from the trunk line would, in view of his low estimate of the strength and continuity of demand for service and his doubt about it, be the most appropriate way of serving Stellenbosch, the Ruler being more optimistic about demand for service and of the opinion that a railway line with heavy works and locomotives was justified. In these circumstances whose view would prevail? The point that I wish to make here is that to the extent that the Ruler overrides the administrator's opinion in such matters, and makes the decisions, the administrator ceases to be the administrator, and ceases to be responsible for covering costs.[28] The Ruler himself becomes responsible, the other person to that extent – if he is told to carry on in accordance with the Ruler's decision and does so – his executive operating under standing orders.

This is not to say that there cannot be more than one administrator contributing to the coordinated decision *ex ante*. The

[27] The difficulty or impossibility of extracting this evidence is understressed, perhaps by speaking of 'the administrator' instead of a number of people contributing to the conjuncture, certainly by speaking of a first-budgeting process and decision instead of to the conjuncture changing over time as anticipations change and rebudgeting occurs. What seems to be required for a perfect scrutiny is a perpetual record of the budgetary thoughts of every person with discretionary responsibility in the undertaking – and capacity in the Ruler to deal with it with less fallibility than that of the administrator! But to what extent and how often administrators would have their thoughts scrutinized, it is for the advocates of the rule, and not for me, to say.

[28] Or, what amounts to the same thing, achieving the additional revenue (equal to the displaced alternative revenue thought likely to accrue from investing the extra resources – required to make the works 'heavier' – elsewhere, in or outside the railway undertaking.)

Ruler or somebody else might, for example, be the medium for coordinating one administrator's anticipated results from investment in one undertaking (e.g. a railway undertaking) with another administrator's anticipated results from investing the same resources elsewhere (e.g. in a chain of saloon bars) instead, i.e. with cost in the proper sense. But it *is* intended to suggest that the terms and method of application of the rule should be explicitly defined, to avoid amongst other things the usurping of administrative authority without accepting responsibility[29] for its results – to say nothing of sanctions for error.[30] And I would add that it is extremely difficult to understand why the Ruler's stamp should be placed upon a proposition simply because the administrator thought that its yield would be equal to the yield of the same resources in some other proposition. It would be much easier to understand that the Ruler should be expected to choose, or confirm a choice, between two alternative propositions, whose expected yields were different – and accept responsibility for doing so.

It is conceivable then that the advocates of the rule intend that the Ruler should be concerned with revenue and cost in the sense of accepted and displaced opportunities; but I suspect that they have not thought rigorously in these terms, but have thought instead of revenue and cost as the two sides of a budget or 'estimated profit calculation'.

2 The application when the relationship refers to the 'estimated profit calculation'

We now become interested, not in two alternative revenues expected to be achievable by the investment of the same resources, but primarily in the money outlays upon factors (as cost), and (as

[29] To say that 'the state' is responsible is to avoid the whole issue: 'the state' has to be given content by an exegesis of the devolution of administrative responsibility upon persons.

[30] In his deliberations on the Administration Chart in *Some Modern Business Problems* (ed. Plant (London 1937)) Mr Paul Wilson suggests that an administrative officer should be subordinated to that higher administrative officer who will stand to suffer most by his likely errors. It is ideas of this kind that should be taken into account in considering the relationship between the Ruler and the administrator and the incidence of sanctions for error.

revenue) the revenue expected to be achievable in *one* of the alternative applications. These two things, the money outlays upon factors expected to be brought into the undertaking, and the revenue expected to be achieved, which are to be the subject of scrutiny, and which – subject to the adjustments for 'opening stock' and 'closing stock' or 'residual assets' which will be mentioned eventually – have to be equal to each other, are the anticipated objective-results in the budget or 'estimated profit calculation' relating to the proposed undertaking (e.g. a railway undertaking). The 'costs' which interest the Ruler are primarily anticipated objective money outlays.[31] That is to say, the administrator is an administrator in that his displacement of alternative opportunities, at any level of deliberation, is not to be queried. All that he has to show is that his expected objective outlays – subject to the same adjustments – are equal to his expected objective revenue. He shows this in a budget which he submits to the Ruler.

I do not propose to raise the issue whether the adoption of this procedure of working upon anticipated objective results (instead of accepted and displaced opportunities) does or does not mean that the rule has lost touch with its purpose of securing the direction of resources into the best social uses. Apart from this question, the most significant aspect of the procedure is the dependence of the Ruler upon the administrator for the accuracy of the administrator's forecasts of the objective results. If the budgetary period were anything like the physical life period of the longest-lived of the physically depreciating assets of a railway concern, the figures for the remoter years would be extremely tentative; and even if the budgetary period for an enterprise which was to possess such assets were shortened, the tentativeness would only be transferred to the administrator's calculation of the money value of the residual assets; but at the same time it would be necessary to produce such figures if the budget was to

---

[31] It should be clear that this budget would not include any outlay which would necessarily measure the value of resources in their best alternative use. It might include, e.g. anticipated objective 'interest' payments on money to be borrowed for a railway undertaking, but these 'interest' payments could not be presumed to measure the yield that would have been expected from borrowing the same money and investing it in a chain of saloon bars.

(pretend to) show that outlays and revenues were to be equal to each other in the end.

The budget that I envisage as being submitted would be of the kind referred to by Machlup as an 'estimated profit calculation', and illustrated in his article.[32] If, however, it had to show the anticipated time dispersion of the outlays and revenues over the budgetary period, its outlays and revenues would not be – or ought not to be – telescoped into annual figures. The statement would show separately the anticipated outlays and revenues as they were expected to occur. A particular outlay (e.g. upon a new set of locomotives) would appear (undivided) at the date at which it was expected to occur. If it were anticipated that there would be residual assets at the end of the budgetary period, the statement would presumably conclude with the anticipated money value of residual assets, in order to show that outlays and revenues would ultimately balance. This money value of residual assets would represent either what the administrator assumed the assets would sell for at the end of the budgetary period, or (what is not strictly an anticipated objective revenue) what he assumed they would be worth in terms of net revenue in subsequent budgetary periods, according to whether it was to be assumed that the enterprise would cease at, or continue after, the end of the budgetary period. If there were non-monetary assets at the beginning of the first budgetary period – and there would be at least the administrator's own services – a similar calculation would have to be made in respect of this 'opening stock' – otherwise the Ruler could not strike the balance (which ought to be nil) in money terms. These calculations would be made by the administrator as such.

If it were deemed to be necessary to break down the budgetary period into 'years', each 'year's' figures purporting to show whether or not a 'profit' was anticipated in respect of that 'year',[33] what would be the appropriate procedure? Clearly the method of charging an outlay undivided at the date at which it was expected

---

[32] Machlup, 'Competition, Pliopoly and Profit', part II.

[33] Cf. Mr T. Wilson's suggestion 'Price and Outlay Policy of State Enterprise', that the principle of covering total costs could not be enforced every year, which seems to imply that some other people think it could be. (This suggestion is specially treated in Appendix II.)

to occur would itself affect the 'fluctuations' in the difference between anticipated outlays and revenues in any 'year', perhaps giving rise to apparent 'deficits' in 'years' of heavy outlays, and apparent 'profits' in others: the outlay might be in respect of a factor (e.g. a new set of locomotives) which was intended to be used over a series of subsequent 'years'. How would this have to be dealt with? The answer is that it would be necessary to insert the administrator's calculation of the money value of the residual assets[34] for the end of each 'year' instead of merely for the end of the budgetary period.

Clearly then to shift the application of the rule to the figures of the 'estimated profit calculation' does not obviate the Ruler's dependence upon the administrator's opinion about what is going to happen in the future – unless the Ruler usurps the administrator's function. But there is still another point. If the Ruler *confines* his scrutiny to the budget, he will have no check upon either the administrator's good faith, or his competence to achieve his ostensibly expected results. To this matter I shall return after considering the application of the rule when the relationship refers to the account.

3 The application when the relationship refers to the account
I now change my assumption, and suppose that it is not the budget at all, but the account only, that the Ruler has to scrutinize. Beyond inspiring fear *ex ante*, and applying any sanctions *ex post*, the Ruler would apparently have no function but to see whether cost and revenue in the sense of realized money outlays and revenues – subject to adjustments for 'opening stock' and 'closing stock' or 'residual assets' – were equal. What are the important issues in this case? One of them is this same difficulty with regard

---

[34] This matter of calculating the money value of residual assets is much the same as that of enterprise valuation, which has received much attention by Bonheight and others. A subjectivist, after working round to the attitude that to get at the value of the enterprise it is necessary to discover what the future revenues (less outlays) are expected to be, must, I think, conclude that 1) to get at these in turn it is necessary to ask the particular administrator of the enterprise what he thinks they will be; 2) that what they are likely to be may depend very much upon the enterprise being run by the particular administrator; 3) that the appropriate 'rate' at which the future figures should be 'discounted' depends, too, upon his views.

to the treatment of opening and residual assets as was encountered in the budget case. An account submitted with opening assets or while there were still significant residual assets would presumably have to have added to it the administrator's calculation for opening or residual assets. It may be asked whether this requirement could not be obviated by the employment of a professional accountant. A professional accountant – if the Ruler were not himself behaving as such – might, and probably would, be employed to ascertain whether the objective results were in fact those which had been reported in the accounts by the administrator to the Ruler: such is the accountant's function. But further than this he cannot go. Without usurping the administrator's function he cannot assess the (net) revenue still to be yielded by the use of residual assets.[35]

So this new shift in the application of the rule – to the account – does not, so far as interim accounts are concerned, obviate the Ruler's dependence upon the administrator's opinion about the future. Again there is another point. Knowing that his realized 'costs' and revenues would be required to be equal, and knowing that whatever his original estimates were they would not be likely to be exactly realized, and because it is probably easier to get rid of an emerging surplus than an emerging deficit, the administrator would probably be inclined to embark only upon undertakings in which, for any period in which he had to show equality of 'costs' and 'revenue', he felt fairly sure of being *able* to make a surplus or 'profit'; that is, he would be disinclined to embark upon undertakings unless, for each such period, he could *budget* for a surplus, and could rely upon being able to avoid the surplus somehow if he subsequently found that he was in danger of realizing it – e.g. by not responding to an upswing of demand to the extent provided for in his undisclosed budget.

A possible addition to the rule: the stipulation that the account should agree with the 'estimated profit calculation'
When the application of the rule shifted to the 'estimated profit calculation', a certain impotence resulted from the lack of the

[35] On 'charging depreciation', see Appendix III.

account; when it shifted to the account, a certain impotence resulted from the lack of the budget. Could potence be restored by requiring that the account should correspond with the budget, the Ruler scrutinizing both?[36] The new requirement – that both the budget and the eventual account should be submitted – would seemingly provide at least a reflection of the accuracy of forecasting – a check or report on efficiency in this sense. But it cannot be left at that. There is something significant to be said arising out of the point that nobody would expect a first budget, constructed with any definiteness of detail, to be exactly realized in the event. I have already pointed out that the figures relating to the remoter future would be extremely tentative. During the course of the budgetary period the administrator would be constantly revising his estimates as he started and continued his 'voyage into the unknown',[37] and corrected his earlier judgements[38] by his fuller realization of the circumstances, which at the first budgeting point of time were circumstances of the relatively remote future. His first estimate would not be likely to be correct. If he had to operate with his own resources, he would not be likely to embark on the venture at all unless he thought that however wrong his estimates were likely to be, he would still realize a profit – or at least as good a living, besides the return of his resources, as he could get elsewhere. It seems reasonable to suppose therefore that, under this new arrangement which requires both budget and account to be submitted, it would have to be understood at the outset that much scope would be allowed to the administrator for subsequent variation of his original figures, revised budgets being constantly submitted to the Ruler.[39] If the administrator were not allowed much scope, it seems likely that he would introduce undisclosed

---

[36] This addendum to the rule may possibly be implied in the idea that if 'the manager' disobeys the order to observe the rule he should be 'dismissed': I do not know. But it certainly is not implied in the mere injunction that cost and revenue should be equal.

[37] I believe I am indebted to Mr Shackle for this phrase.

[38] Subject to the limitations (e.g. by the acquisition of specificities) that he has already imposed upon himself. His later knowledge might suggest that he ought to have adopted a different technical structure (e.g. a different route for a railway), but it does not *follow* that he ought then to change it.

[39] If *perpetual* submission is conceived of, so that *all* alterations in plans are app-

safety margins[40] into his estimates amounting in effect to very much the same thing as budgeting for a surplus – in much the same way as, I believe, Ministers of Finance do, only in our case the administrator would take care to avoid the surplus if it tended to emerge. In other words, the administrator might be very unwilling to embark upon an undertaking unless behind the disclosed budget showing no profit he had a secret budget with a profit which he intended to lose if his anticipation proved correct. The item 'money value of residual assets' might often, I suppose, be a very useful medium for introducing his safety margins. It might also be used for temporarily hiding an impending deficit.

APPENDIX I

On the application of the rule when it requires the equation of marginal cost with something else. If we are contemplating the investment of liquid resources in a railway undertaking, the alternative opportunity to be displaced being a chain of saloon bars, what[41] is the marginal cost of producing, say, the final ton-mile of railway service which is expected to yield, say, a penny-halfpenny as marginal revenue, following the investment of an additional penny of liquid resources?[42] The marginal cost must be regarded as the displaced marginal revenue,[43] say a penny-farthing, which might be expected to accrue from the investment of the same penny in the production of, say, an extra pony of beer, instead of the final ton-mile of railway service.

If the rule is intended to be applied to marginal cost in this

roved before being executed, the eventual accounts must, I think, be identical to the approved revised budgets – if we abstract from the results of 'acts of God', breaches of standing orders, and any variations allowed to sub-administrators, executives and operatives by standing orders (e.g. a standing order to buy a material at a certain rate per unit of time so long as the price did not vary outside certain defined limits). Cf. my 'The Subjective Theory of Value and Accounting "Cost" ', reprinted here, pages, 135-61.

[40] On the introduction of safety margins into estimated profit calculations, see Machlup, 'Competition, Pliopoly and Profit', part II.

[41] Abstracting from the *time* at which the marginal unit will emerge.

[42] Since decimalization $5p \equiv 12d$.

[43] Strictly, the relative significance of the displaced marginal revenue.

sense, the marginal cost will escape the Ruler's observation in the same way as total cost in this sense escaped the Ruler's observation: the prospective alternative revenue is displaced by the decision, and will never be realized. From this point of view the same remarks apply to marginal cost as were applied to total cost.

If the rule is intended to be applied to 'cost' in the sense of anticipated objective outlays, the marginal outlay in the example will be a penny, against marginal revenue a penny-halfpenny. To disclose this to the Ruler, it would be necessary to submit, or at least to prepare, two budgets or 'estimated profit calculations', the one relating to a higher, the other to a lower, level of contemplated output. The penny (marginal outlay) would be the *difference between* total outlays in the two budgets; the penny-halfpenny the *difference between* total revenues in the two budgets. In other words, the 'estimated profit calculation' relating to the margin would be 'marginal outlay, a penny; marginal revenue, a penny-halfpenny'. So apparently marginal 'cost' in this sense might be budgeted.

If the rule is intended to be applied to 'cost' in the sense of *realized* objective outlays (in the account) it *cannot* be so applied, because only one level of output is, or, in the particular situation of time and place, can be, produced: no *variation* from that level occurs to show the required *difference between* the realized objective outlays of one level of output and another.[44]

---

[44] It might, of course, be retorted that at this stage it would be a fairly simple matter for the ruler to calculate what extra 'costs' and what extra revenue *would* have been involved in the production of an additional 'unit'. But this retort is unsound. Calculations of this kind could not be accepted as satisfactory without allowing for imponderable subjective or administrative elements. An alternative retort might be that the ruler would get his results by experimenting: changing the output and watching the results. But obviously this method is not generally satisfactory either, not only because the administrative imponderables might be overridden, but also because the different outputs would be produced at different times. It cannot be assumed that the circumstances affecting 'costs' and revenue are the same at different times. The overriding of the administrative imponderables is easily illustrated. *Illustration.* In response to a request from the ruler, who wishes to observe the results of increasing the output of a particular product of a particular firm, the general manager of the firm issues a peremptory order to increase output by twenty-five per cent. (He would not be likely to behave in this way in the ordinary course of business: it is for the purpose of demonstration that I assume that he does so.) The Ruler, subsequently passing through the firm's premises, encounters the sales manager and the production manager. A discussion ensues in which

It will be remembered that, when the application of the rule shifted to the 'estimated profit calculation', where this referred to *total* outlays and revenue, a certain impotence resulted from the lack of the account. Now that the calculation refers to marginal outlays, potence certainly cannot be restored by requiring that the account should correspond with the budget, because the account cannot exist.

So the objection to the proposed application of the rule to the total apply to its proposed application to the margin *a fortiori*.

APPENDIX II

1 It has been suggested[45] that the principle of covering total costs cannot be enforced 'every year if there are general fluctuations in trade', and that it 'should rather be applied over a period with surpluses in good years and deficits in bad'. Ignoring for the moment the doubt about the possibility of satisfactorily identifying and measuring the 'total costs' and 'total revenues' that are to be equalized over a period during which they fluctuate in relation to each other, would it be stretching analogy too far to suggest that the concession to allow 'surpluses in good years' to compensate for 'deficits in bad' might be extended to allow surpluses in good *transactions* and in good *markets* to compensate for deficits on bad transactions and in bad markets? It is difficult to see why, if allowance should be made for these 'general fluctuations in trade', allowance should not be made for *particular* fluctuations affecting the *particular* undertaking too.[46] Silence on the matter gives ground to suspect an implicit assumption that (apart from these 'general fluctuations') the administrator operates in conditions

the sales manager informs the ruler that he could have told him in advance what the approximate effect of the increased output on revenue would be: it was his job to be able to do that. The production manager tells him that the stepping-up of output involved delaying the execution of a remunerative order, which required the use of the same machines. The sales manager tells him that this order has now been cancelled. (Surely the loss of this job is a cost element – but it will not appear in objective outlays).

[45] T. Wilson, 'Price and Outlay Policy of State Enterprise', section 2 (d).

[46] Incidentally it would often be difficult to distinguish with any exactness the effect of the general fluctuation from the effect of a particular fluctuation.

akin to stationary equilibrium (supporting itself by its own boot-straps!), or that he has little or nothing of difficulty to do in the way of trying to discover how market conditions are going to change, of being prepared for and adjusting to the changes in advance, and of making allowance – particularly in the choice of technical structure – for the inevitability of uncertainty and error.

But if concessions for particular 'fluctuations' are to be made, how does the rule apply? When ends the long run, and where ends the group of transactions (or markets) to which the rule is to apply? Appropriate extension of the idea of permitting 'surpluses in good years' to compensate for 'deficits in bad', to allow for the inevitability of uncertainty and error, seems to render quite indefinite the limits of time and range of operations within which equality of 'surpluses' and 'deficits' was to be achieved.

2 The quandary that one is led into by the inadequate definition of the terms and method of application of the rule can be shown by examining closely Mr Wilson's suggestion,[47] following the one for an allowance for 'general fluctuations in trade', for dealing with a 'permanent decline in the demand' for a socialized industry's product. In order not to be misled by the telescoping of the *ex ante* with the *ex post*, I shall translate some of his statements into terms which I have used before. The industry is 'faced' with this permanent decline in demand. I take this to mean that the administrator is rebudgeting and working on the assumption that demand for the product will for the remaining future be permanently lower than he expected it would be when he originally budgeted. 'In these circumstances', Mr Wilson tells us, 'private firms will go on producing so long as the excess over prime costs is greater than the interest on the scrap value of the equip-ment.' This I adjust to mean that the administrator would, if he were a private firm, decide to continue production providing that he valued his anticipated revenues higher than cost in the proper sense, i.e. his reckoning of the best yield, from all the resources which he contemplated using (including, of course, the 'equip-ment') if he transferred them to his best contemplated alternative

[47] 'Price and Outlay Policy of State Enterprise', in the remainder of his section 2 (d).

opportunities of use – which might be to the production, by himself, of a different product. The cost of using existing equipment cannot be deemed to be adequately described by the expression 'interest on its scrap value'. Mr Wilson then remarks that the socialized industry might at this time have 'a large fixed-interest obligation', and refers to this as (being included in?) 'total costs' (thus telescoping past outlays – i.e. money 'capital' invested – and money payments already contracted to be made – i.e. 'interest' on the 'capital' – with outlays neither made nor contracted to be made). Having done this, he suggests that 'it would be better [than to adopt Mr Lerner's principles] to write down the capital of the industry . . . and then tell the manager to cover total costs at the reduced level'. But what are these 'total costs at the reduced level'? I can only interpret 'total costs' as being intended to mean cost in the proper sense plus either *nil* (if the 'capital of the industry' were written down to the level of the excess of cost in the proper sense over anticipated objective outlays)[48] or a *positive amount* (if the 'capital of the industry' were written down to a smaller extent). But what could this positive amount be other than a surplus of anticipated revenue over cost in the proper sense? And how much surplus would be allowed?[49] That from the output promising the *maximum* surplus? Or that from some other output, and if so, which? And according to what principle would it be chosen? If it is the output with the *maximum* surplus that

[48] It should be clear that these anticipated objective outlays are different from cost in the proper sense, which would include, for example, the value of existing equipment in an alternative use. That Mr Wilson has in mind (as 'costs', excluding the 'fixed interest obligation') something over and above anticipated objective outlays is apparent from his analogy with private enterprise in which he includes 'interest on the scrap value of the equipment' in what a private firm will require to be covered by revenue. The 'capital of the industry' would not be entirely written off unless it were anticipated objective outlays which were to be (only just) covered by revenue.

[49] Let revenue (r) minus cost in the proper sense (c) be x, and let c minus anticipated objective outlays (a) on the same budget (excluding, of course, those outlays which are already contractual obligations) be y, so that anticipated objective surplus on the budget is $(r-c)+(c-a)=r-a=y+x$.

Then Mr Wilson's 'total costs' appears to mean *either* c, if the 'capital of the industry' is written down to y, *or* $c+x$, if the 'capital of the industry' is written down to $y+x$.

But x (and, of course y, a, c and r) will be different according to what *output* is planned.

should be chosen, so long as even this choice still involves writing down the 'capital of the industry', why obscure the issue by referring to the choice as telling 'the manager to cover total costs at the reduced level', without defining the principle for determining what the 'reduced level' is?

Mr Wilson follows up with[50] the statement than 'in general, undertakings which *can* cover total costs should be made to do so', thus 1) obviously telescoping the *ex post* – the 'fixed interest obligation' or 'capital of the industry' – with the *ex ante*, and 2) implicitly asserting that at this rebudgeting point of time the principle to be observed, at least to the extent that this is necessary to meet the 'fixed interest obligation', is that of maximizing the surplus of revenue over cost in the proper sense.

But he concedes the possibility of an exception to this rule being made 'in the case of some old industries where capital is a very large proportion of total costs and where there is little likelihood of new investment', so as to allow the expansion of output beyond the point at which surplus is maximized to the point, presumably, at which marginal cost is supposed to be equal to 'price' ('. . . output could be expanded till it approximated more closely to the theoretical optimum'). The subsidy of 'fixed amount' which for this purpose, he states, 'might sometimes be justifiable' would, I presume, though this is not explicitly stated, be the amount by which the expansion of output caused a deficit in the amount required to meet the 'fixed interest obligation' (i.e. in anticipated revenue minus anticipated objective outlays). The subsidy having been given, 'the management should then be told to cover total costs less the subsidy'. But 'in no circumstances . . . should the State adopt Mr Lerner's policy, and offer to make good whatever deficit emerged as long as marginal costs and price were equated'. Upon this I must make two comments. First, if it is Mr Wilson's point that his desired output differs from Mr Lerner's, I am at a loss to know in what respect. Secondly, if his point is that Mr Lerner's policy would be conducive to carelessness about covering 'total costs', whereas Mr Wilson's would not, I would point out that, unless the Ruler, and not 'the management', were the

[50] 'Price and Outlay Policy of State Enterprise', in section 2 (e).

administrator, the Ruler would, under Mr Wilson's policy, be dependent upon 'the management's' estimates for fixing the amount of the subsidy. Possibly Mr Wilson has this idea at the back of his mind when, in his concluding paragraph, he remarks that 'this policy implies a degree of understanding and discrimination which may well be absent in practice'. It would be interesting to know whether, if he developed his views, explaining precisely what was to be understood by the terms 'costs' and 'revenue', untelescoping time so as to distinguish the *ex ante* from the *ex post* and elaborating the administrative arrangements and their functioning, he would discover that in this second respect he was, after all, in the same boat with Mr Lerner.

By pursuing this untelescoping and substitution of terminology I have endeavoured to show that the proposal to write down a 'fixed interest obligation', and instruct a 'manager' to cover 'total costs' as so reduced, avoids the issue as to the extent to which the 'fixed interest obligation' is to be written down or, what amounts to the same thing, it avoids the issue whether 'the manager' (or whoever is the administrator in the circumstances) is or is not to have a free hand to try to maximize his net returns ('fixed interest obligation' excluded). The proposal fails at this stage to define the principle of operation, although a subsequent reference to it seems to imply the principle of maximizing net returns.

Two other difficulties emerge when it is suggested that this proposal might in some cases be modified to allow subsidized expansion of output. The first is some obscurity on the matter of whether the proposed output is or is not that which would equate marginal cost and price. The second, and critical, difficulty lies in failure, at this point, to notice (or at least to make clear) that the fixing of the subsidy depends upon administrative estimates, and that if administration resides in the management, the Ruler is in the management's hands – a situation which, presumably, it is sought to avoid.

APPENDIX III[51]

In considering the application of the rule when the cost–revenue

[51] Cf. a discussion of 'depreciation' in section III of my 'Permanent Resources'.

relationship referred to the account, I suggested that, without usurping the administrator's function, a professional accountant could not independently assess the (net) revenue still to be yielded by the use of residual assets. But cannot he avoid having to do this by independently apportioning to an interim accounting period part of any outlay upon an asset which has an unexpired (residual) use at the end of the interim period? The answer is that all such apportionments must be unsatisfactory. To understand why this is so it is necessary to revert to the decision to acquire the asset.

Suppose the administrator is faced with the problem of deciding whether to buy an asset for £5,000. Let us assume for simplicity that 1) the asset would be completely specific to the production of a particular product of the particular undertaking, and that if it were to be used at an unvarying rate (considered by the administrator to be the optimum rate) over a period of four years it would still at the end of that period have a residual physical 'life' (reckoned on the basis of the same unvarying rate of use) of one year; 2) the administrator expects that the demand for the product will cease suddenly at the end of the fourth year, but by that time the use of the asset and the sale of the product will, in terms of net revenue, yielded at an unvarying rate, have recovered the £5,000, and he thinks the best thing to do[52] is to acquire the asset; 3) the administrator acquires the asset, produces at the expected rate over the first year – during which his expectations about demand have so far proved correct and, for the future, have not changed.

Now let us suppose that the first interim accounting period ends with the first year, and that the professional accountant attempts to apportion part of the outlay of £5,000 to that interim accounting period. Observing, presumably with the help of an engineer – that the asset has during the year been used up at a rate which if maintained will consume its whole physical 'life' by the end of the fifth year, he 'charges' against revenues one fifth of

[52] In order, we may assume, not to maximize net revenue, but to make outlays and revenue equal.

£5,000 = £1,000 as 'depreciation' of the asset.[53] Clearly, because one fourth of £5,000 = £1,250 has been recovered as revenue (net, before charging 'depreciation') the interim account will show a 'profit', and get the administrator called over the coals.[54]

Possibly the accountant would reply that the remaining £250 would be 'charged' as 'obsolescence'. But the point is that to ascertain what the figure for obsolescence is amounts to exactly the same thing as obtaining from the administrator his calculation of the money value of the residual assets.

[53] I do not of course wish to suggest that this method exhausts accounting methods of 'charging depreciation'. I wish only to suggest that all 'objective' methods – all methods which do not involve appeal to the administrator's calculation of the money value of the residue of the asset – are unsatisfactory.

[54] I might well have added that if such accounting apportionments of outlays (or charges for 'depreciation') were conventionally adopted, the administrator knowing in advance that they would be, and knowing that he would be required to have made his 'costs' (including such apportionments) and revenue equal in the interim account, would be likely to try to adjust his *ex ante* plans accordingly. (In the above example he probably would not have bought the asset at all, because, in order to come out in the end, he would, on the assumptions made, have been faced with having to show a 'profit' in the first four years and a 'loss' in the fifth.) Production would be distorted by the adoption of an accounting convention: technical specialism would be cutting across, or imposing a rigidity upon, administration. (If it were urged that the imposition of this convention amounted to the laying down of a standing order by a higher authority, and that 'the accountant' was therefore taking part in administration. I should probably accept the correction. But it would still be open to economists to consider the effect of such a standing order upon production.)

8

The economist's description of business behaviour

G. F. THIRLBY

First published in *Economica* (May 1952).

I THE FIRST APPROXIMATION

The subject of this paper is the idea that the businessman fixes his output at that level at which the surplus of his total revenue over his total cost is maximized, and accordingly at which his marginal cost and marginal revenue have been brought nearly[1] to equality. It is (sometimes) admitted or asserted that this description is only a first approximation to a description of actual behaviour. I shall accordingly, and for brevity's sake, refer to it as 'the first approximation'. I propose to discuss its limitations, and what we have to do with it before we have something which really comes anywhere near to being a description of a businessman's and a business organization's behaviour.

At each step I shall first examine the shortcomings of the first approximation as a description of the behaviour of the business-man who has no human associates in the business, and then proceed to discuss their significance for the situation in which the business consists of more than one man, that is to say, where the business consists of an organization of human beings. Economists – I am speaking rather of economists operating in the realm of pure theory, and using this marginal cost–marginal revenue 'technique' – do sometimes speak of a 'firm', but rarely does the 'firm' become anything really different from the man combining factors. It is true that one of these factors is 'labour', but labour is thought of as if it were a substance of which the owner sells a quan-

[1] I say 'nearly' because we say that 'marginal cost *equals* marginal revenue' only when we forget 1) that the position of equality is a position of indifference and 2) the *minimum sensible*. In administrative theory both these things are important.

tity to the 'man' ('entrepreneur') or 'firm'. After this moment of sale the previous owner of the labour (the labourer) appears to be decisionless with respect to the use of the labour that he has sold: there is still only one man concerned with the 'firm's' planning operations which dispose of that labour.

Yet it is not always true that there is only one man taking part in the 'firm's' planning. Sometimes another person, just as much as the first, is a planner, making responsible decisions, based on uncertain estimates of future events, and taking his part in the determination of the organization's plan and executory operations. The neglect of this case in economic theory is due, I imagine, to some inhibition in economists against recognizing the existence of an organization of men. In oral discussion with colleagues I have noticed the tendency to dismiss the relationships between the contributory decision-maker and the other members of the organization as matters of internal politics. Whether the organizational relationships which develops a 'maximized' cost–revenue situation are politics, while the market relationships which develop a price are economics, does not seem to me to matter. What does matter, and is distressing, is that the organizational relationships should fall between two stools (economics and politics), and make it necessary to establish a new subject called administrative theory.

The first approximation is probably so-called partly because the costs and revenues are supposed to be money, while it is admitted that a businessman is not necessarily striving always and exclusively for a maximum surplus of money revenue over money cost. In other words the implicit statement of the man's value judgement, or policy-making judgement, is not quite correct. This value judgement and other subjective judgements we shall have to discuss. They become particularly significant when we come to study the organization. But it would be better to return to them after we have referred to the timeless equilibrium setting of the marginal cost–marginal revenue 'equation'.

G. F. Thirlby

II THE TIMELESS EQUILIBRIUM SETTING OF THE
EQUATION. THE SUPPRESSION OF THE PLANNING
OPERATION AND THE EVASION OF DOCTRINE. THE
SUPPRESSION OF 'THE ORGANIZATION' AND THE
CONCEPTS WHICH ITS TREATMENT REQUIRES.
AUTHORITY AND AUTHORITARIANISM

To make the equation conform to anything like business reality, this timeless equilibrium setting has to be seriously altered. The businessman does not make a decision about a situation with which he is already 'in equilibrium' : while out of equilibrium with the situation, he makes a decision to bring himself into equilibrium with it.[2] Neither are his results achieved simultaneously with the making of his decision nor in a state of timelessness: a period of time elapses between the making of the decision and the achievement of the results. To put this matter right it is necessary to substitute for the timeless situation a situation in which there is a planner who plans for a period ahead, proceeds to carry out that plan, and is in equilibrium while, and to the extent that, he continues to do so, that is to say, so long as, in the course of the period, nothing happens to render him unable to continue to carry out his plan, or to cause him to change his plan.[3] As I see it, this continuing, or period, equilibrium corresponds exactly with what we understand in business administration by production under *standing orders*. In execution of the standing orders, various conversions of money into factors, factors into products, and products into money may occur *in equilibrium*, that is, with no new decision following the decision which laid down the standing orders, or with no change of plan.

But my main object in insisting on the introduction of the time dimension is to stress the planning operations preceding the period of execution. A mental deliberation or planning operation, followed by a decision, precedes the business operations which are so planned. I think this should be more definitely stressed even where we are speaking of one-man businesses. To do so would keep in front of our minds the high degree of subjectivity in the maximization process, performed as it must be in advance of the

[2] On this, see Mises, *Human Action* (1949).
[3] Cf. Hayek: 'Economics and Knowledge', reprinted here, pages 43-68.

market operations, and based as it must be on advance calculations, or forecasts, of the market conditions (factor and product prices) that will obtain when those market operations occur. It would prevent our attributing, as we are so prone to do, a false objectivity to the cost and revenue figures to which the businessman is supposed to respond. 'Uncertainty', so often completely forgotten, or regarded as a 'trimming', by economists, is something that it would be disastrous not to introduce into administrative theory at the outset. If money revenue is the businessman's sole aim, cost, as well as revenue, is always somebody's uncertain, fallible estimate or projection of future prices[4] and is a 'function' of that particular person's mind. If the first approximation allows us to forget this, it becomes a 'vicious abstraction'.[5]

To fail to bring the planning stage to the surface perhaps does not matter so much – though I rather think it does – while we are still confining our attention to the one-man business. To continue to suppress it when we are supposed to be talking of an organization – whether this be an English joint-stock company, or whether it be Russia – is to neglect more than half of the problem. It is to do more than this. It is to fail to provide a discipline for a vast literature which concerns itself with business 'organization', 'efficiency', 'planning', 'costing' and so on, but which has often proceeded without benefit of the notion of maximization, or without adequate recognition of it. Moreover it allows, by default, the emergence of the view that the large organization operates under a single planning mind, and, by not looking into the nature of the organization's authority relationships, allows to persist, if it does not propagate, authoritarian views of a very naïve order. The persistent '*he* will adjust his output . . .', *he* will do this and *he* will do that, coming from teachers and students alike, is extremely irritating and provoking to anybody who has made a disciplined inquiry into these matters.

The situation that we have to face, and introduce into our discussion, as a first step in the direction of describing organization

---

[4] This does *not* contradict my assertion, below, that costs are not necessarily *actor* prices.

[5] A term I have taken from Bradley.

behaviour, is one which fulfils the following conditions. The work of planning leading to the plan which is calculated to maximize the surplus of revenue over cost is shared by a number of people. Their tentative plans have to be coordinated with one another. A's (definite) plan will depend on what B's tentative planning is: B's (definite) plan will depend on what A's tentative planning is. For example, a sales *schedule* (A's) has to be coordinated with a purchases *schedule* (B's). This has to happen before the organization's maximized plan, and each member's sectional plan, becomes definite and settled by a *composite decision* or co-ordinated decision *ex ante*.[6] Each of these people has necessarily to make uncertain forecasts of what is going to happen, and be responsible for those forecasts. It is impossible that A should know all that B knows about the situation that B has to deal with (say the buying market), and it is impossible that B should know all that A knows about the situation that A has to deal with (say the selling market). Thus willy nilly, A has to trust B and his uncertain judgements, and B has to trust A and his uncertain judgements. That is to say, it is recognized that the total situation is beyond the capacity of either A or B to deal with. And of course it is implied that A and B feel that they are better off if they work together as an organization than they would be if they worked separately.

This is the situation that, as I see it, has to be brought into any satisfactory description of the business organization. It incidentally raises the authority issues. The crucial issues, or some of them, can be forced to the front by assuming that A and B are equal partners and the only members of the organization. If authority is a property of organization, there must be authority here, for this is an organization. The organization's maximized plan becomes the organization's standing orders. The *composite decision* which settles the plan operates as an order to carry out the plan: in this case an order by A and B as a committee issued to A and to B as subordinates to it. But, although the order issues from above (the

---

[6] Professor H. A. Simon uses the expression 'composite decision'. This is equivalent to the expression 'coordinated decision *ex ante*' which I have used elsewhere. (See H. A. Simon, *Administrative Behavior* (1947), and my 'The Subjective Theory of Value and Accounting "Cost" ', reprinted here, pages 135-61.

committee), the authority, or authoritativeness, of the plan, and hence of the order, *moves up from below*, that is to say, from A and B as subordinate planners in 'the organization'. For it is implicit in the assumptions that in the planning and coordination process A cannot expect to override B's judgement within B's sphere, and B cannot expect to override A's judgement within A's sphere. Arbitrary attempts so to override one another on committee would interfere with the development of an order (the committee decision) which would be accepted by A and B *without psychological resistance* – the harmony condition of authority.

I have little doubt that at this point many people would wish to substitute for the committee a third person, X, whose job it is to 'manage' A and B. If we make this substitution, either we assume that X usurps the functions which we have given to A and B or we do not assume this. If we *do*, then the 'larger' the organization ('larger' referring to the degree to which the planning and uncertain judgements surpass the capacity of one man) the nearer we come to assuming the omniprescient head – unsustainable authoritarianism. If we do *not* assume that X usurps A and B, then we are driven to admit that X must get his purchases and sales figures from the minds of A and B – and trust those people. Authority still moves up from below.

Of course X might have a 'staff-man' to collect the figures for him. Then either the 'staff-man' usurps the functions of A and/or B, or he does not. If he does – this sometimes happens – the position is the same as before : the staff-man *becomes* A and/or B. If the 'staff-man' does not usurp A or B, then he must get the figures from their minds. Authority still moves up from below.

I shall not here attempt to explain how X and his 'staff-man' may make a show of 'managing' by short-circuiting the minds of A and B, and using records (some of them pseudo or 'conventional') instead. But I have no doubt that this procedure goes a long way to explain why some people receive the impression that firms adjust their market operations in a way which appears to defeat or ignore the marginal principle.

My illustration is highly abstract and inadequate, and leaves me open to attack at many points. But it does suggest some of the issues that the first approximation slurs over when it abstracts altogether from the planning operations of the organization.

III THE OBSCURITY ABOUT COST. A RESTATEMENT

In the last section I referred to the businessman's decision to conduct a series of planned operations over the future. This planned course of action might be a course of action to produce, not necessarily only one product, but possibly a number of different products, and to produce them in different proportions on a number of different dates. And possibly it would include lending and borrowing operations as well. This particular plan is simply the one chosen from possibly many contemplated alternative particular arrangements or distributions of *the same resources*. It is necessary to define this entity 'the same resources'.

How are we to define the resources as they exist for the man's planning purposes, *independently of*, or prior to, the cost and revenue calculations which determined the chosen distribution? They must, I think, be deemed to include the following elements:

1 Such money and goods as the man has at the outset.

2 His 'knowledge' or 'prescience' (including uncertain judgements and mistaken beliefs) concerning the loans that he might be able to negotiate, and the factors and products into which he might be able to convert his original assets and these loans. The 'knowledge' will include his views about the (future) prices of the loans, factors and products. If the man knows John Smith, a dealer in linen thread, and feels fairly certain that John Smith would sell him a certain quantity of linen thread next week at a price which he feels fairly certain about too, he has this 'knowledge' as part of his resources. How much of such knowledge he possesses will depend very much upon his unique business experience and the scope of his unique relationships with other people in 'the market', and the qualities and limitations of himself as a unique person. Any such assumption as that all factors and products of every conceivable kind are 'priced', and that all these (future!) prices are known, or 'given', to anybody who chooses to

read them off, must be rejected out of hand. We are dealing, not with a master-mind (or alternatively with an automatic response to a 'price system'), but with a fallible and unique individual who is trying to discern the future, and whose range of observation of even the past and present is limited.

3 The loans and factors themselves. That is to say, any loans and factors that the man thinks or believes would be in existence and available to him to acquire or buy if he wanted them for any production that he might plan. In the event some of them might prove not to be in existence or available. None the less his belief that they would be is a planning datum, and must be included for this purpose in 'the same resources'.

These loans and factors will, or may be, available only as a set of alternatives from which to choose. That is to say, if he plans to acquire some, he may not be able to plan to acquire others. This for the obvious reason that his original assets and (so far as the acquisition of factors is concerned) the loans that he contemplates might be inadequate to secure them all. It would not be surprising therefore if plan A contemplated the use of linen thread but no brass tacks, while an alternative plan B contemplated the use of brass tacks but no linen thread. The idea that the two plans are alternative distributions of the same resources is not destroyed by this possibility. Both the linen thread and the brass tacks (and the man's knowledge about them) are part of 'the same resources' that, in the man's opinion, are available for his planning activity.

Nor is the idea destroyed by the possibility that some of these resources (loans, at least) may be available for some purposes (e.g. work in which the man has special skill) but not for others. They are part of 'the same resources' that in the man's opinion are available for his planning activity.

Thus 'the same resources' are largely ideational in character, and would be irritatingly non-measurable to an external observer who felt that he ought to be able to measure them. They are very much in the way of being a 'function' of the man's mind. Their limits are much to do with the limits of the man's mind.

I have said, then, that the man adopts one particular distribution of 'the same resources' as his plan or accepted course of action, and that this plan will contemplate the *use*, for the purpose of earning revenue, of some or all of 'the same resources'. The 'revenue' that we think of in the first approximation is, or should be regarded as, the revenue that the man expects to accrue to him from the carrying out of this plan. This is the ideational, imaginary, planned or expected revenue whose surplus over cost he deems in the planning stage to be maximized. What then is the 'cost'?

It is often very difficult to understand what economists mean by cost when they are discussing the marginal cost–marginal revenue equation. But it is probable that at least sometimes what is meant is the sum of the prices of the 'factors' to be used in the chosen course of action. These prices may be buying or selling prices, according to whether the factors are to be bought or are already owned. It is extremely difficult to know sometimes whether *all* the resources that are to be used, including the man's own capacity, and money, are supposed to be included in the factors so priced. However, this meaning (factor prices) is not, I maintain, an appropriate meaning of cost for the purpose in hand. Or, at the best, these factor prices represent only one of the various alternative opportunities that might be confronting the man when he is about to make his decision. The appropriate meaning of cost is the *revenue*, from an alternative distribution of 'the same resources', that he would expect to achieve if, instead of his accepted course of action, he adopted that course which would yield the second highest revenue. It is the (greatest) estimated alternative productivity of 'the same resources', rather than their prices as factors, that we have to regard as cost. The two things might conceivably be one and the same: the best alternative to taking the accepted course of action might be to sell (or not buy) 'the same resources' or their services as such. But this is not necessarily so. The best alternative could be an alternative complex of activities to produce an alternative complex of the same products or different products or some of each. Consequently we need to adopt a meaning for cost which covers the cases where the best alternative is, not to sell (or not buy) 'the same resources', but to do something else with them. And we need to do this notwithstanding anything that may be said to the contrary in 'static', or other, equilibrium analysis. We are not assuming that the man is planning or operating in any kind of equilibrium, or other, conditions that require these two things to be the same.[7] We do not say how many different opportunities of making money he sees, or thinks he sees, in the rest of the 'system'. Consequently we define cost as his best alternative revenue rather than as the sum of the factor prices. If any adjustment is implied, I would make just this amount of adjustment to Professor Lionel C. Robbins's description of opportunity cost in his 'Certain Aspects of the Theory of Costs'.[8] Otherwise I would adopt his definition.

I would emphasize that this adjustment of the meaning of cost from factor prices to rejected alternative revenue does not in any way rule out the relevance of factor prices in planning or in the determination of cost.[9] Whether the man will include the *use* of John Smith's linen thread in one alternative plan or another will surely depend partly upon the level of the price that he contemplates having to pay for it. For the level of this price will be one determinant of. the quantity of linen thread that he will be able to get with a given input of money. Hence it may be one determinant of the size of an output (of say, boots). Hence it may be a determinant of revenue from this output – on plan A. And, as the sacrifice of this revenue may be the cost of achieving a revenue on an alternative plan B (which incidentally may not contemplate the *use* of linen thread at all), the (expected) price of linen thread may be a determinant of cost.

---

[7] If there is any profound reason why this implies that the man will not be able to carry out his plan, I should like to point out that I have not anywhere stated that he *will* be able to carry out his plan.

[8] Reprinted here, pages 21-41.

[9] Neither is it intended to belittle the significance of estimating future factor prices and calculating variations in prices and their sums which would be expected to accompany variations in planned production processes and outputs (production functions). Quite the contrary. But it is intended to take care of the situation in which the business man's cost calculation with respect to a particular product is not completed until he has looked at his *alternative product* demand curves as well as his factor supply curves, and calculated all the revenue he expects to lose by devoting resources (total or marginal) to this product instead of doing something else with them. It incidentally takes care of all interdependencies, including interdependencies of demand curves.

I have not yet said what *marginal* cost is. A marginal cost is simply the revenue that the man expects to lose in one direction (to be set against the revenue that he expects to gain in another direction – the marginal revenue) by shifting his proposed application of *some part* of 'the same resources', for example, by shifting some from product A to product B, or from the money market to a product, or from personal consumption[10] to business investment, or from investment on day 1 to investment on day 2, or from 'idleness' to investment. Clearly one such shift occurs in moving from the 'second-best' plan to the 'best' plan. Clearly the marginal revenue involved is greater than the marginal cost involved: net revenue is positive. Or, reversing the process, the marginal revenue involved in moving from the 'best' to the 'second-best' plan is less than the marginal cost involved: net revenue is negative.

Up to this point I have spoken of the man's aim as being the maximization of the surplus of revenue over cost. It is now no longer necessary – indeed it is very nearly erroneous – to do this. It is enough to speak of maximizing revenue. To maximize revenue is to choose the best or greatest of all the alternative revenues that are in mind. There is a surplus of the best over the next best (cost), but to speak of maximizing this surplus is to contradict the assertion that the two revenues are the best and the next best.[11] Let us henceforward speak simply of maximizing revenue.

[10] It should be noticed that, because the maximization of the surplus of money revenue over money cost is the man's single end, he will, apparently, reserve to himself 'leisure' and resources for food and other personal consumption only in so far as he thinks that to do so will indirectly increase the size of his ultimate money surplus.

[11] I should have no objection to allowing cost to mean the 'worst' (or some other) revenue, instead of the 'next best' revenue, and so making sense of the expression 'maximize the *surplus* of revenue over cost'. (And if one of the alternative behaviours were holding idle, the expected outcome being money so held idle, I should of course be willing to include this outcome in the list of alternative revenues, and should have no objection to regarding it as cost.) I should have no objection to this provided that everybody agreed that 'cost' did still mean revenue (or the idle money outcome) and not the resources that the man has at the outset, as such.

It would be possible to go further and allow cost to mean these resources as such. I should have no objection to this either, provided that everybody agreed that cost did mean this, and that nobody then tried to subtract cost from revenue to give profit or net revenue or income. The resources never are homogeneous: the man has at least himself as well as any money he may have. To begin to 'price' the

I come now to the substitution of 'the organization' for the 'man'. Cost, for the organization, would still refer to the revenue of the 'best' of the rejected alternative plans that were under consideration in the planning stage and rejected by the composite decision. But the constitution of this rejected plan, like the constitution of the accepted plan, would be the result of the planning activity and (interpersonal) coordination of a number of collaborating minds, instead of being merely the result of the coordination of the processes of a single mind. Hence 'discovery' of the cost, and how it was arrived at, would have to overcome corresponding complexities. Marginal cost would still refer to the revenue expected to be lost in one direction by shifting the proposed application of some part of 'the same resources' – possibly now by shifting it from one member's use to another member's use. 'The same resources' and their application would have to be thought of in the same way for the organization as for the man, except that 1) the limit to 'the same resources' would depend on the capacities and views of a number of collaborating people instead of one person, and 2) we should have to bear in mind that the amount of the organization member's personal resources that becomes organization resources (and consequently the amount of personal 'leisure' and so on that he sacrifices) is fixed by bargain and contract between that member as a person and the other organization members or the organization as such. So is the member's remuneration for what he so contributes, whether this remuneration is a definite sum, whether it is the residual revenue that is to be maximized, or whether it is a definite share in that residual revenue.

IV THE SUPPRESSED VALUE JUDGEMENTS. NON MONETARY ENDS AND MARGINAL COSTS. INTRA AND ULTRA VIRES POLICY-MAKING AS AFFECTING THE OPERATION OF THE MARGINAL PRINCIPLE IN THE ORGANIZATION. IDENTIFICATION

We can now return to the value judgements which the first

resources in order to make them summable, is to begin to convert them into the money yield (revenue) that the man thinks he could get for them. It is either this or much-practised pseudo-objective nonsense!

approximation obscures. I have already referred to the assumption that the man's single aim is to maximize money revenue, and to the admission that this assumption may not be quite correct. A man may relax this valued aim somewhat to allow, say, for his preference for producing the kind of product that he 'likes', or for his preference for 'leisure' or food (valued because he 'likes' them as ends, and not merely as indirect means to maximize his money revenue) or even for his preference for being benevolent towards other people. His 'net satisfactions' may be greater if he does so. In other words the man may have other ultimate ends, or rather other ends *pen*ultimate to 'value', besides the end of money revenue.

The significance of the possible presence of these other ends is just this. In so far as the man has them, his pursuit of money-revenue maximization will be restricted by marginal costs which will be, not exclusively alternative marginal money revenue, but his valuation of the marginal achievement of these other ends – e.g. additional 'leisure' to be enjoyed as a valued end. Or revenues will be 'weighted' by the other valued ends that the man expects to achieve in the process of earning the revenues – e.g. when he 'likes' making one product more than another. In either case his resources will be partly devoted to the achievement of ends other than revenue maximization. This is the main point. But we should notice incidentally that if in these circumstances we desired a concise expression to describe the man's optimum distribution of his resources, and to indicate what we meant by cost, we should be driven to say that he adopts a course of action which maximizes his *value*,[12] and that the cost is the *value*,[12] from an alternative distribution of 'the same resources', that he would expect to achieve if, instead of his accepted course of action, he adopted that course which would yield the second highest *value*.[12] This is what happens to us when we remove the oversimplification in the assumption that the man's value judgement makes revenue maximization his single end. We get back to the old-fashioned description of rational behaviour.[13]

[12] Or values or satisfaction or utility or ophelimity or something like that.
[13] See Mises, *Human Action*.

I want now to suggest how the introduction of these other valued ends affects *organization* behaviour.

To make a value judgement as part of an effective decision is to make policy. Whether it can be distinguished in practice or not, this act of policy-making can be distinguished in thought from the acts of administration and execution which implement the policy. When the subject of our inquiry is the man working alone, this distinction may not be a matter of great significance. The man is assumed to approve what he decides to do and does. That is the end of the matter. There is no problem of whether his decisions and actions are in accord with his policy. If they were not, he would be presumed to be irrational or mad.[14]

When the subject is the organization, however, we are in a different position. It is obviously possible for an organization member to make a decision which is inconsistent with the policy or approved aims of the organization, that is to say, to allow his personal value judgements to intrude, or to allow his misguided 'identification'[15] with a department, person or practice to intrude. For example, he might decide to make product A, rather than product B, because he personally 'liked' making product A, or because he was 'identified' with the product-A department, although he thought product B would yield more revenue, and although the organization policy was to maximize revenue regardless of product. Such a person is not necessarily irrational (mad), although in such circumstances 'the organization' may be.[16]

But this *deliberate* intrusion of personal values, and this misplaced identification, are not the only aspects of the matter. It is often very difficult to see how administrative decision-making can be delegated without driving the administrator into making policy himself. Suppose, for example, that it was the organization's policy to make product A rather than other products, even at *some* loss of revenue, because it (or its policy-makers) had a special 'liking' for making product A. Then the problem of devising a policy-directive giving the weights to attach to the A marginal revenues

14 See Mises, *Human Action.*
15 For a fuller discussion of 'identification' see H. A. Simon *Administrative Behavior.*
16 Fortunately for us it has not been possible to put organizations into lunatic asylums.

so as to allow the administrator to measure them against the marginal revenues of other products would be difficult if not insuperable. Again suppose that it was the policy of the organization to provide some 'welfare' at the expense of some revenue, that is to say, because it 'liked' providing welfare and not merely because it regarded the provision of 'welfare' as a means of increasing revenue. Here again the problem of devising a policy-directive giving *the descriptions of tangibles*[17] that were supposed to yield 'welfare', and the weights to attach to them, so as to allow administrators to measure them against the marginal revenues of products, would be difficult if not insuperable. The only rational way out of the difficulty would seem to be to provide for discussion between administrators and policy-makers proper, and for *tentative administrative plans to be submitted for confirmation to policy-makers proper*. There is then a meeting of minds and a two-way flow of ideas. Policy-makers can eventually 'value' and select from the alternative plans which the administrators submit to them. Administrators thus have the means of making their plans definite without themselves making policy.

It might be thought that another way out of this difficulty would be to delegate policy-making itself to the administrator. The members of a company might be thought to delegate policy-making to its board of directors. But this situation is surely morally intolerable. To delegate policy-making is to permit somebody else to make one's ethical judgements for one. A person joining an organization accepts, not any aim that some other member chooses to adopt subsequently, but the aim which he and all other members at that time accept in common. He accepts ethical or moral responsibility for pursuing that aim. It would seem, then, that the making, or changing, of policy without common consent is necessarily a change *ultra vires* – that policy-making cannot be delegated.[18] If policy-making could be delegated, and if a company delegated policy-making to its board of directors, the

[17] This cannot be avoided by a directive which simply allows so much money to be allotted to undefined 'welfare'. Under such a directive the administrator could define 'welfare' as putting the money into his own pocket.
[18] This is not to say that there cannot be a considerable degree of common

board would be at liberty to devote all the resources of the company to charitable works, or whatever else it saw fit to regard as 'good'.[19]

So far then I have suggested that what the organization's output is, and what are the *marginal costs*, or marginal *values*, that are determining it, may depend partly upon the presence of *ultra vires* policy-making within the body of the organization, either because of the intrusion of personal values or because of misguided identification or because administrators without appropriate policy-directives are driven to make policy. A serious inquiry into the determination of a business organization's 'output' would have to be prepared to 'discover' whether influences of this kind were at work. It should be noticed incidentally that if it did find these influences at work, it would not have disproved the marginal *principle*[20] though it would have discovered marginal costs and marginal values whose introduction rendered the organization behaviour irrational.

Such an inquiry would not be easy. Even in the one-man business, it would be difficult enough to discover from the man's mind how far he was forecasting achievements of other ends than revenue, and setting the forecasts against, or adding them to, his forecasted achievements of revenue. Indeed he might himself be only partly conscious of what he was doing. In an organization a

understanding of what policy is, even though no explicit policy statements or directives are issued: no doubt a man joining a business firm assumes that it is there largely to make money. The point is rather this. When the number of members is large, it becomes difficult to get and maintain common consent to a common policy which binds members to pursue a common end. But if the many try to leave policy determination to the few, the moral issue arises. When I say that policy-making (as distinct from administration) cannot be delegated, I mean that A who directs B to pursue A's ends for him cannot be presumed not to have defined or determined those ends, and valued, approved of or accepted moral responsibility for those ends as fit to be pursued. (If A were a group, perhaps including B, I should say this of each person in the group. This personal responsibility cannot, I suggest, be eliminated simply because the persons have formed an organization.)

[19] To assume that the board is the policy-maker (and consequently that the shareholders are infants without moral responsibility) does not dispose of the issue in question, but only shifts its locus to the relationship between the board and the subordinates to whom the board delegates administration.

[20] If economists want to study organization pathology, they should go about it in the right way, and not be too ready to scrap principles of their own which some of them have ceased to understand.

serious inquiry would be much more complex. It would have to probe the minds of more than one person. It would have to study the effects of meetings of minds. These meetings, whether for the purpose of securing the administrative composite decision,[21] or for the purpose of reconciling administration and policy, would not necessarily proceed through formal committee meetings: as likely as not the link-up would occur in informal discussions.

The investigation would have to be wary of misplaced identification. This I have mentioned before, but it needs further stress. n an organization people are *necessarily* in some sense specialized: to say this is to say no more than that the organizations activities are divided amongst the people in it. A man, or a 'department' of men, might be specialized to the production of a 'product' or to plant maintenance or to 'welfare' activities or to 'accounting'. Either because they personally like the activity, or because they get their living at it, or for some other reason, people so specialized sometimes 'identify' themselves with the departmental end rather than the organization's end, and, when they are before the coordinating body, 'push' their departmental end, and press for resources to achieve it. Incidentally they are likely to develop standards or practices relating to their specialism, and push these, even sometimes where they are inappropriate. Sometimes these standards or practices are those of a profession to which the people belong and with which they are 'identified', recognizing the profession as a group or organization superordinate to the business organization in which they are working. It is notorious that accountants are 'identified' with the practice of 'attaching' and 'expiring' : I have written about that elsewhere.[22] At least some of them develop a pseudo-objective 'cost' calculation, which includes these arbitrary attachments, and which an unwary and uninitiated investigator might be led into substituting for the estimates of alternative revenues (and alternative 'values') that I have been discussing. Misleading inferences about how output was determined might follow. I have no

---

[21] Economists, who appreciate the abstraction of a 'market price', should have no difficulty in grasping the idea of a composite decision as a similar abstraction.

[22] 'The Subjective Theory of Value and Accounting "Cost" ', reprinted here, pages, 135-61.

hesitation in adding that it is to such 'cost' calculations that I was referring, in section II, when I spoke of the behaviour (which I should now describe as organizationally irrational) of the 'manager' and his 'staff-man'.

V OTHER SUPPRESSED SUBJECTIVE JUDGEMENTS. TIME PREFERENCE. POLICY-MAKING AND ADMINISTRATIVE JUDGEMENTS AFFECTING MARGINAL COST

In the last section I supposed the value judgement to be relaxed so as to allow the man to be pursuing another end besides money revenue. Sometimes it is admitted that, even though money revenue is deemed to be the single end, another value judgement intrudes as soon as we think of maximization of revenue *over time*. This appears in the determination of what is known as the rate at which future revenues are discounted. Money may be planned to come in (or go out) at different times and in different quantities over the future. These planned times and quantities may be varied. The man may prefer a pound at one date to a pound at another date, and plan to get it at one date rather than the other. This relative preference affects the meaning of maximization, even given that money is otherwise the single aim.

But to understand how much of this preference is of the value judgement nature – how much of it is 'policy' – we have to analyse it a little. Let us momentarily abstract from all elements of uncertainty about the possibility of accrual of the pound at either of the two alternative dates. Then the preference for the pound at one date rather than the other can be due to one of two things.

First, the man may prefer the pound at one date rather than the other because he 'likes' or 'values' it more at that date, possibly because he wants to withdraw money for personal consumption at that date rather than at the other – for personal consumption over and above what he requires to enable him to maximize revenue. This preferred date may be the date of the planned termination of the operating period (or infinity!) or the planned date of some interim drawing. My suggestion is that the decision settling the date of the termination of the period (the termination of the business operations) and the decision settling the date of interim drawings (which can be regarded as partial terminations of the business) are of the nature of value judgements (policy decisions) which are necessary adjuncts to the simple statement which says that the aim is to maximize revenue, but which says nothing about the length of the operating period. It would follow that if *in an organization* (e.g. a company) the policy-making body (e.g. a body including shareholders) was distinguishable from the administrative final coordinating centre (e.g. the board of directors), these decisions should be made by the policy-making body, and that the administrators should administer in accordance with the decisions so made.[23] This would require either a policy-directive laying down the time preference for revenue withdrawals, or the kind of discussion between administrators and policy-makers, and joint settlement of plans, to which I referred before. Otherwise administrators would be driven into policy-making. It should hardly be necessary for me to add that the introduction of this time preference affects marginal costs: a pound earnable at one date is no longer necessarily equivalent to a pound earnable at another date.

Secondly, the man may prefer the accrual of the pound at one date rather than the other on the ground that he expects its accrual at that date to lead, through better opportunities for its reinvestment, to greater revenue in the end, or according to his scale of preference with regard to dates of withdrawal. In this case there appears to be no (additional) value judgement involved: the case is covered by the decision, and the value judgement involved in it, to maximize revenue in the end, or according to the scale of preference for withdrawals. This would mean that in the organization no additional policy-directive to administrators would be required, and that they could make this type of decision without reference back to the policy-makers. That is to

---

[23] Whether or not this view is correct, it should be clear that administrative behaviour should be *coordinated* to secure that all administrators are working to the same range of preference regarding the dates at which revenue is to accrue or be maximized: otherwise an administrator of one section of the total plan might be working to maximize at the day after tomorrow, while another was working to maximize ten years later.

say, given the policy-makers' scale of preference with regard to dates of withdrawal, the administrators would make the dis-investment and reinvestment decisions. Once again marginal cost is affected, this time by an administrative judgement which appraises the revenue to be sacrificed by an earlier or later disinvestment and reinvestment.

I would emphasize that neither of these preferences for a pound at one date rather than the other has anything to do with relative uncertainty of accrual. I have abstracted from this matter, not because it is of small importance, but because these relative uncertainties about accruals at *alternative* times can be regarded – from the point of view of whether the decision about them involves another value judgement—in the same way as relative uncertainties about alternative accruals at the *same* time. It is to this problem that I now turn.

Let us suppose that our businessman is concerned with a choice between two alternative courses of action which he believes would yield revenue. He states that if he took the first course he would be surprised if its revenue fell outside the limits of ten and twenty; if he took the second course he would be surprised if its revenue fell outside the limits of five and thirty.

I take the view that the question of which of these prospective revenues is the greater is not capable of being answered objectively, and consequently that the simple statement of the aim to maximize revenue has to be modified or elaborated to allow for the subjective judgement about which is the better risk to take or uncertainty to face. In this case, in which the lower and higher limits of the one revenue fall respectively below and above those of the other revenue, the man's decision seems to depend upon how much he 'likes' risk-taking, and accordingly involves a new value judgement, affecting what is meant by maximization of revenue and by marginal cost. It would seem to follow that in an organization a decision of this type would require the expression of the preference of policy-makers. I do not profess to know how a policy-directive could be framed for the purpose!

Now let us alter the example. Let it be otherwise the same, but let the revenue limits be ten and twenty for one course of action and twenty-five and thirty-five for the other. It seems to be clear that in this case the man in pursuit of revenue maximization could firmly choose the twenty-five to thirty-five alternative without making any new value judgement.

There is of course a subjective judgement involved. Uncertainty is involved. As far as we know, it is only *he* who is relatively certain that the limits are twenty-five and thirty-five: only *he* who would be surprised if the revenue fell outside those limits. If other people instead of this man were in his decision position at the time he was, their opinions might be different from his. And he (or they) might be wrong in the event. Similarly for the administrator in the organization. It would seem that decisions of this type, which do not depend on the decision-maker's special taste for risks, could be delegated by the organization's policy-makers to administrators, and that the subjective judgement involved is the element of judgement which is always involved in *administration*, but which is perhaps distinguishable from the value judgement involved in *policy-making*.[24]

This section might be summarized thus. What the man working alone would mean by maximation or revenue and hence by marginal cost, would depend, not only upon his (*administrative*) views about when he should disinvest in order to reinvest, but also upon his *policy* defining the time or times at which he wished to withdraw revenue; not only upon his uncertain *administrative* judgement about revenues he could achieve in the future, but also upon his *policy* towards risk-taking. The meaning of maximization of revenue by an *organization* would depend upon the same administrative and policy-making judgements, with added complexities. These judgements are not all made by one person. The difficulties of disentangling administration and policy-making, and of devising appropriate policy-directives would probably lead to *ultra vires* policy-making. The alternative

---

[24] The influence of G. L. S. Shackle in these last few paragraphs will be apparent. Professor Shackle, who kindly read this paper in draft, suggested that the illustration of the distinction between administrative decisions and policy-making decisions might be compared with the distinction, in his *Expectation in Economics*, (1949), between deciding on the shape of a 'potential surprise curve', and choosing between two points on a 'gambler-indifference map'.

to the policy-directive, as a provision against *ultra vires* policy-making, is constant contact between policy-makers and administrators. I might add that this would limit the size of the organization in terms of numbers of members.[25]

[25] For helpful comment on the draft of this paper, I should like to thank particularly Mr Jack Wiseman and Professors G. L. S. Shackle, H. A. Simon and H. M. Robertson.

9

Uncertainty, costs, and collectivist economic planning

JACK WISEMAN

First published in *Economica* (May 1953).

I INTRODUCTION

The purpose of this paper is to consider the possibility, in conditions of uncertainty, of utilizing a marginal-cost 'rule' to distribute resources between uses in an economy in which there is consumers' sovereignty, with freedom of choice of goods and occupations, but in which factors of production cannot be privately owned and exploited.[1]

It will be argued that in conditions of uncertainty (i.e. once the fact of time is admitted), the marginal-cost rule, as normally framed, gives no clear guidance to those responsible for the organization of production in such an economy. Attempts to re-interpret the rule in such a way as to take account of uncertainty preclude the possibility of a direct check on the efficiency of collectivist managers in obeying that rule. Any indirect, *objective,* check used as a supplement to the marginal rule will in fact supplant that rule as the directive for managerial effort, and in any case no completely objective check is possible. Further, what-ever rule or check is adopted, imperfectly competitive behaviour is to be expected in the absence of detailed regulation to control it.

In these circumstances the most satisfactory distribution of resources seems likely to be obtained by an instruction to collectiv-ist managers similar to the profit-maximization 'rule' of the market economy. Identification of the managerial and the public interest would then have to be sought through the detailed regulation of managerial behaviour, in much the way that the government in a

[1] Such an economy will be referred to hereafter as a 'liberal collectivist' economy.

market economy attempts to regulate imperfectly competitive behaviour by entrepeneurs.[2]

The competitive market economy

The 'rule' to be discussed derives from the classical model of the perfectly competitive market economy, and is best understood in relation to that model. It was elucidated in the course of controversy as to the possibility of distributing productive factors efficiently between uses in an economy in which such factors were owned collectively.[3]

In this competitive market economy resources are privately owned and exploited. They are also, in the perfectly competitive model, perfectly divisible and perfectly mobile between uses. Producers are assumed to act in the light of known data; i.e. their task is the combination of factors of production with known prices in the production of products to be sold at known prices. The distribution of resources between uses is carried out by an administrative mechanism, the characteristics of which are profit maximization and a system of competitive markets in which buyers and sellers compete. With such a mechanism producers' decisions about the use of resources are determined by *opportunity cost*; i.e. the use of resources in the chosen way is the result of an assessment of the revenues to be obtained by their use in any other way, the greatest of these forgone alternative revenues being the opportunity cost.

---

[2] While the argument presented is related to the functioning of a liberal collectivist economy, it has a direct bearing on problems arising in a 'mixed' society such as our own. It is relevant, for example, to a consideration of the pricing policy of public utilities which is normally discussed in relation to similar rules. This is a question the writer hopes to take up in a later paper.

[3] Much of the early discussion has been brought together in two sets of reprints of relevant articles: *Collectivist Economic Planning*, ed. F. A. Hayek (which includes L. von Mises's pioneer article, 'Economic Calculus in the Socialist Commonwealth') and *On the Economic Theory of Socialism*, ed. Benjamin E. Lipincott (which includes reprints of articles by O. Lange and F. M. Taylor suggesting and elaborating the use of marginal criteria). A number of other papers on the subject were published in the *Economic Journal* and *Review of Economic Studies* during the 1930s, and a marginal 'rule' was elaborated by (*inter alia*) A. P. Lerner in *Economics of Control* (1944).

With the conditions of the model the process described must result in an 'efficient' distribution of resources between uses in the sense that, with given consumer incomes, no reallocation of factors or products between uses could increase the satisfaction of any one consumer without reducing that of another. Since all relevant factor and product values are assumed known, there is no *doubt* about the production decisions to be taken by individual producers. The subjective (opportunity) costs have an objective counterpart in lists of known factor prices, which are in effect the sole content of the opportunity-cost decision. The producers' task is simply the pricing of money inputs (i.e. sums of known factor prices) and product outputs, in the case of some production plan, and the relating of this certain result to the money values of products forgone, the prices of these products also being known. Different individuals in similar circumstances should make identical assessments and reach identical decisions. That is, the opportunity-cost concept in such conditions is merely a reassertion of the fundamental economic problem of *scarcity*; it contains no element either of uncertainty or of judgement.

The competitive model as normally set out nevertheless contains an indirect check on efficiency in resource distribution, implicit in the mechanism of competitive profit maximization. It is a property of the ideally efficient situation that producers' total money revenues will equal their total money outlays (including payment for their own services). Inefficiency in production (and hence in resource distribution) results in a money loss which indicates a need to redistribute resources. That is, the final check on the efficiency of the individual firm would be the bankruptcy court. However, the idea that firms can be 'extra-marginal' (in this sense of money outlays exceeding money revenues) requires the introduction of time into the analysis in some form, since otherwise it is difficult to explain, in the light of the assumptions of the competitive model, how the resources came to be in that use or why there is not an instantaneous readjustment removing all extra-marginal production. This difficulty is usually circumvented, not by introducing a problem of *judgement* by relaxing the assumptions about knowledge, but by retaining the assumptions about knowledge and introducing time only as a modification of the assumptions about mobility. Only some of the productive factors are now fully free to move; losses can therefore be incurred as a result of the use of temporarily immobile factors, if the data on which the decisions were taken change after that use was decided upon.

A solution along these lines is uncomfortable in two important and related respects. The producer plans his productive activities in terms of factor and product prices of which it is assumed he has knowledge. It appears that he does not take possible future changes into account in reaching his decisions. If this is because the assumptions imply *knowledge* of future prices, and these are the prices which influence decisions whenever relevant, then how can the data change so as to create extra-marginality, since the change was foreseen? If, on the other hand, future conditions are not assumed known, then how can the producer plan in terms of known prices? Associated with this problem is the difficulty of establishing a precise relationship between mobility and time: the concept of the long period as a period in which all factors are free to move seems to make sense only if regarded as a planning period – i.e. a subjective notion about future activity sufficiently distant for all resource uses to be replanned. But such an interpretation appears to imply the need for foresight and judgement, which are ruled out by the perfect-competition assumptions.

The liberal collectivist economy

This then is the model from which the cost rule of the liberal collectivist economy derives. As has been said, a liberal collectivist economy is one in which resources cannot be privately owned and exploited. With this reservation the same freedom of choice of goods and occupations pertains as in a competitive market economy.[4]

The administrative mechanism of profit maximization is replaced in the liberal collectivist economy by a 'marginal rule'.

[4] An economy of this kind is discussed (e.g.) by A. P. Lerner, *Economics of Control*, and E. F. M. Durbin, *Problems of Economic Planning*.

This rule has several formulations;[5] the most general one is the rule that managers of collectivist enterprises, working through a system of competitive markets similar to that of the market economy, should produce that output which makes marginal (money) cost equal to price. The origins of this rule are to be found in the model of the competitive market economy. It is a property of the 'efficient' situation in such an economy that marginal money cost (i.e. the sum of known prices of marginal factor inputs) of producing each product must be equal to the price for which the product can be sold. This equality is merely another way of expressing the fact that profit is being maximized, since in the conditions postulated a maximum profit (excess of revenues over outlays) is made when marginal cost is equal to price.

This is a *property of the market economy model*, an incidental result of the operation of the administrative mechanism of profit maximization in the rarified conditions of perfect competition. It is no one's purpose to make marginal cost equal to price. But in the liberal collectivist economy this incidental property becomes a principle of administration, by following which, it is argued[6] a liberal collectivist economy could not only effect an efficient distribution of resources, but could do so more quickly and accurately than a market economy, because a broader survey of the data relevant to his decisions could be made available to each collectivist manager.

III TIME AND UNCERTAINTY

Once we admit that the future is unknown, analysis of the behaviour of producers in terms of adaptation to *known* future conditions becomes irrelevant. It is therefore necessary to ask how the admission of time and uncertainty affects the administrative mechanism of the market economy and of the liberal collectivist

---

[5] e.g. Lerner, *Economics of Control*, formulates five conditions relating marginal private and social benefit, cost, etc. Durbin, *Problems of Economic Planning*, (paper VIII), has suggested the use of marginal-value products. These differences do not affect the substance of the argument.

[6] e.g. Lange (in *On the Economic Theory of Socialism* pp. 89-90,) Durbin (*Problems of Economic Planning*, p. 50), P. M. Sweezy, *Socialism*, p. 231.

economy. The task of the producer is now to decide, on the basis of *his own estimates* about likely future conditions, between the possible alternative courses of action open to him at any point in time. Present prices and conditions are relevant only in so far as they provide a basis for judgements about the future. There is now no reason to suppose that individuals in similar circumstances will make the same assessments and hence reach the same decisions.

The administrative mechanism of competitive profit maximization can still function in the market economy, but the 'efficient' distribution of resources between uses must now take account of the use of *new* resources and of the development of *new* products. An excess of money revenues over money outlays, once the element of judgement inevitable with uncertainty is admitted, is no longer necessary evidence of an inefficient distribution of resources; it may be due simply to exceptional skill in forecasting. But at the same time the fact of uncertainty makes the association of competitive behaviour and profit maximization, on which the market-economy model depends, less generally acceptable. The desire to reduce uncertainty by gaining control of the uncertain variables must be an important motive in attempts to eliminate competition. Uncertainty thus implies the need for positive government policy to ensure *competitive* behaviour in pursuit of profit maximization, since only such behaviour conduces to an efficient distribution of resources. The difficulty in framing such a policy lies in distinguishing those factors which are the inevitable accompaniment of ignorance and uncertainty and those which arise simply out of a desire to maximize net revenue in an environment characterized by these things.

It is no longer possible, once uncertainty is admitted, to interpret the opportunity-cost problem as one of scarcity alone, to be solved by a choice between alternative factor inputs and product outputs with all prices known. That is, opportunity cost is no longer a simple question of summation and comparison of known data. Prices and other variables have to be estimated: opportunity-cost decisions involve uncertainty (and therefore judgement) as well as scarcity. The cost problem now arises as a *choice between alternative plans of action*, i.e. a choice between a series of estimates of the outlays likely to be incurred and the revenues likely to be obtained as a result of the adoption of particular alternative courses of action. Costs are in fact incurred when decisions are made; to understand the use of resources over time it is necessary to go back to the decisions which decided that use, and to understand cost requires consideration of the *estimated forgone alternative revenue* associated with the decision when taken. These forgone alternatives (i.e. discarded plans) not then implemented may in fact never be implemented at all.[7] But in the circumstances of the market economy errors in the alternatives considered by any one producer do tend to be adjusted by the ability of others to take advantage of his oversight.

Since opportunity costs cannot be treated simply as known money costs, but must be considered as estimates of forgone alternative revenues, it is no longer very useful in conditions of uncertainty to speak of equality of marginal money cost and price as a property of an efficient resource distribution. This is unimportant in a market economy, since the equality comprises no part of its administrative mechanism. Uncertainty creates conditions in which it is to be expected that the mechanism of profit maximization in competitive markets will function imperfectly and will require positive government action to support it. But the final check on efficiency is still the bankruptcy court, and difficulties about the interpretation of the marginal-cost–price equation are unimportant to its functioning. In fact the admission of uncertainty disposes of those difficulties of the comptetitive market economy model which arise out of the association of time with resource mobility only. Once the assumptions about knowledge are dropped, 'extra-marginality' becomes reasonable; it is a function both of accuracy in forecasting and of speed of reaction to change (i.e. flexibility in coordination and the replanning of activities).

The problem is of greater importance in a liberal collectivist

---

[7] A decision to build a particular type of bridge over a river, for example, is likely to mean that alternative plans concerned with other types of bridges, considered *ex ante*, will never be implemented.

economy: it follows from the nature of the opportunity-cost problem that an instruction to equate marginal money cost and money price in conditions of uncertainty gives no clear guidance to collectivist managers as to their productive behaviour. Thus the rule requires reformulation. The most appropriate reformulation would appear to be in terms of *anticipated objective outlays*. The marginal cost of any decision must be the displaced alternative revenue which would have accrued from some alternative use of the resources concerned. To obtain this figure requires a comparison of alternative sets of *ex ante* budget calculations. Each set of calculations gives the expected revenues and outlays involved in the production of each of the two relevant outputs of some product. The *budgeted* marginal cost is the difference between the outlay and revenue calculations in the case of the best forgone alternative budget.[8]

The question is whether the rule, thus reinterpreted, can provide an unambiguous guide for collectivist managers, and whether it enables a check to be made on the efficiency of the distribution of resources between uses similar to that provided by profit in the market economy.

IV THE RULE AS REFORMULATED

If no rule other than the marginal cost rule is used,[9] and that rule is interpreted as a relationship between *budgeted* marginal cost (as defined) and *budgeted* price, is there any check on the efficiency of the distribution of resources between uses?

A *direct* check on efficiency requires a check on decisions in relation to results. But only one of the *budgeted* outlays becomes a *realized objective* outlay, since only one plan can in fact be decided upon. Thus the 'marginal cost' with which we are concerned rests upon a judgement by the manager as to the accuracy of his estimates about the revenues which would have accrued had the forgone alternatives in fact been chosen. That is,

[8] This formulation is based upon that used by G. F. Thirlby, 'The Ruler', reprinted here, pages 163-98.

[9] i.e. no relation between total revenues and total outlays is postulated (see section VI).

estimation of marginal cost involves an inevitable element of personal judgement. There may in some cases be a check upon the 'reasonableness' of estimates. This is the more likely to be so the more the alternatives considered relate to the production of known things by known methods. The imponderables, and with them the difficulty of a direct check on efficiency, become the greater the more unique or novel are the matters with which decisions are concerned. All decisions about new and major investments of resources seem likely to involve important imponderables of this kind; it appears that those decisions likely to be most important to efficiency will be those upon which no adequate check can be made with the rule as now interpreted.

There is a further difficulty not yet considered. How is it to be decided whether the plans considered are the relevant ones? Suppose, for example, there is a difference of opinion about market prospects between the manager and the checking authority. If the checking authority can impose its views on the manager, then decisions about resource distribution (i.e. about costs) inhere in the checking authority; the decisions of that authority become the ones relevant to a check on efficiency, and the same questions have to be asked about them as about the decisions of the collectivist manager. The removal of investment decisions from managers robs them of their primary function from an economic viewpoint: the concentration of decisions in another authority shifts the relevance of the analysis towards that authority. It becomes appropriate to consider the *joint* decisions of the two bodies, in so far as any decisions are left with the manager at all. In effect, the vesting of such powers in the checking authority carries with it the need to abandon rules of the kind considered here, and to adopt some kind of centralist scheme[10] for the distribution of resources.

If the check is made at intervals, it must also be taken into account by the checking authority that estimates are subject to

[10] Cf. H. D. Dickinson, 'Price Formation in a Socialist Economy', *Economic Journal* (December 1943), and *The Economics of Socialism*, pp. 104-5, and M. Dobb, *Political Economy and Capitalism*, chapter VIII. Dobb advocates such a scheme in preference to the competitive solution using a marginal rule; Dickinson merely suggests it as a possible practical alternative.

constant revision; skill and speed in revision must in effect be recognized as factors in efficient behaviour. But the existence of, and need for, such revision of plans is a further obstacle to a sensible check by an outside authority.

Thus, if the only criterion used is a marginal-cost – marginal-revenue relationship, as now defined, there can be no possibility of an unambiguous check on managerial efficiency through the use of these magnitudes. The most that can be done is to check efficiency, in the limited sense of correct forecasting, in the plan actually chosen. If both the manager's *planned* results and his *realized* results can be stated in unambiguously objective (empirical) terms, and if the plan is unambiguously his own, the comparison of planned and realized results provides (*ex post*) a check on *forecasting* efficiency *in respect only of the plan actually chosen*. But this provides only a very partial check, since it cannot explain whether that plan should have been chosen at all.

There seems little possibility of a direct check upon whether the marginal-cost rule has been obeyed: can the liberal collectivist economy then function without such a check? There are two possibilities: abandonment of any attempt to check obedience to the rule and the use of some other indirect check in the form of a relationship between total revenues and total outlays, *ex post*, arising out of the plan actually implemented.

V THE RULE WITHOUT A CHECK

The rule as reformulated does not carry with it any relationship between total revenues and total outlays. In the absence of some further instruction there seems no reason why a manager should not obey it whilst producing continuously at a loss.[11] The manager can check his own efficiency (i.e. the extent to which his activity conduces to an efficient distribution of resources, as defined), or can have it checked by someone else, only through the fulfilment or non-fulfilment of the plans he elects to implement. And even the meaning of the results of this limited check is not un-

---

[11] i.e. if no plan considered is expected to yield a surplus of revenues over outlays.

ambiguous: what degree of nonfulfilment should suggest to a manager (e.g.) that he should cease producing?

The manager is not told what things to take into account in drawing up budgets. As a result, it is to be expected that he will often base his policy partly upon judgements about the policy of his close rivals, since he considers this to be realistic budgeting, unless he is instructed to ignore such related policies when compiling his own. But how could such an instruction be formulated or enforced? Would it be conducive to efficiency in any case to attempt to make managers act on the basis of assumptions they believed to be unrealistic? But, in the absence of any guidance or control beyond the 'rule', it is a short step from this 'ogliopolistic competition' to attempts to make budgeting easier by reaching policy agreements with rivals – that is, to collusive, imperfectly competitive behaviour.

Knowledge of rivals' reactions gained in this way is not, of course, what is envisaged by those who suggest that a liberal collectivist economy could reach an equilibrium more quickly and efficiently because more data on which to base decisions could be placed at the disposal of each manager. Their argument is quite other: its basis is the idea that more information could be made available to all managers by the use of some kind of central information service. But there is a logical fallacy here. What each manager wants is knowledge of the firm plans of other managers, on which to base his own plans. But plainly not *all* managers can have such information unless either all plans are imposed from above (a possibility already rejected) or the plans are made *jointly* through some form of collusive (non-competitive) behaviour.

If there is to be no check on the efficiency of managers in attempting to obey the 'rule', the choice of the managers themselves becomes particularly important to efficiency. The market economy depends, for the correction of errors of judgement, upon the ability of any producer to take advantage of the oversights of others. From this point of view, any restriction of the field of choice of managers is a restriction upon possibly useful entrants and hence a curb upon efficiency. On the other hand, if *anyone* can be a collectivist manager, how are the managers of banking institutions to decide who is to have control over liquid resources, and how much?[12] Presumably they would have to try to judge whether the applicant was capable of equating marginal cost and marginal revenue, although, once the funds have been granted and used, those granting them become dependent upon the applicants' view as to whether this has been done or not.

It has sometimes been suggested, as an alternative, that managers should qualify by some kind of competitive examination.[13] Apart from the difficulty of formulating a suitable test, it still has to be decided what those who have qualified become entitled to. Can they all demand control over the same volume of liquid resources or does the volume controlled vary with seniority or is there some other means of deciding?

In the absence of a check on the *outcome* of managerial behaviour, then, managers will be uncertain as to the implications of the consequences of their own act, no other authority will be in a position to check the efficiency of those acts, oligopolistic and collusive behaviour is to be expected, and there is no clear criterion for the allocation of control over resources between managers. Therefore, while there can be no direct check on efficiency in resource distribution through the marginal relationship, an indirect objective check is plainy desirable; the problem is to discover one.

VI CHECKS THROUGH NET REVENUE

Since the marginal check is ineffective, the only possibility remaining lies in a check on efficiency depending upon the relationship between total money revenues and total money outlays. There are two possible relationships between total revenues and total outlays which might be accepted as a standard of efficiency: equality of total outlays and total revenues, and maximization of the excess of receipts over outlays.

[12] I leave aside the question of where *these* managers come from, and whether they can interpret the marginal rule, if they are expected to follow it.

[13] e.g. Durbin appears to envisage 'planning' of this kind being taken care of by extension of the Civil Service: *Problems of Economic Planning*, paper VI.

The equality criterion is indicative of an efficient resource distribution only in the conditions of the perfectly competitive model. Uncertainty introduces the possibility of a difference between revenues and outlays due to exceptional ability in forecasting, and such a difference cannot be considered incompatible with efficiency. Thus to use such a check might entail the abandonment of plans which producers would expect to yield greater revenues for the same outlays. Since such plans would be implemented if the marginal rule were followed, a criterion of equality of total revenues and total outlays is incompatible with the marginal rule, as reformulated to take account of uncertainty. A check on the equality of total revenues and total outlays would not operate as a supplement, for the checking authority, to the marginal rule to be followed by managers, but would in fact replace that marginal rule as the directive to managerial effort.

The most likely result of the use of an equality criterion is secret budgeting for revenue surpluses on the part of managers. These surpluses can then be 'lost' if they seem likely to materialize, so that the required equality is always achieved. There is also an inducement to non-competitive behaviour. Oligopolistic situations arise for reasons already argued, and the realization of interdependence must lead to a realization that the equality of total revenues and total outlays is more easily budgeted for and achieved if some variables can be ruled out of account by collusive action.

The seeming objectivity of a check on the equality of total receipts and total outlays is in any case misleading. The check must by its nature be periodic, and to obtain the requisite receipt and outlay figures for any period it is necessary to place a valuation upon the *physical resources* of the organization at the beginning and end of the period concerned. This valuation rests upon a judgement about possibilities of future revenues from the use of the resources in question – a judgement incapable of complete check by another person or body.[14]

An instruction to managers to maximize the excess of money

[14] A valuation problem similar to this arises, of course, in a market economy. In either economy there is more possibility of an approximate check than was the case with the marginal rule, since wide fluctuations in successive valuations of particular assets appear reasonably clearly and need to be explained.

receipts over money outlays raises fewer problems. It is compatible with the marginal rule, in that the latter would lead to the same choice of plan as does the instruction to maximize net revenues. But the marginal rule is no longer needed; once net revenue is accepted as the guide, the marginal rule is no more important to a check on efficiency than it is in the market economy. On grounds of convenience it is therefore better dispensed with. There is with this revenue rule some kind of check on efficiency, in the size of the net revenue, and some possibility of formulating a criterion for the allocation of resources between producers, probably in terms of the size of past net revenues. The utility of the net-revenue rule does, however, depend upon two preconditions.[15] First there must be similar opportunity for individual producers to take advantage of the oversight of others as was the case in the market economy, so that absence of net revenue is a clear indication of a need to redistribute resources and its persistence in the case of any one manager an indication of the inefficiency of that manager. Second, the behaviour of managers in maximizing net revenue must be conducive to efficiency, i.e. it must be competitive. But since in conditions of uncertainty the net-revenue rule provides the same kind of incentive to imperfectly competitive, collusive and monopolistic behaviour as in the market economy, the net-revenue rule could only hope to function reasonably efficiently given detailed government regulation of revenue maximizing behaviour of kinds incompatible with efficiency in the distribution of resources.

VII CONCLUSIONS

The most effective general rule for managers of enterprises in a liberal collectivist economy seems to be one similar in nature to the profit-maximization 'rule' of the market economy. This appears to be the only rule offering the possibility of any external check on managerial efficiency; the 'marginal' rule is of no value in this respect. The 'net-revenue' rule also makes possible the

[15] It also depends upon a reasonably satisfactory solution of the valuation problem, which is still relevant (see note 15 above).

formulation of a criterion for the allocation of resources to producers in the future in terms of achieved past net revenues. The use of the 'net-revenue' rule (or, for that matter, any other of the rules examined) provides an incentive for non-competitive behaviour on the part of producers, which would need to be tackled by detailed regulation similar to that required in a market economy.[16]

It may be that imperfectly competitive behaviour would be less of a problem in a liberal collectivist economy, because the link between personal income and net revenue is less direct and the desire to act in the public interest more important. But it must be borne in mind that in the case of joint-stock organization the link is also indirect, and also that it is implicit in the whole liberal collectivist pattern that the incentive to obey the rule (in this case to maximize net revenue), whatever that incentive might be, is such that producers treat it seriously.

If the preceding argument is sound, and the need for a net-revenue rule is accepted, then the only difference of economic importance between the two systems lies in this possibility of greater simplicity in the control of imperfectly competitive behaviour in the liberal collectivist economy, balanced against the loss of the 'unparalleled simplicity and force' of the motive of private profit in the market economy. It becomes relevant at least to consider whether a competitive market economy might not function more efficiently even while accepting such impairment of the force of the profit motive as resulted from policies of income redistribution satisfactory to collectivists.[17]

[16] Where, in the nature of things, competition cannot function (e.g. for technological reasons), revenue maximization with detailed regulation may be unsatisfactory; a combination of regulation and some given net-revenue objective might operate more efficiently. This is the public utility pricing problem of the market economy.

[17] I am particularly indebted to the valuable suggestions and criticisms of Mr G. F. Thirlby, and to my colleagues who commented on the article in draft.

10

The theory of public utility price—
an empty box

JACK WISEMAN

First published in *Oxford Economic Papers*
(Oxford University Press, 1957), ix.

Criticism of the analytical validity of public-utility pricing 'rules' has resulted over a period of years in the introduction of successive modifications to the original simple (though not unambiguous) marginal-cost 'rule', culminating in advocacy of the two-part tariff and of the 'club' principle.[1] While these pricing rules have been regarded with scepticism as practical guides to public-utility pricing policy,[2] however, there has perhaps been a less general appreciation of the cumulative weight of the theoretical objections to all such rules; there is still interest in the discovery of a 'right' rule, and in the estimation of the 'marginal' or other costs of particular public-utility enterprises.

It will be argued in this article that no general pricing rule or

---

[1] There is a good deal of literature on this subject. For a useful first list the reader is referred to the end of the lucid survey of the topic by Professor E. H. Phelps Brown in chapter viii of his book, *A Course in Applied Economics*. Cf. also G. F. Thirlby, 'The Ruler', reprinted here, pages 163-98; William Vickrey, 'Some Objections to Marginal Cost Pricing', *Journal of Political Economy*, 56 (1948); Gabriel Dessus, 'The General Principles of Rate Fixing in Public Utilities', *International Economic Papers*, No. 1 (translation of a report presented to the Congress of the Union Internationale des Producteurs et Distributeurs d'Énergie Électrique, 1949); and T. Wilson, 'The Inadequacy of the Theory of the Firm as a Branch of Welfare Economics', *Oxford Economic Papers* (February 1952). This list is not comprehensive.

The historical development of the rules and their analytical origins is set out in two articles by Nancy Ruggles: 'The Welfare Basis of the Marginal Cost Pricing Principle' and 'Recent Developments in the Theory of Marginal Cost Pricing', *Review of Economic Studies*, Nos. 42 and 43, (1949-50).

Specific references have been given in the text only where articles are of particular relevance to the issue concerned.

[2] The scepticism is by no means universal: e.g. The *Report of the Committee on National Policy for the use of Fuel and Power Resources* (Cmd. 8647), 1952 (Ridley Report), considered the question of whether coal should be priced at marginal cost, and half the members of the Committee in fact favoured the use of some form of marginal-cost pricing.

rules can be held unambiguously to bring about an 'optimum' use of resources by public utilities even in theory. Indeed, failing some universally acceptable theory of the public economy, the economist can offer no *general* guidance at all to a government having to decide a price policy for such utilities. To demonstrate this, it will be necessary to begin with a brief survey of the criticisms of the simple marginal-cost rule. This will provide the basis for a demonstration of the possibly less familiar (though no less decisive) analytical shortcomings of the two-part tariff rule both in its simple form and as modified by a club principle. In conclusion the effect of uncertainty on the analysis will be examined, and the broad implications of the whole argument for public policy will be suggested.

I THE MARGINAL-COST RULE

Any discussion of a 'right' price presupposes criteria of the public interest against which alternative suggested prices can be judged. The criteria from which the marginal-cost rule stems are derived from the analytical model of a perfectly competitive market economy, in which entrepreneurs are assumed to have perfect foresight[3] and it is a property of the long run equilibrium situation that, given the distribution of income between consumers, no transfer of factors between uses could increase the satisfactions of one consumer without reducing those of another. The optimum conditions of 'economic welfare' are consequently said to be fulfilled by the model. For the competitive firm it is an incidental property of the long-run situation that marginal cost (money outlay on factors)=average cost=price of product. Consequently this equality can be regarded as evidence of the existence of an 'ideal' situation, and pricing at marginal cost has accordingly been proposed as a general pricing rule (e.g. as the 'principle of

[3] This assumption is of course highly unrealistic; there are also tenable arguments for the view that it is internally inconsistent (cf., e.g., my 'Uncertainty, Costs, and Collectivist Economic Planning', reprinted here, pages 227-43. For the purposes of this article, the model is accepted for the present and criticism is developed within its assumptions. Section III discusses the consequences of relaxation of the foresight assumption.

administration' of a collectivist economy).[4] But public utility enter-prises are not perfectly competitive firms. By the usual definition an important part of the factors they employ are not perfectly divisible; they can be obtained only in large physical units, or in a durable or specific form, or both. Also the technically efficient production unit is large relative to the possible size of the market, and the utilities are public bodies, often with considerable powers of monopoly protected by law. In such circumstances there may be no possible price equal both to marginal cost (the money out-lay required to increase output marginally) and average cost (which includes outlays on the 'indivisible' factors excluded from marginal cost). It therefore appears to be necessary to decide whether price should be fixed equal to the one or to the other.

The argument for pricing such public-utility products at average cost is simply that 'each tub should stand on its own bottom'; all money outlays which would have been avoided if a product had not been produced should be recovered in the price charged by the utility. But the advocates of marginal-cost pricing find this unconvincing. Some of the outlays included in average cost, they argue, are not current opportunity costs but are either payments for technically indivisible factors or past out-payments for durable and specific factors. The inclusion of these outlays in the price charged therefore prevents the achievement of the optimum welfare conditions, which (it is said) require that additional consumption of a good or service should be possible at a price not greater than the additional costs (money outlays) necessarily incurred in providing for that consumption. Accord-ingly such outlays should be ignored, and the product priced at marginal cost, even though the enterprise runs at a loss as a result.

Clearly the proposal for pricing at marginal cost requires an explanation of how the consequent losses are to be financed. Hotelling, who originated much of the discussion,[5] suggested the

[4] For a critique of this collectivist 'rule' and of the model from which it derives, cf. my 'Uncertainty, Costs and Collectivist Economic Planning'.

[5] H. Hotelling, 'The General Welfare in Relation to Problems of Taxation and of Railway and Utility Rates', *Econometrica*, (1938). Hotelling's paper was stimu-lated by the much earlier work of Dupuit, around 1844. The relevant papers have been collected and reprinted with comments by Mario di Bernardi and Luigi Einaudi, 'De l'utilite et de sa mesure', *La Riforma soziale* (Turin 1932). One of the

use of particular types of taxes. The inclusion of charges for 'overheads' (past outlays on indivisible factors) was itself, he said, of the nature of a tax. But there were other and preferable taxes (lumpsum taxes on inheritance, income taxes, etc.) which did not offend against the welfare criteria since they affected only the *distribution* and not the *size* of the national income. If such taxes were used, and public-utility prices were equated with marginal cost, the optimum welfare conditions would be achieved. Later writers have been justifiably sceptical of the possibility of a tax system that would meet Hotelling's conditions.[6] In particular income taxes (on which he expected to have to rely) can be shown to affect the marginal welfare conditions directly. In any case the proposal is open to an even more fundamental objection: the welfare 'ideal' relates to a *given* distribution of income, and that distribution of income must be altered by the proposed taxes (unless these fall on consumers of public-utility products in proportion to their consumption, which is effectively a return to average-cost pricing). Thus to advocate marginal-cost pricing and the meeting of losses out of taxation is to advocate acceptance of income redistribution from non-consumers to consumers of public utility products. The welfare criteria provide no justification for an interpersonal comparison of this kind. In other words any government deciding upon a pricing policy for public utilities has to take simultaneously into account the effects of its decisions upon the fulfilment of the welfare optima (and hence the size of the national product) and upon the distribution of incomes, and there is nothing in the welfare analysis that provides guidance as to the 'right' policy about the second of these.[7]

most interesting papers, 'On the Measurement of Utility of Public Works', *Annales des Ponts et Chaussees*, (1844), is published in translation in *International Economic papers*, No. 2.

[6] Cf. (*inter alia*) J. E. Meade, 'Price and Output Policy of State Enterprise', *Economic Journal* (1944), pp. 321-8, and 'Rejoinder' pp. 337-9; P. A. Samuelson, *The Foundations of Economic Analysis*, p. 240; R. H. Coase, 'The Marginal Cost Controversy', *Economica*, N. S. (1946), pp. 169-82; H. P. Wald, 'The Classical Indictment of Indirect Taxation', *Quarterly Journal of Economics* (1945), pp. 577-97; I. M. D. Little, 'Direct v. Indirect Taxes', *Economic Journal* (1951), pp. 577-84.

[7] There is implicit in Hotelling's argument (and in that of writers who have supported him) the view that the welfare criteria can be extended to cover situations involving changes in the distribution of income. Some attempt has been

The reason why marginal-cost pricing raises these difficulties is to be found in the fact that the arguments for the marginal-cost rule are logically unsatisfactory in that they attempt to apply welfare criteria derived from an analysis concerned with marginal variations in factor use to a problem whose essence is discrete change; the whole basis of the public-utility discussion is the indivisibility of the factors employed by such utilities. The results of this attempt are not only of dubious relevance to policy; they are also uncertain in themselves.

The type of indivisibility most emphasized in the discussion is that created by the durability and specificity of factors (*temporal* indivisibility).[8] It is enlightening to examine the nature of such indivisibility more closely. It has been shown that the marginal-cost 'rule' distinguishes between 'current' and 'past' opportunity-cost problems. Once the sacrifices necessary to create a durable and specific asset have been made, it is argued, no further opportunity costs are created by its later use. The opportunity costs having been borne in the past, no account should be taken of them in deciding current prices,[9] even though, as has been demonstrated,

made to support this position by reformulating the compensation principle (that a decision about a particular measure can be made only if all who would lose by it can be, and in fact are, compensated for their loss) in such a way that only the *possibility* and not the *fact* of compensation is necessary for an economic policy to be accepted as beneficial. However, it has been amply demonstrated that interpersonal comparisons cannot be avoided in this way (cf. M. W. Reder, *Studies in the Theory of Welfare Economics*; I. M. D. Little, *Critique of Welfare Economics*; W. J. Baumol, *Welfare Economics and the Theory of the State*, and the references cited therein). The debate will not be discussed in the text; all that has to be established is that the simultaneous decisions referred to therein are unavoidable, and that the welfare criteria provide guidance about only one of these decisions.

[8] The distinction between this type of indivisibility and *technical* indivisibility is not always made clear in the literature (for a clear separation, cf. e.g. Phelps Brown, *A Course in Applied Economics*, and Coase ,'The Marginal Cost Controversy').

In contrast with the present section, the discussion of the club principle in Section II will be conducted with reference mainly to technical indivisibility. Such indivisibility amounts to no more than the fact that the whole of a productive factor must be employed in order to obtain *any part* of the total product of that factor, so that if the factor is an economic good it must have *current* alternative uses, and therefore a price (e.g. if a railway carriage can be attached to different trains, opportunity costs are incurred in attaching it to any one train. But no opportunity costs may be incurred in allowing one more passenger to travel once the carriage is attached).

[9] Dupuit's argument against bridge tolls ('De l'utilité et de sa mesure') is the *locus classicus* of this argument.

this results in losses and in income redistribution. Such an argument rests upon a dubious interpretation of the welfare criteria. The long period, from which the welfare postulates derive, is a situation in which all factors of production are considered to be perfectly mobile; this would seem to imply consideration of a time period at least as long as the lowest common multiple of the life span of all the factors of production concerned. If the marginal-cost rule is conceived in terms of a time period shorter than this, then not all the opportunity costs requisite to the manufacture of the product concerned can be imputed to that product, and the time period chosen must itself be arbitrary, so that the marginal-cost rule becomes simply a statement that outlays on factors of some specified durability should be ignored in deciding prices (i.e. should be treated as 'past' outlays). The figure treated as marginal cost will thus depend upon the time period selected.[10]

The division of outlays into 'past' and 'current' is clearly unsatisfactory, and the implications of durability and specificity become less obscure if such a division is abandoned and the problem is presented in the form of a planning process through time. All opportunity-cost decisions, taken at one moment in time, fix the use of factors during some future period of time. All factors embodied in plans implemented by entrepreneurs, that is, become durable and specific to some degree; new opportunity costs arise in respect of them only when their use can be replanned. This being so, it is not possible to separate opportunity costs into two groups, 'past' and 'current'. The most that can be said is that some kinds of factors lend themselves more readily than do others to frequent replanning. There is a difference, for example, between the extent to which factor use will be 'fixed' over time by the implementation of a decision to build a railway bridge and by a decision to hire a railway porter. But the difference is one not of kind but of degree; it is possible to conceive of an 'ordering' of opportunity-costs decisions in accordance with the length of time for which they commit factors to particular uses (i.e. create

[10] Cf. T. Wilson, 'The Inadequacy of the Theory of the Firm as a Branch of Welfare Economics'.

specificity and durability), but it is not possible to divide such decisions into a group that involves a commitment over time and another group that does not.

Marginal (opportunity) cost in these circumstances is represented by a forgone revenue. The use of factors of production in the entrepreneur's selected plan excludes them from use in some other plan; marginal cost is the forgone marginal revenue from the best plan necessarily excluded because the chosen plan is selected. But the alternative uses to which factors can be put, and hence the opportunity-cost valuation imputed to them in the planning process, will depend on the time period in terms of which the entrepreneur's plans are themselves conceived; marginal cost will consequently vary according to the time span of the production plans considered. Thus the meaning and results of an instruction to equate marginal cost and price will be determined by the length of the planning period to which the marginal cost is intended to refer. At one extreme the period chosen may be as long as the lowest common multiple of the life periods of the assets required to produce the public-utility product, and the marginal-cost rule would then give a price that took into account the whole of the sacrifice of alternative consumption caused by the implementation of plans to manufacture the utility product. At the other extreme the consideration of 'current' opportunity costs only, if interpreted rigorously, would seem to require that products should be given away. Between these two extremes there is a range of possible marginal-cost rules, differing from each other in the planning time period chosen as appropriate and hence in the 'durable' assets they ignore and in the opportunity costs they treat as relevant to decisions about price and output.

The only time period in which all factor-use can be clearly attributed is one as long as the lowest common multiple of the life period of the assets concerned; the designation of any other (shorter) time period as the one appropriate to the rule must involve both an arbitrary decision that that period is one relevant to the computation of marginal cost and a value judgement that income should be redistributed over time towards the consumers of goods produced with relatively durable assets. The marginal cost principle thus becomes, not the assertion of a general welfare 'ideal' *but the expression of a particular value judgement, that certain long-run opportunity costs for the community as a whole should be ignored in the interests of the greater short-run utilization by consumers of specific factors of some stated degree of durability.*[11]

The only defence offered against criticism of the marginal-cost rule on such grounds lies in the introduction of a supplementary criterion: the investment principle. This requires that marginal-cost pricing should be used to decide the selling prices of public-utility products once the utilities are in existence, but that the public investment necessary to create a utility initially should be considered justified only if a perfectly discriminating monopolist could (notionally) recover its cost by charging prices that would maximize his returns. The need for such a supplementary principle to a 'general' rule is implausible. In any case the investment principle does not answer the criticisms. It still has to be decided which economic decisions are to be treated as 'investment' decisions and which as subject to the marginal cost-rule, and no principle has been suggested by reference to which such decisions might be made. Further, since the prices actually charged are to be determined by the marginal-cost rule the discussion of the effects of that rule (e.g. on income distribution) is unaffected by the introduction of the supplementary principle. It is worth pointing out further that the investment criterion itself has redistributive implications: certainly it does not appear to meet the welfare conditions in the same fashion as would a perfectly competitive market.[12]

[11] It will be appreciated that arguments based on *technical* indivisibility raise similar considerations.

[12] In the competitive market case all consumers are faced with the same system of prices: in Wicksteed's phrase, the 'terms on which alternatives are offered' are the same for all. In the other, since discrimination is admitted, each individual is considered to be faced with a different price for the purpose of deciding whether or not to make the investment. If such prices were subsequently charged, they would involve a change in the distribution of real income, and would fall under the same strictures about interpersonal comparison as the marginal-cost rule. That is, a decision taken in accordance with the investment principle might be considered as being partly concerned with the consequences for consumption of the public-utility product in question of a change in the distribution of real income. But it

The foregoing criticisms of marginal-cost pricing have been fairly widely accepted, although the precise nature of the value judgements implied in the treatment of temporal indivisibility is perhaps not generally recognized. Despite this acceptance, there still seems to be considerable support for marginal-cost pricing from those who feel that policies affecting only the *distribution* of the national income both are possible and are in some sense superior to alternative policies that would also affect its *size*. In the absence of some generally acceptable basis for preference between different income distributions, it is clear that such a position cannot be supported by logic. The two issues cannot be separated, and policies desirable in terms of the welfare criteria may therefore reasonably be rejected because a government chooses to obtain a preferred distribution of income even at the cost of some diminution of its total size. There is no escape from the very special value judgements that marginal-cost pricing implies.[13]

II THE MULTI-PART TARIFF AND THE 'CLUB'

The two- (or more) part tariff is intended to avoid the anomalies of marginal-cost pricing, in that it is designed to meet the marginal 'welfare' conditions and also to avoid problems of interpersonal comparison by raising revenues large enough to cover all outlays. The essence of the proposal is that the price to be charged should by the sum of two parts:[14] a 'marginal-cost' element determined by the increase in costs necessarily incurred in providing further consumption for an individual consumer, and a 'fixed charge' to

appears that in this respect, as with the advocacy of marginal-cost pricing, the income redistribution is treated as a problem separable from, and in some way inferior to, that of income size (as expressed in the welfare 'ideal').

[13] An illustration may help to make the point clear: A government, having decided to build a bridge out of revenue raised by taxation, might offer the services of the bridge free and ignore the source of the initial revenues in framing subsequent tax policy. Alternatively it might decide to charge tolls for (say) twenty years, accepting the reduction in use (i.e. in total income) in the interests of compensating those who had to make the initial sacrifice, or it might decide upon some other combination of current financing and compensation. The economist is without adequate criteria to judge between these alternatives.

[14] There could of course be more than two parts, depending upon the nature of the fixed factors. To introduce more simply adds complexity without affecting the logic of the argument.

cover costs which do not vary with consumption but which must be incurred if the consumer in question is to be enabled to consume at all. In this way total costs are covered and the payments made for additional consumption are kept equal to the extra costs of provision (marginal cost) alone. The problem appears to be solved, since the 'welfare' conditions are satisfied and no income redistribution seems to be implied.[15]

Unfortunately multi-part pricing provides an unambiguous solution only if the two types of costs concerned can be clearly imputed to individual consumers. In fact, when this can be done, the two parts of the price can logically be treated as the prices of separate products, each capable of clear determination by a normal market process. When these conditions do not obtain, however, the situation becomes very different. This can be seen by introducing the possibility of common costs. If problems of time are disregarded, these are simply current costs that do not vary with total output, but are necessarily incurred if *any* output is to be produced at all and *are not imputable directly to individual consumers*.[16] How should these current 'fixed and common' costs be shared between consumers? In principle limits can be set to the charges that individual consumers can and should be asked to pay, by reference to the cost of providing the indivisible service

[15] A model used by R. H. Coase, 'The Marginal Cost Controversy', gives the essentials of the argument very clearly. The model is concerned with current (technical) indivisibility only, problems of time and of common costs being abstracted therefrom. In the model a number of roads radiate from a central market and there is one consumer on each road. All costs are assumed to be currently incurred, and each consumer purchases a combination of the market product and the transport service necessary to deliver it. Transport units are sufficiently large to carry any one consumer's requirements. Thus, while the transport service is *indivisible,* in that extra units of product can be carried without cost, there are *no common costs* since one van serves only one customer and the transport cost is attributable to that consumer. In these conditions, Coase argued, the price charged should comprise a fixed charge for the transport service and a price per unit for the product. Total costs are then covered, and the additional payment for extra consumption is equal to the price of the product only (i.e. to marginal cost).

[16] Indivisibility need not imply the existence of such costs, though their presence must imply indivisibility.

The nature of the complications caused by common costs can be illustrated by replacing Coase's road-system (note 15 above) by a ring road, with the market at the centre and one van serving a number of customers around the circumference, which the van can join at any point. Clearly the pricing problem now becomes much more complex.

for them if other consumers ceased to consume, on the one hand, and the minimum possible cost of providing their addition to total consumption on the other.[17] But there may still remain a variety of possible methods of charging, and some non-arbitrary means of choosing between them is required if the multi-part tariff is to provide an unambiguous solution to the public-utility pricing problem.[18]

There is a suggested means of meeting this common-cost problem that seems to be fairly widely accepted. This is the use of the 'club' principle. This principle is not usually stated with precision; its essence appears to be the proposition that the consumers of the utility product can be treated as a club, created by the consumers to arrange both the amount of the good each individual shall consume and the amount that he shall pay for it. Then, if all 'members' (potential consumers) are asked what they would voluntarily pay as a fixed charge rather than go without the possibility of consuming a particular product at a price per unit equal to marginal cost (money outlay), and if the sum of the amounts offered would be great enough to cover the total outlays required, the service should be provided and each consumer charged that part of the common cost that he has stated his willingness to bear. It follows that the 'club' principle is likely to give rise to price discrimination, in that different individuals need not be required to pay the same amount for a similar volume of consumption. That is, the principle must imply a redistribution of real income, since consumers with given money incomes purchase

[17] In the conditions of the modification of the Coase model (note 16 above), these limits (for any one consumer) would be the total cost of providing the service ('indivisible' transport cost plus cost of goods purchased), on the one hand, and the cost of the goods alone on the other. If there were also variable costs associated with the transport service (e.g. petrol cost), then the lower limit would have to be increased by the minimum cost of transport between the consumer in question and the next nearest consumer.

[18] The problem becomes even more intractable if time is introduced into the analysis, so that the 'common costs' being considered can become past outlays on *temporally* indivisible assets. This kind of question cannot suitably be discussed without relaxing the assumptions of the competitive model. The present section therefore ignores these questions of time, which are more fully treated in the following section of the article. It will be appreciated that the criticisms of the two-part tariff and the 'club' principle in the present section are in no way invalidated by this simplification.

a technically homogeneous product at money prices differing from one consumer to another. But, it is argued, the 'club' principle allows consumers themselves to make a voluntary decision whether to accept the good and the consequent income redistribution in preference to having neither. If they, as consumers, take the first course, then this must produce a more satisfactory situation from the point of view of consumers' choice, and the optimum welfare conditions must therefore be better satisfied as a result of the use of the 'club' principle despite the consequent redistribution of income.

The 'club' principle has deficiencies serious enough to make the extent of its acceptance a matter for some surprise. The deficiencies are of two kinds. First, the value judgements being made in relation to income redistribution are difficult to justify. Second, the 'club' proposals require an unusual (and peculiar) interpretation of the concept of voluntary choice.

Income redistribution and the 'club' principle
No one suggests that the 'club' principle avoids the need for value judgements about income distribution.[19] Rather, what is implied is that 'welfare' can unambiguously be said to have been improved by a policy which meets the marginal welfare conditions, even though there is a consequent change in the distribution of income, *provided that the changed income distribution is the consequence of the 'voluntary' action of consumers*. This extension of the welfare criteria is less innocuous than might at first appear. Economic welfare, as normally defined, is concerned solely with the optimum conditions of individual choice, given the distribution of income; the objective of the public-utility discussion might be described as the discovery of a pricing policy to meet those conditions, in the special circumstances of public-utility produc-

---

[19] The 'club' argument might indeed be stated in the form that there is some distribution of income, different from the existing one, which would induce consumers to cover the costs of the utility without the need for differential charges, and that this distribution must be superior to the existing one because consumers will 'voluntarily' bring it about if allowed to do so. This form of statement brings out the similarity between the 'club' principle and the investment criterion and compensation principle (note 7 above) discussed earlier; it is therefore not surprising to find that they have similar weaknesses.

tion. But if a suggested principle of pricing would affect economic magnitudes other than the conditions of choice, then it becomes necessary to establish further policy criteria concerned with these other magnitudes, by reference to which the proposed principle can be assessed. In the present case, since income distribution is affected by the 'club' principle, criteria for choice between income distributions are required. Moreover these criteria must take the form of a statement about the *income-redistributive objectives of a government,* since it has to be recognized that the public-utility discussion (although itself conceived in relation to the conditions of individual choice) is concerned to recommend policies to be implemented by a government. *That is, income distribution is a question of public policy, and it is the attitude of the government to it, and not the attitude of particular groups of consumers, that is of significance for policy.* The value judgement implied in the 'club' principle is that if the members of the public-utility 'club' agree to a particular redistribution of income, then the government must necessarily think such a redistribution desirable. This is not plausible; there are likely to be many cases in which the 'voluntary' redistribution would be of a kind that the government dis-approved.[20] In short, once a government is committed, by the creation of a utility and the existence of common costs, to a decision about income distribution, there is no reason why it should prefer public-utility pricing policies that cover total costs by use of the 'club' principle to other policies which may or may not cover costs, but which accord better with its own attitude to redistribution. A government permitting utilities to use the 'club' principle in effect substitutes the authorities of the utility for itself as the final arbiter in matters of income distribution in this particular context.[21]

[20] An illustration used by Phelps Brown (*A Course in Applied Economics,* p. 260) makes the point very well; poor families in an area may be willing to pay more towards the provision of a playground than richer families in the same area, but there is no presumption that a government will agree that they should. The welfare criteria provide no guidance in such cases since they offer no means of choice between income distributions.

[21] These criticisms are the more striking when the restrictive assumptions of the analysis are recalled; the 'offers' made by consumers must be quite independent, since otherwise there may be no possibility of an 'agreed' set of prices because

'Voluntary' choice and the 'Club' principle

The argument for the 'club' principle depends upon the fact that the charges to which it gives rise are 'voluntarily' agreed by consumers. In general this agreement will be 'voluntary' only in the special sense that a malefactor voluntarily goes away to prison after a judge has sentenced him; he chooses the best alternative still available. To appreciate this, it is necessary to look more closely at the form these 'clubs' can take and at the nature of their 'regulations' (i.e. the powers they have to take and enforce decisions about such matters as the payments to be made by members). Three broad types of 'club' can be envisaged.

The first type might be called the *direct production club*: it is created and administered by the consumers themselves. Thus, if factor services are available for purchase in free competitive markets, groups of consumers may find it convenient to join together to hire certain services whose products will be consumed by all the group, although it would not be worth the while of individual consumers to hire them separately. Effectively the consumers *ask themselves* whether it is worth their while to create a 'club' to provide the good concerned, and agree together (in

'club' members insist on relating their own offers to the amounts others will be expected to pay. Further, there is no *logical* reason why only one system of prices should satisfy the 'club' principle; what happens, e.g. if the amounts offered to meet standing charges are greater than the total of common costs, but only total cost is to be recovered? In these cases, where more than one set of prices would satisfy the conditions, someone will have to choose between them. Value judgements must be made in the process, and it is difficult to understand why the government should accept those of the utility as superior to its own.

The false plausibility of the argument for voluntary redistribution through the 'club' arises from the application of a logical system concerned solely with individual choice and taking no account of the existence of a government with coercive powers, to a situation where governments have to take decisions involving economic matters outside the scope of individual choice. Some attempt has indeed been made to 'fit' the behaviour of the public economy into the individual choice (welfare) analysis, by treating the whole of the economy as a 'club'. This brings out the weakness and unrealism of the 'club' argument even more forcefully than the discussion above; it leads to advocacy of an 'ethically neutral' system of government income and expenditure, such that the size of the taxes paid and the public services consumed by individuals would be determined by the free agreement of the citizens (taxpayers and consumers) themselves, and to the suggestion that those unwilling to pay such taxes should be treated as 'pathological' (see F. Benham, 'Notes on the Pure Theory of Public Finance', *Economica*, (1934), pp. 453-4, and, for a critical discussion, Musgrave, 'The Voluntary Exchange Theory of the Public Economy', *Quarterly Journal of Economics* (November 1949).

deciding to create it) upon the volume of their individual consumption and upon the payments each shall make. The illustrations given of the 'club' principle are usually of this direct-production character.[22] Provided that there are alternative competing means of satisfying the demand in question without recourse to a 'club', then the possibility of forming a 'club' simply represents a widening in the range of choices made available by the competitive market, and so increases satisfactions ('welfare').[23] This is true even though members of the 'club' pay different amounts for what is technically the same service. However, such cases of direct production would seem unlikely to be of widespread importance, though there may be special instances in which the conditions are quite well satisfied.[24]

The second form that the 'club' might take is one in which the organization of production is undertaken, not by the eventual consumers, but by independent producers, who find the use of standing charges advantageous but whose freedom in deciding the charges that consumers ('members') shall be asked to pay is restricted by the presence in the market of other, similar clubs competing for the consumer's membership. An example of this type of 'club' (the *competitive-producer club*) is provided by the book clubs, offering supplies of books at differential rates related to total guaranteed consumption, but with the discretion of any

[22] If, for example, a man wishes to fly to Scotland to visit a sick relative, but cannot quite afford to charter an aeroplane at £30 for the trip, it may be possible to find a prospective rail traveller who is willing to pay £10 to share the air trip. The same (physical) service thus costs each traveller a different amount, but each prefers to make the payment and take the service rather than take the services to be obtained by using the market in any other way.

[23] e.g., in the illustration given (note 22 above) the travellers could themselves decide whether to travel separately or together, could choose between a variety of competing means of transport, and could decide between various offers of aeroplanes for hire.

[24] A good example is given in part III (pp. 94-145) of R. S. Edwards, *Co-operative Industrial Research*. Here the common service is research for a group of firms with a common interest in the results. Firms can, within broad limits, control the direction of research activity, the distribution of benefits between members, and the methods by which common costs are covered. There is also a possibility of using the market as an alternative to the 'club'. But it is also not without interest, in view of the earlier argument about the role of government (see p. 259), that a decision had to be made as to whether membership should be made compulsory, because the benefits of the cooperative research are not always easily confined to members of the 'club'.

one club in deciding its rates circumscribed by the policies adopted (or able to be adopted) by the other book clubs, and by the ability of consumers to transfer their 'membership'. There is a case for the existence of this type of 'club' also, on grounds of economic welfare. But it must be noticed that the consumers are not now taking decisions about how much they are willing to contribute to a venture in joint production; their 'voluntary' decisions are concerned solely with the nature and amount of their personal consumption at the prices thrown up by the market. The production decisions are taken by independent producers, and the fulfilment of the welfare conditions depends upon the protection provided for the consumers by competition between these producers.[25]

The third type of 'club', *the discriminating-monopoly club,* occurs when neither direct production (with factor services provided by a competitive market) nor competition between 'club'-type producers is present. Only one 'club' is in a position to provide the good or service, so that consumers must join this 'club' and pay the discriminatory charges asked, or go without the good. In such cases, where the producer has a considerable degree of monopoly power, it is difficult to see how discriminatory charges can be justified by appeal to the 'club' principle. The differential charges are fixed by the producer without reference to consumers, who must accept them as a datum when deciding how much to consume – the only 'voluntary' decision left with them. Consumers in these circumstances are protected neither by direct association with pricing and production decisions nor by the existence of competition among producers of the good concerned. The distinction between this last formulation of the 'club' principle and the earlier ones is clear; it is the difference between my offer (choice) to pay two thirds of the cost of a particular taxi shared with a friend, in preference to travelling by bus, and my choice whether or not to consume electricity at the particular set of discriminatory prices that a monopolistic electricity utility decides

[25] The difference between the two types of 'club' might be put in this way: in the second type, unlike the first, the members of the 'club' are not automatically members of the committee, although they are still in a strong position to influence its decisions.

to apply to me. Cases of the latter type are clearly not justifiable on 'welfare' grounds; if all that is required to satisfy the 'club' principle is that some consumers should pay rather than go without, then any private discriminating monopolist might meet the conditions.

Unfortunately it is only the last and most unsatisfactory type of 'club' that is likely to be relevant to the pricing policy of public utilities, whose products often have no close substitutes and whose monopoly power is protected by law, so that the 'club' becomes effectively a method of coercion operated by a sole producer.

In summary, there are clear arguments for a multi-part pricing rule only where the services of the indivisible factors (and therefore the 'standing charges') can be imputed directly to individual consumers. In such conditions the method avoids the need for interpersonal utility comparisons. This is not so if there are common costs, which is likely to be the general case. In these cases the decision taken about the prices to be charged must involve a value judgement about the distribution of income, and this cannot in general be avoided by an instruction to make use of the 'club' principle.

III THE WELFARE MODEL AND UNCERTAINTY [26]

In the simplified conditions of the competitive model so far postulated, the pricing 'rules' could be implemented simply on the basis of objective cost computations made by utility managers. The assumptions about knowledge that lie behind the model are such that it does not matter who takes the decisions about the use of factors in production, nor is there any need for economic activity concerned with the discovery of information, framing of expectations, or considering and choosing between alternative and speculative courses of action. Any departure from the 'ideal' situation in which the price of any factor (including 'entrepreneurship' as rewarded by normal profit) is equal to its value in another

[26] The method of analysis adopted in this section is similar to that used by G. F. Thirlby, 'The Ruler'. Cf. also T. Wilson, 'The Inadequacy of the Theory of the Firm as a Branch of Welfare Economics', and my 'Uncertainty, Costs and Collectivist Economic Planning'.

use or to another user must be explained solely by reference to the short-term immobility of factors of production.

A simple model of this kind is inadequate for the derivation of pricing rules intended to have relevance to practical policy. This can be seen by considering the effects of uncertainty.[27] Once uncertainty is admitted, it becomes necessary to distinguish between the process of decision-taking by which the use of resources is determined (the *ex ante* planning process), and the *ex post* distribution of factors between uses that is the consequence of that process. The opportunity-cost problems arise at the *ex ante* planning stage: costs are incurred when decisions committing factors to particular uses are taken. With uncertainty this *ex ante* planning process must involve judgement as well as a capacity for arithmetic; there is no longer any reason why different individuals, working as they must in an atmosphere of doubt and with incomplete information, should make the same assessments or reach the same decisions even in the unlikely event of their acting on the basis of identical data. That is, the *ex post* distribution of factors between uses at any time is determined not only by factor mobility but also by the skill of those who plan the use of those factors *ex ante*.

In these circumstances the entrepreneurial function cannot be treated simply as a factor of production rewarded in similar fashion to other factors. The decision-taking process is concerned with the selection and implementation of the production plans which, in the view of those taking the decisions, offer combinations of riskiness and expected net revenue superior to those offered by any alternative plans considered. But the implementation of any plan at all involves a risk that the actual revenues and outlays achieved *ex post* will differ from the *ex ante* forecasts that

[27] It is not suggested that the unsatisfactory treatment of uncertainty is the only reason for objection to the perfectly competitive model and to the welfare criteria. In particular, there has been considerable and cogent criticism of the validity of the simple welfare model as an explanation of the process and nature of individual choice (cf. e.g. I. M. D. Little, *Critique of Welfare Economics*, and W. J. Baumol, *Welfare Economics and the Theory of State*). However, such criticism need not concern us here. There is still point in discussing the use of resources in terms of choice, and the logic of the 'rules' can be destroyed even accepting the conceptions of the simplest welfare analysis.

provided a basis for action. This risk is borne by those whose resources are utilized in implementing the plan (the 'owners'). The 'owners' and the 'decision-takers' need not be identical. The possible combinations of the functions of ownership and planning control (decision-taking) are clearly very numerous, and the returns to risk-bearing and to the planning function are difficult if not impossible to separate in practice, since individuals may share both functions in varying degrees. But the separation is clear in principle.

The reward of the decision-taking function will be that part of the earnings of decision-takers that is not directly dependent upon the *ex post* success of their *ex ante* planning activities. So regarded, the return to such decision-taking can be treated, like normal profit in the competitive model, as an outlay on a productive factor. But the rewards offered to individual decision-takers will reflect the view taken by owners of their relative abilities; there can be no question of their being treated as homogeneous. The return to risk-bearing, on the other hand, cannot be treated as an outlay at all; its reward is the *ex post* (achieved) excess of revenues over outlays (net revenue) in plans actually implemented. It is in no sense a hire payment for a factor, depending as it does upon the ability to obtain a return from the utilization of factors greater than the hire payments that have to be made to those factors. The size of the return obtained is directly determined by the efficiency with which planning decisions are taken *ex ante* and by the attitude of risk-bearers to ventures of different degrees of riskiness.

Since net revenue is the return to the essential economic function of risk-bearing, but cannot be treated as an outlay on a factor, it follows that, if factors of production are to be ideally distributed between uses, the total revenues obtained by firms (*ex post*) should be greater than their total outlays and not equal to such outlays as in the conditions of the perfectly competitive model. Also the 'normal profit' principle cannot be satisfactorily replaced, as a condition of the welfare 'ideal' by a requirement that the net revenues obtained by different firms should be equated *ex post.* The competitive process does provide a check on the undue divergence of the net revenues actually obtained from different kinds of productive activity, by directing activity towards avenues in which large net revenues seem likely. But even with complete freedom for potential producers to enter any market they wish there is no reason to expect that competition will, or (from the point of view of an 'ideal' factor distribution) should, result in a general equality of achieved net revenues. Net revenue depends upon the individual skill of risk-bearers and decision-takers and upon their attitude to risk. If the abilities and risk attitudes of these individuals differ, then net revenues must also be expected to differ. A welfare principle of net-revenue equalization, in accord with the general principle of factor-price equalization, would thus be valid only in a society in which risk-bearers and decision-takers were of precisely equal ability and took the same attitude to risk. Such a situation being unlikely, it seems better to substitute the more realistic, if less precise, formula that some net revenue must be obtained if the employment of factors of production in any use is to be justified, and that some means (such as the competitive process) is necessary to limit the extent of the divergences between the net revenue obtained from different kinds of productive activity.

If this argument is accepted, then a new dilemma arises for public utility pricing policy. The need for skill in making production plans, and the risks involved in implementing those plans, are not peculiar to one form of economic organization. They do not disappear because an industry becomes a public utility; simply the risks are transferred from private owners to the community as a whole. In respect of decision-taking no insuperable difficulties need arise; so long as there is a large private sector, suitable individuals can be hired at prices determined by their earnings in private industry, and their hire prices treated as outlays. The only difficulty in this respect is the discovery of an incentive to efficient *ex ante* planning activity that will replace the association of reward with achieved net revenue generally used in private industry. But risk payments cannot be treated in this way; they are not simply factor outlays. If public utilities are not expected to earn some net revenue, as is the case with the 'rules' so far discussed, then factors of production will be utilized in plans that would not be implemented in private industry because the expected returns were too small. On the other hand, public utilities will often have considerable powers of monopoly, so that the competitive process is not available as a check upon the means utilized to obtain revenues. Consequently, if they are required to earn a net revenue, utilities may do so simply by using their monopoly power to raise prices. Some increase in *ex ante* planning efficiency may (but need not) also be stimulated by the need to reach a more difficult target. Thus there appears to be some justification for the view that if a public utility, required to achieve a specified net revenue, did so solely by exercise of its monopoly power over prices, yet the need to raise the revenue might serve a useful 'welfare' purpose by checking the over-expansion of the public-utility enterprise relative to enterprises in private industry of a similar degree of riskiness. But there seems to be no 'right' net revenue that all utilities should be required to earn in all circumstances, since public utilities differ both in riskiness and in the extent of their monopoly power.

The introduction of considerations of uncertainty also draws attention to the problems that would arise for utility managers concerned with interpreting and administering 'rules' of the type so far discussed. These problems are particularly important in the case of rules that do not require costs to be covered. For example, the investment principle, interpreted in *ex ante* planning terms, requires that managers, when deciding whether or not to create an asset, should base their revenue estimate upon the system of prices (discriminatory or not) that they would expect to maximize such revenues. The asset should be created if any plan shows a potential (*ex ante*) excess of revenues over outlays. But if no charge is made for the use of the asset once created, then the plans that prompted its creation will never be implemented. There will therefore be no means of checking upon the efficiency with which the investment decisions are made. This position will be aggravated by the fact that once charges for the use of durable assets cease to be made, no guidance can be obtained from the success of *ex post* (implemented) plans when considering newly current (*ex ante*) plans, since the revenues obtained from implemented plans are not an indication of the valuations placed upon the durable factors by consumers. It is difficult to believe that such a situation would be conducive to efficiency in planning the use of factors and hence in the *ex post* (achieved) distribution of factors between uses. Similar problems arise with the marginal-cost rule. The marginal-cost – price relationship becomes a manager's opinion about the results of a marginal increase in factor use in the alternative *ex ante* plans considered by him.[28] There is consequently no possibility of any outside authority checking upon whether a general instruction to implement the marginal-cost rule is being followed, quite apart from the other shortcomings of such a policy. Considered together with the proposition advanced earlier, that what is treated as marginal cost must depend upon the length of the planning period specified, this suggests that the marginal-cost rule could only be made intelligible in an environment of uncertainty if the general rule were replaced by specific individual directions to managers. Such directions would take the form of an instruction to ignore the estimated replacement costs of particular specified durable assets when deciding price policy, which should otherwise aim at the recovery of all outlays. But this would amount to the replacement of the marginal-cost rule by average cost (or multi-part) pricing, associated with a specific subsidy.

SUMMARY AND CONCLUSIONS

It must be concluded that the welfare criteria give rise to no unambiguous general rule for the price and output policy of public utilities, such that for the given distribution of income to which the welfare model refers obedience to that rule must achieve an

---

[28] For further discussion of this cf. T. Wilson, 'The Inadequacy of the Theory of the Firm as a Branch of Welfare Economics.,' and 'Price and Outlay Policy of State Enterprise', *Economic Journal*, (December 1945), G. F. Thirlby, 'The Ruler', and my 'Uncertainty, Costs and Collectivist Economic Planning'.

ideal use of resources by the utility. An instruction to price at marginal cost, if it was to be intelligible, would need to be supplemented by a specific statement of what costs were to be ignored when fixing prices, in the case of each utility, so that 'he general 'rule' would effectively be replaced by average cost (or multi-part) pricing and specific subsidies decided separately for each utility. Furthermore value judgements about income distribution are unavoidable with marginal-cost pricing. Average cost or multi-part pricing can solve some of the problems, but only if there are no important common costs, or if the 'club' principle can be justified in individual cases. In any case any policy 'rule' adopted would need adjustment to take account of uncertainty; an optimum use of resources requires that utilities should earn an excess of revenues over outlays, and there is no simple principle by reference to which the appropriate net revenue to be earned on account of the risk factor can be decided. Failure to require an excess of revenues over outlays encourages the use of resources by utilities that could be better employed elsewhere, but a net-revenue requirement may be met by the exploitation of the monopolistic position of the utility concerned. Consequently uncertainty considerations also require the abandonment of general 'rules' and the separate determination of pricing policy in respect of each individual utility.

These negative conclusions have an important positive aspect. The failure to establish general pricing rules does not mean that the government need take no pricing decisions. Rather, given the existence of public utilities, it has to consider each utility individually, and decide policy in respect of some or all of the following matters in respect of each one :

1. The net revenue that the utility should be expected to earn.

2. Whether it is considered desirable explicitly to encourage the short-period use of particular durable and specific factors and, if so, what form the requisite subsidy shall take.[29]

[29] In general the desire of governments to give this type of encouragement seems likely to be greater the longer the relevant planning period and the more random and imprecise the distribution of the benefits and losses concerned.

An example of a suitable case might be a change of a permanent nature in the geographical environment, as through the diversion of a river.

3. The nature and extent of the discriminatory pricing to be permitted. That is, if there are common costs, whether these can be satisfactorily allocated by the free use of a 'club' principle without this implying a compulsory and undesirable redistribution of income by the utility managers. If the 'club' principle is not appropriate, then a decision has to be taken as to what system of charges would best accord with the government's general policy in regard to income distribution.

4. Whether, quite apart from the considerations at 2) and 3), the industry concerned is thought suitable for use as a means of redistributing income, as a part of the general system of indirect taxes and subsidies. In this regard of course public utilities differ from other industries only in that they are more likely to become the subject of government policy for other reasons,[30] and in that they provide a convenient method of achieving those 'indirect' income redistributions that some economists consider must be one of the purposes of public finance.[31]

Clearly the decisions taken in the case of each utility must be a reflection of the particular attitude of the government concerned. It would therefore appear that, failing some universally acceptable theory of the *public* economy by reference to which policy could be decided (and the possibility of such a theory is doubtful), economists would find their efforts better rewarded if they ceased to seek after general pricing rules and devoted attention to the examination of the policies actually adopted by governments, in order to discover their effects and make clear to the government and to the electorate the nature and consequences of the policies actually being pursued. That is, the economists' *general* recommendations need to be concerned not with general pricing rules,

---

[30] A question of this type inevitably arises, e.g. when a utility ceases to be able to cover costs at its present size as a consequence of changes in the economic environment, so that a decision has to be taken as to whether it should be subsidized, or should simply cease to be treated as a public utility at all, and competition allowed to determine its future size and operations. This is perhaps a not unrealistic way of describing the current position of the British railway industry.

[31] Cf., e.g., J. Margolis, 'A Comment on the Pure Theory of Public Expenditures', *Review of Economics and Statistics*, (November 1955).

but rather with the availability of information about policy and with the methods adopted to keep that policy under review.[32]

[32] The preceeding analysis would appear to furnish sound arguments, for example, for treating British public utility pricing policy as part of indirect tax policy, and (possibly), for providing opportunity for review and discussions of the policies of important utilities along with the rest of tax policy at the time of the annual budget.

I am grateful to Professor H. G. Johnson, to Mr T. Wilson and to colleagues at L.S.E. for reading and criticizing drafts of this article.

11

Economists' cost rules and equilibrium theory

G. F. THIRLBY

First published in *Economica* (May 1960).

This is an article about rules, devised and advocated by certain economists, for the control of business and other undertakings: rules, such as the one which says that marginal cost ought to be equal to price, which prescribe what are claimed to be correct relationships between an undertaking's cost and revenue. I have attacked the rules before in a paper[1] which has received some notice.[2] The following observations on four crucial and inter-connected issues succeed a re-scrutiny of some of the fundamental theoretical literature[3] which must have guided me in the preparation of that article and one which immediately preceded it.[4] While I am still following the same line of attack, seeking to expose the non-objectivity and non-implementability of the rules, I am this time offering a little more than a hint that the rules ought to fall away with the ground on which they were built, that is to say, with the notion of perfect competition or competitive equilibrium. This notion requires, I believe, to be replaced by a different notion of equilibrium which was, I feel, implicitly recognized in the earlier of my two articles to which I have just referred.

I CONFLICTING NOTIONS OF RATIONALITY

In economics the human being is supposed to pursue ends, valued

[1] 'The Ruler', reprinted here pages 163-98.

[2] Latterly in J. Wiseman, 'The Theory of Public Utility Price: An Empty Box', reprinted here, pages 245-71.

[3] Particularly Lionel Robbins, *The Nature and Significance of Economic Science*, 2nd ed (1935); Lionel Robbins, 'Remarks upon Certain Aspects of the Theory of Costs' reprinted here, pages 19-41; F. A. Hayek, 'Economics and Knowledge' reprinted here, pages 43-68 F. A. Hayek, 'Scientism and the Study of Society', *Economica* (August 1942, February 1943 and February 1944).

[4] 'The Subjective Theory of Value and Accounting "Cost" ', reprinted here, pages 135-61.

and chosen by himself, with the use of means of some kind.[5] This behaviour, including the choice, is spoken of as rational behaviour. But the content of the conception of rationality varies. Sometimes it is adjusted to admit the behaviour of the ordinary, sane, human being who is limited in his knowledge,[6] and can make mistakes in the processes whereby he selects and pursues his ends. Sometimes it is something less fallible than this, in that it includes knowledge that the behaving subject does not possess, or objective data of which the behaving subject may be unaware.[7] At the extreme it is something which is omniscient and infallible: something which has, or is, perfect foresight.[8] It was, I believe, because of an attitude which tacitly assumed that the behaving subject was possessed of a rationality which transcended his actual state[9] that

[5] Cf. Lionel Robbins, *The Nature and Significance of Economic Science*, p. 18.

[6] It is so adjusted in the following statement, 'It may be irrational to be completely consistent as between commodities . . . just because the time and attention which such exact comparisons require are (in the opinion of the economic subject concerned) better spent in other ways. In other words, there may be an opportunity cost of "internal arbitrage" which, beyond a certain point, outweighs the gain' (Robbins, *The Nature and Significance of Economic Science*, p. 92). This opportunity cost of 'internal arbitage', which is introduced to limit the pursuit of maximization, is referred to alternatively as 'the marginal utility of not bothering about marginal utility'.

[7] Robbins appears to switch to this view of rationality in giving an instance of inconsistency which can be shown up by economics: the inconsistency of wishing to satisfy consumers' demands fully and at the same time wishing to impede the import of foreign goods by tariffs, (Robbins, *The Nature and Significance of Economic Science*, p. 92.) He refers to this as irrationality. It would seem to be open to an advocate for the person having these inconsistent wishes to plead that the person had not the knowledge to show that the wishes were inconsistent, that he preferred (to the marginal utility of the extra knowledge) the marginal utility of not bothering about it, and that consequently he was rational according to Robbins's earlier view. (See note 6 above.) At least we may say that if in this instance the behaving subject is irrational through ignorance, rationality implies knowledge greater than the behaving subject possesses, and consequently we are able to call a man rational or irrational according to which of Robbins's conceptions we use.

[8] The fact is of course that the assumption of perfect rationality in the sense of complete consistency is simply one of a number of assumptions of a psychological nature which are introduced into economic analysis at various stages of approximation to reality. The perfect foresight, which it is sometimes convenient to postulate, is an assumption of a similar nature; and 'Rationality in choice is nothing more and nothing less than choice with complete awareness of the alternatives rejected'. (Robbins, *The Nature and Significance of Economic Science*, pp. 93-4, and p. 152 respectively.)

[9] And possibly, confused the rationality of the behaving subject with the rationality of an observing economist, who was assumed to be omniscient. See Hayek's discussion of the confusion about the data, or facts, of the demand schedules, where

it became possible to put forward the rules as implementable controls. The appropriate assumption is the other one: that the human being is limited and fallible.

The act of choice, which is part of the rational behaviour, involves the rejection of a course of action to achieve a value which is called 'cost', and the selection of a course of action to achieve another value which, in the context of the rules, is often caled 'revenue'. These two values, 'cost' and 'revenue', are the subject of the rules.

II CONFUSION ON THE MEANING OF 'COST'

In the consideration of the behaviour of isolated man in the non-market environment (Robinson Crusoe), it is admitted that the two values compared (the 'cost' and the other one) are values of alternative end products that might be achieved by the use of the same resources. The full application of the same doctrine to the entrepreneur in the exchange economy would require the cost to be regarded as the entrepreneur's own valuation of the outcome of a course of action that he rejects. And because, as a first approximation, money revenue is regarded as the entrepreneur's single aim, this outcome would be an alternative money revenue.[10] But the doctrine is not always fully applied in this way. The rejected course of action with its outcome of money revenue tends to be ignored, and to be replaced (as the 'cost' element to be compared with the 'revenue' element) by the entrepreneur's resources themselves (these being assumed to consist of money) or,

he raises 'the question whether the facts referred to are supposed to be given to the observing economist, or to the persons whose actions he wants to explain, and if the latter, whether it is assumed that the same facts are known to all the different persons in the system, or whether the "data" for the different persons may be different' (F. A. Hayek, 'Economics and Knowledge', p. 52).

[10] Which, if 1) the entrepreneur were allowed to be considering the production of a second product, besides the alternative of disposing of his resources in the resource markets, and 2) cost were regarded as being the *best* of the rejected alternatives, could be the contemplated revenue from one of the products. Further, if the calculations were marginal calculations (which might incidentally lead to the selection and subsequent production of some of each product, so that the entrepreneur became a 'multi-product' entrepreneur), marginal cost could be the contemplated (extra-) marginal revenue from one of the products.

what amounts to the same thing, by the 'prices' of the factors to be bought and used in the accepted course of action.[11] At this point, 'cost', defined as money resource input, or outlay, relinquishes its connection with the end value of the use of the entrepreneur's resources in an alternative course of action, and consequently with the entrepreneur's act of choice.

But this is not all. The subtle change in the meaning of cost, from the valuation of his *own* displaced end product to the money input required for the selected course of action, is a change leading to still another conception, which carries with it the suspicion that it is to be regarded as a social cost. It resembles the first meaning of cost, in that it is supposed to be an alternative value displaced, but differs from it in that it is not the entrepreneur's *own* valuation of his *own* displaced end product, but other people's (consumers') valuations of products which might have been produced by other entrepreneurs had they not been displaced. This further conception arises in this way. The money-resource input (or 'factor prices') of the first entrepreneur is now supposed to 'reflect' these other people's valuations. It reflects these valuations because any one of the factor prices is supposed to be the limit (it should strictly be regarded as being *above* the limit) that the excluded bidder (another entrepreneur) would be willing to pay for the factor in order to produce a product himself, and accordingly to reflect its contribution to the value of that product to consumers.[12]

---

[11] Space does not permit me to enlarge either upon how this replacement might be permissible as a conceivable limiting case, or upon the necessity for rejecting the money input concept on the ground that money is not the entrepreneur's only resource.

[12] My account of the transition from 1) the isolated producer's end-product value, regarded as cost, to 2) the entrepreneur's money input or factor prices, regarded as cost, and regarded also as something which reflects the value of excluded products, is offered as a fair statement of what occurs in Robbins's 'Remarks upon Certain Aspects of the Theory of Costs', section I, pp. 22–7. I cannot accuse him of actually calling the value of the excluded products a social cost, but the suggestion seems to be there, particularly, perhaps, in his insistence that the excluded products *themselves*, as distinct from their values, are *not* to be regarded as cost. For doubt cast upon the validity of the method of transition from the individual situation to the social situation, see Hayek's discussion in which he stated he had 'long felt that the concept of equilibrium itself and the methods which we employ in pure analysis have a clear meaning only when confined to the analysis of the action of a single

So now it appears that the meaning of cost, in an instruction to an entrepreneur to observe a certain relationship between cost and revenue, could be any one of these three. The very doubt about which meaning to apply would impede the proper implementation of the rule, for clearly both controller and controlled would in this respect have to be at one. However, this obstacle to the control is supplemented, so as to reduce the idea to absurdity, by the realities that are obscured by the manner of discussion of the conditions of equilibrium.

III NEGLECT OF TIME AND UNCERTAINTY IN EQUILIBRIUM ANALYSIS

The presentation of the conditions of equilibrium[13] proceeds in such manner as to suggest that the act of choice and the complete implementation of it occurred simultaneously. There is no apparent gap in time either between the selection of a course of action with its advance reckoning of cost and revenue, or between the beginning of the actual expenditure of resources and the termination of the achievement of the valued outcomes of the course of action taken. The rational choice which plans the achievement of a 'revenue', by the disposition of resources, at a 'cost' in some sense, virtually disappears from view, or becomes merged in the actual disposition of resources and the actual achievement

person, and that we are really passing into a different sphere and silently introducing a new element of altogether different character when we apply it to the explanation of the interaction of a number of different individuals', and in which he stated that 'the data which formed the starting point for the tautological transformations of the Pure Logic of Choice . . . meant . . . only the facts . . . which were present in the mind of the acting person . . . But in the transition from the analysis of the action of an individual to the analysis of the situation in a society the concept [of "datum"] has undergone an insidious change of meaning' (Hayek, 'Economics and Knowledge', pages 47 and 51 respectively.)

[13] My comments in this paragraph are supposed to reflect fairly upon Robbins's discussion of the conditions of equilibrium in the 'Remarks upon Certain Aspects of the Theory of Costs', but are not supposed to suggest that he is oblivious of time and uncertainty, either elsewhere in that paper, or in *The Nature and Significance of Economic Science*. In *The Nature and Significance* uncertainty appears, e.g. in references to the theory of profit. In the 'Remarks. . .', it appears to belong to references to disequilibrium and equilibration (and to criticisms of Marshall), rather than to the discussion of the theory of costs in its competitive-equilibrium setting. (And it was surely competitive equilibrium that set the standard for the special rules about the cost/revenue relationship.)

of the actual 'revenue'. The termination of the achievement of the valued outcomes ('revenue'), which in reality may occur only at the end of a long means–ends chain of events (purchases, conversions into outputs, sales and the like) occurring over a long period of time, appears to be simultaneous with a single-resource input. This procedure of telescoping time out of existence tends to obscure two things, which, brought into light, are devastating to any supposition that the rule under criticism could be implemented.

First it obscures the fact that any cost in the sense of a displaced alternative value or revenue (the imagined outcome of a course of action which is *not* taken) will never have an actual, realized, counterpart, observed as achieved results, to compare with the imagined outcome. This absence of an actual counterpart is a necessary condition of the situation, whether we are referring to the entrepreneur's *own* cost, or whether we are referring to the 'social' cost[14] (both of which I have explained in section II above), and is a condition which would obviously prevent the rule from being implemented in a manner which required *results* to be looked at to see whether the rule had been observed.

The second thing that is obscured and has to be brought to light is something which stands in the way of implementation of the rule, not at the time of the checking of results, but at the earlier time of the generation of the rational choice in the mind of the maker of it, that is to say, at the time when the controller would, presumably, want to know whether the planned course of action was in accordance with the rule. This is the uncertainty, or limited rationality,[15] of the entrepreneur or anybody who tries to supersede or control him. When it is understood that a reckoning of cost, according to any one of the three concepts[16] referred to in

[14] And, where the cost referred to in the rule is a *marginal* cost, whether we are referring to either of these or to the money input concept. Cf. 'The Ruler', page 191.

[15] The significance of it will not be fully realized unless it is seen that the period of time between the rational choice and the achievement of the outcome of the accepted course of action may be, not just a minute or less, but anything between a minute or less and ten years or more. The degree of uncertainty will often be extremely high.

[16] It should be clear that this obstacle to implementation would remain if the meaning of cost were money (or other) resource input. However short the period

section II, depends upon the forecasting of events and outcomes of the future, and when it is understood that any individual is uniquely situated in relation to past events on which such forecasts are based, it becomes clear that the result of the reckoning is dependent for what it is upon the unique knowledge and attitude (towards uncertainty or risk) of the unique and uniquely situated individual who calculates it, and that the validity, correctness or authoritativeness of an overriding calculation by somebody else would often be dubious in the extreme. The cost (as well as the revenue) calculation, or residual elements in it, is ultimately a matter of subjective opinion, and, where one person is trying to control the other, is likely to be a matter of differences of opinion. To the extent that this conflict arises and remains, the substitution of one opinion (the controller's) for another (the controlled's) as the authoritative one can be regarded as effecting also a transfer of the responsibility for the calculation. The prevailing opinion itself then escapes control, and it, instead of the other one, has to be taken on trust.

I have related these obscurities to the timelessness that appears in the statement of the conditions of equilibrium. This notion of equilibrium was attacked, and a different notion substituted, by F. A. Hayek in 1937.[17] His attack was directed largely against the assumption of perfect knowledge (or what I have referred to as the omniscient type of rationality),[18] and against the use of the

of time between the cost calculation and the occurrence of the events which were the subject of it, the cost calculation would be uncertain and a matter of subjective opinion. While, in pure equilibrium analysis, 'it is simply assumed that the subjective data coincide with the objective facts' (Hayek, 'Economics and Knowledge' page 56.

[17] Ibid. And see also his, in many ways, supporting series of articles, 'Scientism and the Study of Society'.

[18] It is significant that in his criticism of the pure equilibrium analysis, Hayek remarks: 'It seems that that skeleton in our cupboard, the "economic man", whom we have exorcised with prayer and fasting, has returned through the back door in the form of a quasi-omniscient individual' (Hayek, 'Economics and Knowledge', page, 58). In his restatement he said: 'It is important to remember that the so-called "data" from which we set out in this sort of analysis are (apart from his tastes) all facts given to the person in question, the things as they are known to (or believed by) him to exist, and not in any sense objective facts' (page 48). The 'data', distinguished from 'the objective real facts' as supposed to be known by the omniscient economist (page 52), are to be conceived of 'in the subjective sense, as things known to the persons whose behaviours we try to explain' (page 52).

propositions of the pure logic of choice (which were supposed to relate to the choice of equilibrium of the single individual) for the purpose of describing an equilibrium (or social choice) of many people working competitively.[19] Thus his attack supports my attitude in this section, and casts doubt on the validity of the use, as the cost concept, of the value to consumers of displaced products that might have been produced by entrepreneurs other than the one having to make the cost calculation – the third concept in section II. His restatement substituted time[20] for time-lessness, and recognized a distinction between the individual's plan (or what I have called rational choice) and the subsequent execution of it. The individual's actions, taken in execution of his plan, were to be regarded as being in equilibrium relationships with one another so long as his actual actions agreed with his planned actions – which[21] means, approximately, so long as the emerging events of the external world, including the actions of other individuals in execution of their own plans, permitted this agreement, or, in other words, so long as the relevant forecasts expressed or implied in his plan proved adequately correct. Similarly for society, or individuals, at large, equilibrium and its continuance depended upon an adequate compatibility of one another's plans[22] and adequately correct forecasting of emerging objective data.[23]

'Subjective data' and 'individual plans' can be used interchangeably (note 11. page 56.)

[19] Cf. note 12 above.

[20] 'Since equilibrium is a relationship between actions, and since the actions of one person must necessarily take place successively in time, it is obvious that the passage of time is essential to give the concept any meaning' ('Economics and Knowledge', page 49).

[21] 'The equilibrium relationship comprises only his actions during the period during which his anticipations prove correct'. ('Economics and Knowledge', page 49).

[22] For a society then we *can* speak of a *state* of equilibrium at a point of time – but it means only that compatibility exists between the different plans which the individuals composing it have made for action in time', 'Economics and Knowledge', page 53).

[23] 'It [equilibrium] will continue . . . so long as the external data [the objective real facts] correspond to the common expectations of all the members of society', ('Economics and Knowledge', page 53).

I should like to add here that presumably a firm would begin to *re*plan as soon as it began to *anticipate* that its original anticipations would, for one reason or

G. F. Thirlby

IV NEGLECT OF DISCONTINUITY OF KNOWLEDGE WITHIN 'THE FIRM'

I referred in section II to the apparent conversion of the individual cost/revenue relationship into a social cost/revenue relationship and in section III to (what amounts to much the same thing) the conversion of the individual choice or equilibrium into a competitive social equilibrium. An objection to the latter conversion, and hence to the former, is that in this competitive social situation there is discontinuity of knowledge, as between the different individuals who, each on the basis of his own particular knowledge, make the forecasts on which in turn their own individual actions are based. Hayek, in raising this objection with regard to the competitive situation in particular, was pointing[24] to the lack of theories relating generally to the communication of knowledge. Regrettably, although many of his general observations were relevant, his interest did not lie specifically in the similar discontinuity of knowledge inside large business organizations. Consequently he was not led to criticize the practice, in the theory of the firm, of drawing no distinction between the one-man firm and the multi-man firm – a practice which ignores the possibility that in the business organization there might be any number of planning individuals ranging from two to as many as would be found in the competitive situation.

The discontinuity of knowledge inside the organization is significant, in the context of economic and administrative theory, for at least two reasons. First it raises the question whether the

another, be falsified – and then act according to the revised plan. So perhaps we can speak of its being out of equilibrium with respect to its old plan and in equilibrium with respect to its revised plan. With this adjustment, the Hayekian notions here expressed supply an amenable milieu – or containing theory – for my own view that the firm's *account* (which I regard as a counterpart statement of realized or actual events) always agrees, or ought to agree, with its *revised* budget (which I regard as its statement of anticipated events, or its plan) though not necessarily with its earlier, or original, budget. See my 'The Ruler', pp. 189-90, note 39, and my 'Notes on the Maximization Process in Company Administration', *Economica*, (August 1950), pp. 268-9 (particularly footnotes) and p. 278. And see the connection between my view and the modern question of what plans of the directors of large organizations should be submitted to the stockholders before they are put into operation ('Notes on the Maximization Process in Company Administration', pp. 276-7, particularly footnotes).

[24] In both 'Economics and Knowledge', and 'Scientism and the Study of Society'.

283

conversion of the idea of an individual cost/revenue relationship into the idea of an overall, or organizational, cost/revenue relationship is worthy of the same scepticism as is the conversion of the idea of an individual cost/revenue relationship into the idea of a social cost/revenue relationship. Secondly it relates to the question whether an internal rule relating to the cost/revenue relationship is non-implementable in the same way as is an externally imposed rule. On this second question, I do not propose to say much more than that what applies to a rule supposed to be imposed by an external controller upon the entrepreneur applies in much the same way to a rule supposed to be imposed by a superior (coordinating) administrator upon a subordinate administrator in the organization. I want to deal briefly with the first question, because I do not wish to leave the impression that if the social relationship goes, the organizational relationship goes with it. Before I do that, it will be well to look at what is left of the cost/revenue relationship after my treatment of it in sections I to III.

It will be seen that, after rejecting the other notions of cost, I am left with the view that cost is the entrepreneur's own second-best outcome-value (second-best 'revenue') reckoned by him according to his own uncertain, highly subjective, calculations, and rejected by him in favour of his own, similarly calculated, best-outcome value (best 'revenue') from the use of the same resources. I am left, too, with the view that, with the multi-product and output-variation ideas introduced, this best outcome-value differs from the second-best outcome value only by a *net* marginal variation. I say '*net*' because the marginal variation in the planned course of action, upon which the change in value is dependent, can be conceived of as having a minus ('marginal cost') effect and a plus ('marginal revenue') effect upon the value – e.g. when the variation in the course of action consists in ideationally reducing the output of one product (and so its revenue) a little, and increasing the output of another product (and so its revenue) a little.[25]

---

[25] I hope to attempt in a subsequent paper a reconciliation of this restatement. and some other aspects of my paper, with certain modern administrative theory.

This view can now be reduced to the simple statement that the entrepreneur's total cost is approximately equal to his total revenue,[26] and his marginal cost is approximately equal to his marginal revenue,[27] but it is a view which allows *the planned revenue, related to the planned resource input (money or mixed) of the selected course of action, to be of any magnitude.*[28] And, to reiterate, it is a view which sees the costs and revenues as subjective data – unrealized planning data belonging to the decisional process preceding action.[29]

Now it appears to me that a rule, based on this theoretical statement of the final situation in the entrepreneur's decisional process, would be not only non-implementable, but also about as instructive and guiding as – and possibly much less intelligible than – an injunction of the order of 'seize your best opportunities!' The statement is not intended to be the basis of a rule to instruct or control the behaving subject: it is rather a theoretical, hypothetical, statement offered as a description of the behaviour of the behaving subject.

I shall now assume that this statement, understood as I have explained it, is as applicable to the organization as to the individual, and that the multi-person organization replaces the one-man entrepreneur as the behaving subject.[30] And I turn to the question whether this conversion is as worthy of criticism as is the conversion of the individual cost/revenue relationship into

[26] That total cost (in some sense) should be equal to total revenue is one of the rules (or part of one).

[27] There is a rule (or part of one) that where marginal revenues differ from price, output should be extended to that point at which marginal cost (in some sense) is equal to price. This rule, I believe, falls away with the 'perfect competition' which is the ground on which it is based. However, with cost defined as I have defined it, it appears to fall away for another reason too. With cost so defined, marginal cost is always displaced alternative marginal revenue, and, consequently, from the point of view of the rule advocates, open to the same stricture as is the selected marginal revenue itself: to get a marginal cost which was independent of autonomous pricing, we should be driven back on to marginal money input.

[28] i.e. there is no 'cost'/revenue equality in this sense.

[29] The statements in this paragraph and the preceding one represent the principles behind the model (in which, however, the entrepreneur is converted into an organization) in my 'The Subjective Theory of Value and Accounting "Cost" '. See note 30 below.

[30] This is the conversion that I effected in 'The Subjective Theory of Value and Accounting "Cost" '. See note 29 above.

the competitive social cost/revenue relationship. On this issue, and in support of the idea of the organization cost/revenue relationship, I can do little more here than point to two significant differences between the competitive situation and the organization:

1 In the organization, the individuals are assumed to be common-goal-oriented.[31] Hence the organization itself, although it has no mind, has to be viewed anthropomorphically,[32] that is to say, *as if* it were behaving rationally, like a man, and has consequently to be assumed, in determining its course of action, to develop an overall, or organizational, cost/revenue relationship. In the competitive situation, on the other hand, the individuals are not assumed to be common-goal-oriented in this way. Consequently the overall (social) cost/revenue relationship is not implied in this way.

2 In the organization the individual decision-makers – the sectional planning administrators – are assumed to declare their plans, for the purpose of interpersonal coordination, before their plans are executed. This behaviour is an essential condition for the acceptance of the view that there is an overall, or organizational, cost/revenue relationship: the relationship is a reflection of this declaration and coordination.[33] In the competitive situation, on the other hand, this *ex ante* declaration and coordination does not occur.

There is now little more that can be done in the space available than to stress that this assumption that the individual declares his plan for the purpose of coordination does not imply that the coordinator perceives and comprehends it with the same exhaustiveness as does the individual who submits it, or that the

[31] It seems to me that common-goal orientation is silently – and perhaps unconsciously – assumed in the economists' practice of using the same cost/revenue diagrammatic apparatus to represent the behaviour of 'the firm' regardless of whether the firm is a one-man or a multi-man set-up.

[32] Hayek, condemning 'an illegitimate use of anthropomorphic concepts', adds in a footnote, 'What is said in the text does of course not preclude the possibility that our study of the way in which individual minds interact may reveal to us a structure which operates in some respects similarly to the individual mind' (Hayek, 'Scientism and the Study of Society' part II, p. 45 and footnote).

[33] The process is illustrated in my 'The Subjective Theory of Value and Accounting "Costs" '.

individual perceives and comprehends the other plans, with which his own have to be coordinated, with the same exhaustiveness as do the other individuals who have to prepare them. In the organization there is discontinuity of knowledge between people of limited rationality, gaps that are filled by reciprocal- (mutual) authority relationships which replace some of the single-minded coordinations which occur when the individual operates alone in a narrower sphere. The individual's plan, though it clearly must disclose the elements which are required to be known for the purpose of coordination,[34] is, as communicated, an authoritative statement whose acceptance is of necessity one which is to a greater or less extent accepted on trust as a communication possessing the potentiality of reasoned elaboration.[35] To say this is not to say either that the reasoned elaboration is never requested, or that the plan can never be 'faked' – any more than that these same assertions would be made of authoritative communications in other spheres. But acceptance on trust has to enter. And within what is so accepted will often be much revealed and unrevealed cost-and-revenue calculation.

[34] For an illustration of what elements would have to be disclosed, see, again, the model in my 'The Subjective Theory of Value and Accounting "Cost" '.
[35] For this expression, see Carl J. Friedrich, 'Authority, Reason, and Discretion', in *Authority*, ed. Carl J. Friedrich, (1958).

Index of Names

Ammon, A., 62n

Bauer, P. T., 177 and n
Baumol, W. J., 251n, 264n
Baxter, W. T., 104n, 113n
Benham, F., 260n
Bernardi, Mario di, 249n
Bigg, W. W., 119–20, 122
Borcherding, T., 16n
Bradley, 206n
Brutzkus, B. D., 144n
Buchanan, J. A., 6, 13, 14n, 15n, 98
Burn, D. L., 159n

Canning, 77, 137
Carter, R. N., 76n
Coase, R. H., 11–12, 12–13, 122 and n, 159n, 250n, 256n, 257n

Davenport, H. J., 14, 22
Dessus, G., 247n
Dickinson, H. D., 231 and n
Dobb, M., 237n
Dupuit, J., 251n
Durbin, E. F. M., 232n, 240n

Edgeworth, F. Y., 22–3n, 29–30 and n, 32 and n
Edwards, R. S., 11, 12–13, 97–8, 99–100, 103–4, 261n
Einaudi, L., 249n

Fells, F. M., 73

Ferrara, F., 14 and n
Fisher, I., 46n
Fowler, R. F., 97–8
Friedrich, C. J., 287n

Garcke, E., 73
Green, D. L., 22

Haberler, G., 24–5 and n, 30
Hatfield, H. R., 113
Hawtrey, R. G., 152n
Hayek, F. A. von, 3, 4, 5, 11, 54n, 55n, 139n, 146n, 177n, 205n, 230n, 275n, 276–7n, 278–9n, 281–3 and n, 286n
Henderson, H, D., 22
Hotelling, H., 249n, 250–1n
Hubbard, L. E., 178n

Johnson, H. G., 271n

Kaldor, N., 61n
Keynes, J. M., 114, 177
Knight, F. H., 9, 13–14, 22, 24–5, 30, 33, 46, 65n
Kreps, T. J., 86

Lacey, K., 158n, 159n
Lange, O., 5, 230n, 233n
Lerner, A. P., 194, 195–6, 230n, 232n, 233n
Lippincott, B. E., 230n
Little, I. M. D., 250n, 251n, 264n